THE
THEOLOGY
OF
HISTORY
IN
ST. BONAVENTURE

THE
THEOLOGY
OF
HISTORY
IN
ST. BONAVENTURE

Joseph
Ratzinger

FRANCISCAN HERALD PRESS

The Theology of History in St. Bonaventure, by Joseph Ratzinger, translated by Zachary Hayes O.F.M. Copyright © 1971 by Franciscan Herald Press, 1434 West 51st Street, Chicago, Illinois 60609. Library of Congress Catalog Card Number: 71-85509; ISBN 8199-0415-5. Made in the United States of America.

NIHIL OBSTAT:
  Mark Hegener O.F.M.
  Censor Deputatus

IMPRIMATUR:
  Rt. Rev. Msgr. Francis W. Byrne
  Vicar General, Archdiocese of Chicago

January 21, 1971

INTRODUCTION

It is above all at times of greatest crisis in human history that we find men concerned with the theology and the philosophy of history.[1] Thus, the first great Christian theology of history, Augustine's *De civitate Dei contra paganos,* emerged from the crisis of the Roman empire, in which the life of that age had found an orderly and apparently definitive form.[2] Since that time, the attempt to come to terms with history theologically has never been foreign to Western theology. In fact, from the viewpoint of the New Testament and its eschatology, history has become basically "critical."[3] The attempt to penetrate history reached a new high-point in the High Middle Ages, and more precisely, in the thirteenth century. One of the reasons for this may be found in the new type of historical prophecy of Abbot Joachim of Fiore.[4] But this prophecy acquired its real incendiary force through the outstanding confirmation which it apparently found in the person and work of St. Francis of Assisi.[5] These two elements developed into that profound questioning of the Medieval form of history from which a new and broadly conceived theology of history could take its rise. Bonaventure's *Collationes in Hexaemeron* represents this new, second high-point in the Christian reflection on history.[6] Therefore, the present study, which is intended to be a presentation of St. Bonaventure's theology of history, will be concerned primarily with analyzing this work. But we must not overlook the relationship of this work to the total literary output of Bonaventure; nor may we bypass the roots which this work has in the intellectual world to which Bonaventure belonged.

Therefore, we can set up the basic structure for this study as follows. First, we must bring to light the statements that pertain to the theology of history and subject them to a precise and detailed analysis. Unfortunately, these statements are not presented systematically in the *Collationes*; they are scattered here and there, and are, for the most part, enigmatic and difficult to interpret (Ch.1). Then, on the basis of these individual statements, we will attempt to bring to light the central idea of Bonaventure's hope for history (Ch.2). This should enable us, then, to place the doctrine of Bonaventure in its proper place within the stream of tradition at least in broad outline (Ch.3). Finally, on the basis of the particular insights gained in this study, we will attempt to make a contribution to the problem of the thought-form of Bonaventure in general, which has again become a disputed question (Ch.4).

CONTENTS

The German edition of this book appeared ten years ago, which may seem to be a very long time when we consider the developments that have taken place in theology and in the Church in the intervening years. Naturally, under such circumstances, I have had to ask myself whether a translation of the unaltered original could be justified; for it was clear to me that I could not undertake a reworking of the text because of the growing number of commitments which have engaged me.

A few brief remarks concerning the genesis and intent of the book are necessary to clarify the fact that I have given an affirmative answer to this question. When I began the preparatory work for this study in the fall of 1953, one of the questions which stood in the foreground of concern within German-speaking, Catholic theological circles was the question of the relation of salvation-history to metaphysics. This was a problem which arose above all from contacts with Protestant theology which, since the time of Luther, has tended to see in metaphysical thought a departure from the specific claim of the Christian faith which directs man not simply to the Eternal but to the God who acts in time and history. Here questions of quite diverse character and of different orders arose. How can that which has taken place historically become present? How can the unique and unrepeatable have a universal significance? But then, on the other hand: Has not the "Hellenization" of Christianity, which attempted to overcome the scandal of the particular by a blending of faith and metaphysics, led to a development in a false direction? Has it not created a static style of thought which cannot do justice to the dynamism of the biblical style?

These questions had a strong influence on me, and I wanted to make a contribution toward answering them. In the light of the accepted tradition of German theology, it was self-evident to me that this could not be done in an *a priori* way. Rather, it could take place only in dialogue with that very theological tradition which was being called into question. Only on the basis of this type of study could any systematic formulation take place. I have attempted to give a tentative sketch of such a formulation in my book *Einführung in das Christentum* which appeared in 1968. Since I had devoted my first study to Augustine, and thus had become somewhat familiar with the world of the Fathers, it seemed natural now to approach the Middle Ages. For the questions with which I was concerned, Bonaventure was naturally a more likely subject for study than Aquinas. Thus, a partner was found for the discussion. The questions which I hoped to direct to this partner were sketched in general terms in the concepts of: revelation — history — metaphysics.

First, I studied the nature of revelation together with the terminology used to express it. On the basis of this material, I attempted to describe the relation between history and metaphysics as Bonaventure understood it. As yet it has been possible to publish only several fragments from the voluminous material which emerged out of this research. Aside from the external reasons involved, there was an internal reason as well. This is to be found in the fact that in formulating the question in this way, we are already approaching Bonaventure with *our* concept of history, whereas it would be important to read Bonaventure within his own framework even though we might discover a perspective which would be entirely foreign to us and which might be meaningless in relation to our present problem. So my attention was concentrated more and more on the theology of history as Bonaventure himself had developed it in the spiritual struggle of his own age. This is the way in which the present volume came to be.

The results were surprising enough. It became apparent that Bonaventure's theology of history presents a struggle to arrive at a proper understanding of eschatology. It is thus anchored in the central issue of the New Testament question itself. It became clear that the discussion which Bonaventure undertook with Joachim of Fiore — the remarkable prophet of that period — led to a change in the concept of eschatology which remains operative even today. Finally, it became obvious that the theology of history does not represent an isolated area of Bonaventure's thought. On the contrary, it is related to the basic philosophical and theological decisions which provided the basis for his participation in the bitter controversies of the 1260's and 1270's. It was in these controversies that the question of philosophy and theology was handled as well as the question of Hellenism and de-Hellenization and the problem as to whether faith could be translated into understanding. In many ways those turbulent years, with the abrupt entrance of Arabian science into the firmly built structure of traditional theology, are similar to the post-Conciliar mood which we are experiencing at the present time. Ten years ago it would not have been difficult to work out applications to the present. The discipline of the historian, however, forbade such a procedure. The task of the historian is to present his findings and nothing but his findings. At times this limitation has disturbed me, but I believe it was and is justified.

Since its publication, the work has been discussed frequently and its conclusions have been refined here and there. Most of the critique seems to center around the question as to whether I have overestimated the influence of Joachim of Fiore. The reviews have been listed in: J. G. Bougerol, *Lexique Saint Bonaventure* (Paris, 1969) 82. I would like to refer, furthermore, to the outstanding presentation of Bonaventure together with comments on my book by F. van Steenberghen, *La philosophie au XIII* siècle (Louvain-Paris, 1966) 190-271. Unfortunately, it is impossible to go into particular points of the discussion. It seems clear to me that Bonaventure *could not* remain silent concerning Joachim since he was Minister General of an Order that was torn almost to the breaking point by the Joachimite question. *Hexaemeron* is the answer he gave to this problem as General of the Order. It is a critical discussion with the Calabrian Abbot and his followers. Without Joachim, the work would be incomprehensible. But the discussion is carried on in such a way that Joachim is interpreted back into tradition while the Joachimites interpreted him against that tradition. Bonaventure does not totally reject Joachim (as Thomas had done); rather, he interprets him in an ecclesial way and thus creates an alternative to the radical Joachimites. On the basis of this alternative, he tries to preserve the unity of the Order.

With this I will return to the original question as to whether a translation of the unchanged original is still meaningful today. I hope that I have learned something from the reviews and other literature that has appeared in the meantime. I would now place many points of emphasis differently and alter many nuances. But the general argument remains untouched, and I see no reason for reworking it. To this extent, a new printing seems to me to be justified from the viewpoint of the historian. I am furthermore convinced that, precisely at the present moment, theology has every reason for remaining in contact with its own history. Without this, it is condemned to wither like a tree cut off from its roots. Therefore, it is my hope that this book will be helpful in this area also, and that it might stimulate others to enter into that dialogue with history which must always be taken up anew.

I cannot end this Foreword to the American edition without expressing my gratitude again to my venerable teacher, Prof. Dr. Gottlieb Söhngen of Munich, who provided the stimulation for this study. He was always a fatherly friend and helper in the numerous external and internal difficulties which I encountered while the book was in the making. Furthermore, I must express my sincere thanks to the translator, Dr. Zachary

Hayes O.F.M. and to the publisher, Fr. Mark Hegener O.F.M. In these years, both have shown me an extraordinary degree of patience which will not be forgotten.

Tübingen, August 15, 1969

JOSEPH RATZINGER

THE
THEOLOGY
OF
HISTORY
IN
ST. BONAVENTURE

CHAPTER I

AN ATTEMPT TO FIND THE STRUCTURE OF THE BONAVENTURIAN THEOLOGY OF HISTORY ON THE BASIS OF THE "COLLATIONES IN HEXAEMERON"

#1. General Remarks concerning the "Collationes in Hexaemeron."

When Bonaventure held his "Lectures on the Hexameron"[1] at the University of Paris early in the summer of 1273, he completed a task which had been sketched already at the time he assumed the office of General. In February 1257, Bonaventure had been called suddenly from his successful activity as professor at Paris in order to replace the departing General, John of Parma.[2] John's withdrawal from office was not entirely voluntary. He had created an extraordinarily difficult situation for the Franciscan Order by his decisive stand in favor of the prophecies of Joachim of Fiore, and the Joachimite-spiritualist concept of the Order in general. The untenability of his position became particularly obvious in the light of the ecclesiastical condemnation (on October 23, 1255) of the *Evangelium aeternum* in which the Franciscan, Gerard of Borgo San Donnino, had attempted to formulate the Franciscan Spiritualism.[3] Certainly the person of the General was not the only difficulty with which the young Order was burdened. The Order had to struggle for an understanding of its own proper nature somewhere between the extremes of a radi-

1

cally eschatological and purely spiritual self-consciousness on the one hand and an all-too complacent formulation according to the already existing forms of the older Orders on the other hand. It seemed that the unadulterated will of the Founder could not be realized on earth. But that which could be realized seemed to be a departure from the will of the Founder.[4]

In this situation, the youthful Master, Bonaventure, who was then teaching at Paris, was called to the highest position in the Order as the seventh successor of St. Francis.[5] He found himself confronted with a task which was entirely new for him. According to the most certain chronology,[6] he had entered the Order in Paris in 1243. At that time, it had been above all his respect for his teacher, Alexander of Hales, which had drawn him. So great was this reverence that he calls Alexander not only *magister,* but also *pater.*[7] Obviously, then, the University of Paris was the spiritual climate for his vocation to the Order. Consequently, his entire approach to Franciscanism has something "Scholastic" about it. (The word "Scholastic" is used here in the most general sense.)[8] Certainly the spirit of a Franciscan soul is always perceptible in the works which Bonaventure wrote even as a Schoolman. But the world in which he lived, thought, and wrote as a teacher was an entirely different world than that world of pure, fundamental religious ardor which was characteristic of early Franciscanism.[9] His problems were different from those which we have just described as the problems of the Order.[10] Apparently Bonaventure sensed this himself. When, in 1259, he withdrew into solitude on Mount Alverna, the holy Mount of the Order, he apparently had no other intention in mind than to allow himself to be drawn more deeply into the spiritual world of Francis in whose place he now stood.[11]

The *Itinerarium mentis in Deum,* which Bonaventure brought with him from these weeks of solitude, is a first sign of a new intellectual direction. From this book onward, the figure of St. Francis enters ever more into the center of his thought; indeed, it is precisely that Francis who has fittingly been called the "Christ-Image of the Middle Ages."[12] This development can be followed further in the *Life of St. Francis* (1260-1263),[13] in the various ascetical and practical writings which come from the time of Bonaventure's Generalate,[14] and above all in a series of sermons which was begun in the year 1267. With this series, Bonaventure returned to the university pulpit ten years after his departure, and he entered again into the arena of doctrinal disputes which were becoming ever more critical. But it was a transformed Bonaventure. He did not return simply to take up a position within the inner-disciplinary debates. Rather, he came back as an outsider to point out the limits of science from the perspective of faith. It is in this context that we must understand the *Collationes de decem praeceptis,* the *Collationes de donis Spiritus Sancti,* and the other Sermons given at Paris at this time.[15] But it is the final work of this period, the *Collationes in Hexaemeron,*[16] written in 1273, that clearly provides us with the synthesis and crown of the whole development. It is first in this work that Bonaventure offers a penetrating exposition of those problems which had led earlier to the downfall of John of Parma. These were the problems which had kept the entire Order in suspense to an ever-increasing degree; namely, the questions of Joachimism and Spiritualism. For this reason, the work, by its very nature, was forced to undertake a fundamental treatment of the theology of history. The unique individuality of this work can be seen in the fact that it is the only work in which a leading Scholastic theologian takes a position relative to that stream of thought characterized by Dempf as Germanic symbolism or perhaps more precisely by J. Leclerq as "moyen âge monastique" (in contrast to the "moyen âge scolastique") in order to attempt a synthesis of historical-symbolic thought with the conceptual-abstract thought of Scholasticism.[17]

Therefore it is understandable that for a long time, the *Hexaemeron* has evoked amazement. It has been called, doubtless not without a bit of exaggeration, "l'ouvrage le plus original, le plus riche et peut-être le plus puissant de la littérature ecclésiastique;"[18] or more properly "un des plus étonnants ouvrages de génie chrétien."[19] Dempf designates it as the "umfassendsten Entwurf einer Summa in ganzen Mittelalter"[20] and as the "bedeutendste Geschichts—und Gemeinschafts philosophie des Mittelalters."[21] Nonetheless, up to the present, it has remained by and large a closed book; an "ager adhuc . . . incultus, in quo ligo numquam fossus est; e via tantum aliqui flosculos de illo collegerunt, at, etsi fertilitatem et pinquedinem cognoverint miratique fuerint, praeterierunt," as Tinivella has expressed it.[22]

There are many reasons for this state of affairs. They lie first of all in the unique character of this work and in its textual tradition. It has already been pointed out that we are here concerned with lectures. We do not possess the original manuscript of the speaker but only the notes of the listeners. This involves a degree of uncertainty in individual formulations which is obvious already in the variety of titles under which the work appears. At times it is referred to as *Illuminationes* (*ecclesiae*); at times it appears as the *Collationes in Hexaemeron.*[23] The edition of a second text recension published by F. Delorme[24] has revealed the inexactness of the textual tradition in a drastic way. It shows, on the one hand, that the basic content of Bonaventure's thought has been faithfully retained; but at the same time, it brings out clearly the freedom of the writers of the recensions regarding the choice of words.

No less difficult for any attempt at interpretation is the fragmentary character of the work which remained incomplete because of Bonaventure's elevation to the cardinalate.[25] Furthermore, Bonaventure merely alludes to many things; and frequently ideas are expressed in a veiled manner. In particular, the predictions of the future are presented in the style of a sort of apocalyptic mystery which may well have been understandable for his hearers because of their knowledge of the situation, but are often almost impenetrable for us.

Consequently, we have attempted to bring together all the related texts and allusions so as to reconstruct the original whole on the basis of the isolated parts in as far as this is possible. In an attempt to achieve a greater degree of certainty, all the analyses were worked out first only on the basis of the text published in the *Opera Omnia,* vol. V, p. 329-449. The comparison with Delorme's text is intended to serve as a check for the correctness of the results. Happily, our interpretation was confirmed and at times complemented by the text of this recension, which is frequently clearer in matters pertaining to the theology of history. The intention of the present study, however, is not to present a properly critical textual comparison of the two recensions. We are concerned rather with an analysis of the content of the Bonaventurian theology of history. The general impression which forced itself upon us from the texts has brought two facts more clearly into focus. In the text of Delorme we find an effort toward clarity. This text designates the historical figures by name and interprets the contexts. It takes references from the field of the liberal arts and expands them to short, formal tracts,[26] and it expands the citation-material. Furthermore, it smoothes over all the offensive passages which could be interpreted as taking sides for Spiritualism and Joachimism. Consequently, the other recension appears basically as the *lectio difficilior*. We will find evidence of this often in the course of our presentation. We hope to take up this question in more detail in a projected bilingual edition of the *Hexaemeron*.* On the basis of what has been said so far, we feel justified for the time being in preferring the text of the *Opera Omnia*. On the whole, it seems to be the better text, and we have taken our citations from it. As often as the Delorme-recension departs substantially from the *Opera Omnia* or offers additions to it, the Delorme-text will be given as well.[27]

#2. A Provisional Delimitation of the Relation between Scripture and History according to the "Hexaemeron."

It is the intention of the *Hexaemeron* to hold up the picture of the true Christian wisdom in the face of the intellectual aberrations of the age. But for Bonaventure, who was entirely a man of his times, wisdom is unthinkable and unintelligible without reference to the historical situation in which it has its place. Consequently, the development of the ideal of wisdom naturally grows into a treatment of the theology of history.

---

* Tr. Note: Since the original publication of the present study, a German translation of the **Hexaemeron** has been prepared by Dr. Wilhelm Nyssen. This translation was read by Dr. Ratzinger prior to publication. A commentary was to appear in a separate volume which was to be prepared by Dr. Nyssen and Dr. Ratzinger. Because of his work as **peritus** at the Second Vatican Council, Dr. Ratzinger has been unable as yet to complete this work.

The unique relationship between any given form of knowledge and the historical situation to which it is related is seen already in the general outline of the work: it distinguishes six levels of knowledge which are interpreted allegorically in relation to the six days of the creation account. At the same time, the six periods of salvation history are related to the six days of creation. For Bonaventure, this double relationship is not chance nor is it arbitrary. Rather, it is a fitting reflection of reality which is characterized by an historical, step-wise growth in knowledge.[1]

In this way, Bonaventure arrives at a new theory of scriptural exegesis which emphasizes the historical character of the scriptural statements in contrast to the exegesis of the Fathers and the Scholastics which had been more clearly directed to the unchangeable and the enduring.

According to Bonaventure, the word of Scripture has, as it were, three levels of meaning. First, there is the *spiritualis intelligentia* which penetrates through the literal sense to the allegorical, tropological, or anagogical meaning.[2] But he is not satisfied with this traditional division. Next to the "spiritual sense" of Scripture as understood above he places a second dimension, the *figurae sacramentales,* with which Scripture speaks of Christ and of the Anti-Christ in all its books.[3] And finally, in the third place, he puts the *multiformes theoriae* of which he says: "Who can know the unlimited number of seeds which exist? For from one single seed, entire forests grow up; and they in turn bring forth innumerable seeds. So it happens that innumerable theories can arise from Scripture which only God can grasp in His knowledge. As new seeds come from plants, so also new theories and new meaning come from Scripture . . . Each of the theories which are derived from Scripture is related to the totality of those theories that are based on Scripture as a drop of water taken from the sea is related to the whole of the sea."[4] It is because of this unlimited potential that the "theories" are distinguished from the spiritual sense and from the *figurae sacramentales*, since both of these remain within a certain clearly established framework.[5]

But the question with which we are here concerned is this: what does Bonaventure mean by these so-called theories? There is no clear definition to be found in his works. But on the basis of the material before us, we can express his idea as follows: The theories are intimations about future times found in Scripture. Scripture points to the future; but only he who has understood the past can grasp the interpretation of the future because the whole of history develops in one unbroken line of meaning in which that which is to come may be grasped in the present on the basis of the past. Therefore, if the theories, strictly speaking, are hidden indications of the future in Scripture, then these theories cannot be determined without a knowledge of the past history of salvation which is the indispensable basis for the understanding of that which is to come.[6]

Thus Bonaventure appropriates the exegesis which Joachim of Fiore had developed in his *Concordia veteris et novi testamenti*; the three-fold explanation of the work of creation is taken from the same work.[7] Bonaventure thus accepts that type of essentially historical understanding of Scripture which was central in the work of Joachim and which was one of the decisively new elements that distinguished the work of the Calabrian abbot from that of the Fathers. With this in mind, we can see the significance of one of the images which already appeared in the text given above. The spiritual sense of Scripture is indicated in the gathering of the waters on the third day of creation; the *figurae sacramentales* are indicated in the command, "Let the earth bring forth vegetation"; and finally, the theories are implied when Scripture speaks of the fruits and the trees that carry seeds within themselves.[8] It is apparent that this amounts to nothing less than a transfer of the theory of *rationes seminales* to Scripture.[9] Certainly Scripture is closed objectively. But its meaning is advancing in a steady growth through history; and this growth is not yet closed. As the physical world contains seeds, so also Scripture contains "seeds"; that is, seeds of meaning. And this meaning develops in a constant process of growth in time. Consequently, we are able to interpret many things which the Fathers could not have known because for them these things still lay in the dark future while for us they are accessible as past history. Still other things remain dark for us.[10] And so, new knowledge arises constantly from Scripture. Something is taking place; and this happening, this history, continues onward as long as there is history at all. This is of fundamental importance for the theologian who explains Scripture. It makes it clear that the theologian cannot abstract from history in his explanation of Scripture; neither from the past nor from the future. In this way, the exegesis of Scripture becomes a theology of history; the clarification of the past leads to prophecy concerning the future.

#3. **The Historical Schemata of the "Hexaemeron."**
    1. **The exclusion of Augustine from the narrower consideration of the theology of history.**

From what has been said, it is clear that in many ways what Bonaventure intended in writing the *Hexaemeron* is similar to intention of Augustine in his *Civitas Dei*; that is, to make the present and the future of the Church understandable from its past. The traditional schema of the seven ages of world history played only a very secondary role in the case of Augustine;[1] his principal point of emphasis is the presentation of world-events in terms of the conflict between the *civitas Dei* and the *civitas terrena,* between the *corpus Christi* and the *corpus Diaboli.* The entire course of human history is brought together in terms of this duality which reaches out over the entire history of man in both directions, to the past and to the future.

It is exactly the opposite with Bonaventure. He mentions Augustine's historical principle at times; for example, when he says: "All the mysteries of Scripture treat of Christ with his Body and of the Anti-Christ and the Devil with his cohorts. This is the meaning of Augustine in his book on the City of God. . ."[2] However, Bonaventure relates this understanding of Scripture not to the *theoriae,* and therefore not to the theology of history, but rather to the *figurae sacramentales* which we might see as a "typology" in contrast to the "allegory" that stands behind the "spiritual sense."[3] Consequently, Augustine is deliberately excluded from the real theology of history right from the start.[4] This fact is not without significance for the proper evaluation of what follows.

2. The new form of the theology of history.

Bonaventure again carries out a careful division of the traditional materials within the realm of the *theoriae*; i.e. as regards that which properly pertains to the historico-theological* consideration of Scripture. He presents here two types of historical schemata:

---

* Tr. Note: Rather than make use of awkward paraphrases, we will consistently translate the adjective "geschichtstheologisch" with the word "historico-theological."

a) The divisions of history in the School-theology, of which three are named:

 a) The doctrine of the seven ages from Adam to Christ, as they were known from Augustine's *City of God.*[5]

 b) A division of world-history into five ages. This was worked out on the basis of Jesus' parable of the workers in the vineyard (Mt. 20,1-16). In this parable, we read about the call in the early morning, as well as at the third, the sixth, the ninth, and the eleventh hour. On the basis of a homily of Gregory the Great,[6] the Middle Ages had seen a doctrine of five world-epochs hidden in this parable. The divisions of history are designated by the names: Adam—Noe—Abraham—Moses—Christ.[7]

 c) Finally, there is the well-known division of history into three ages: the time of the law of nature; the law of Scripture; and the law of Grace.[8] We mention in passing that the three numbers 7, 5, and 3 are finally added together and the number 15 which results from this process is likewise given a mysterious meaning.[9]

b) Bonaventure uses none of these schemata as his own; not even the seven-schema, as a superficial study might lead one to believe. Instead, he contrasts all these constructs with an idea from Joachim's *Concordia* which was to become decisive for his own conception. The knowledge of history arises in the interplay between the Old and the New Testament. These are the two Cherubim over the mercy seat; they are the two divisions of historical time which are similar in form. Accordingly, there is not only a correspondence between the seven days of

creation and the seven ages from Adam to Christ, as Augustine
had taught; but there is also a correspondence between the
history of the Old Testament and that of the New Testament.
Not only had Augustine not taught this; he had clearly rejected the idea.[10] The Old and New Testaments are related
to each other "as tree to tree; as letter to letter; as seed to seed.
And as a tree comes from a tree, a seed from a seed, and a
letter from a letter, so one Testament comes from the other
Testament."[11] Thus, a double relation is seen between the
Testaments. The first is a dynamic relation whereby one Testament comes from the other and emerges out of the other. The
second is a more static relation in which one Testament stands
over against the other. A further duality stands in the background: the Pauline determination of the relation between the
Testaments as *littera* and *spiritus* remains here in as far as the
one "tree" is designated as the *littera* and the other "tree" is
seen as *spiritus*.[12] The original Pauline comparison is transformed, however, by the comparison "ut littera ad litteram."
This comparison is given precedence, and it provides a new
form for the older comparison. The presuppositions, meaning, and consequences of this procedure will be treated in
detail later (##4 and 5).

In this approach, the emphasis is on the exegetical element
known as the *theoriae*, for only this element allows for real
statements concerning the future of the Church, which is the
primary concern of the "theories." Since there is a multiplicity
of "theories" hidden in Scripture, we are not restricted to one
particular schema; the relation of the Testaments can be treated
on the basis of all the numbers from 1 to 7. In this way, seven
new historical schemata arise.

a) If we work on the basis of the number 1, we arrive at the Pauline relationship

— servitus .... libertas

— timor .... amor

— littera .... spiritus

— figura .... veritas

— nox .... dies[13]

b) In this schema, the new meaning given to this way of thinking is not yet apparent. It becomes clear, however, in the relationship which arises when we work on the basis of the number two. This involves two periods of time for each of the Testaments so that the following picture arises:

Ante legem+sub lege ....

vocatio gentium+vocatio Iudaeorum.[14]

Here already the primary significance of the *theoriae* is realized, that is, a projection into the future; for the call of the Jews into the Church of Christ is yet to be realized. But abstracting from the testimony of Scripture which promises this fact, it can be seen also from the necessary correspondence of the Testaments. It thus becomes apparent that the present time is not a time of perfect fulfillment. "This time is not yet here. If it were already here, then the saying of Isaias would be fulfilled: 'Nation shall not lift up sword against nation, nor shall they learn war anymore' (Is. 2, 4). As yet, that is still unfulfilled; for two kinds of swords are still being raised. There is still war waged with weapons; and there is still the spiritual war against heresy."[15] Here Bonaventure raises a new, innerwordly, inner-historical messianic hope. He rejects the view that with Christ the highest degree of inner-historical fulfillment is already realized so that there is nothing left but an eschatological hope for that which lies beyond all history. Bonaventure believes in a new salvation in history, within the limits of this time. This is a very significant shift in the understanding of history, and must be seen as the central historico-theological problem of the *Hexaemeron*. It is expressed for the first time unequivocally here; but it becomes more and more clear from schema to schema.

c) The following picture arises when we use the number 3 as the basis:

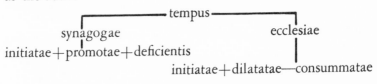

While in the previous schema, the prophecy of the future does not go beyond the general statements of Scripture, here it takes on a more precise form. It is the "fulfillment" of the church, which is still to come. After Lea—who from antiquity had been the picture of the *vita activa*—had given birth to her sons, Rachel—who is the picture of the *vita contemplativa*—had to bring the last sons to the world, namely Joseph and Benjamin. In other words, the completed church, the *ecclesia contemplativa,* is yet to come.[16]

Here again we meet the same hope of an inner-historical transformation of the church. Details of this section which may still seem unclear will be treated more extensively later.

d) The same interpretation pointing to a contemplative, monastic church arises from the schemata based on the numbers four and five. These will be treated explicitly in relationship to Bonaventure's hope regarding revelation (Ch. 2); we can, therefore, bypass them for the present. They close with the announcement of Elias, "who will restore all things," (Mk. 9, 12; Mal. 3, 22f) and with a vision of the great final tribulation.[17]

e) For Bonaventure, all of these schemata have a merely provisional character. Each one emphasizes only particular aspects, all of which are brought together in his own, proper schema which is built on the numbers six and seven. This demands a special treatment. In dealing with it, we move into the center of the Bonaventurian theology of history.

#4. **The Central Form of the Bonaventurian Theology of History: the 2 x 7 Time-Schema.**

1. **Time-schemata built on six and seven in tradition and in Bonaventure.**

a) In line with the tradition of his time, Bonaventure sees no distinction between the time-schema built on six and that built on seven. In this tradition, we find a peculiar union of elements from late Judaism and early Christianity together with philosophical, speculative concepts. Late Judaic thought had developed the notion of a world-week that was to last six-thousand years; the eternal kingdom of God would follow as the seventh day. Presumably it was the Christian transgression and destruction of the Judaic notions about the Sabbath which helped to form the new notion of the eighth day of the Resurrection as distinct from the Sabbath.[1]

A certain tension between the seventh day and the eighth day is noticeable[2] until a solution is found in the axiom: Septima aetas currit cum sexta.[3] Bonaventure appropriates this axiom as his own, and understands it in such a way that the seventh epoch is found in those who now enter into heavenly glory between the Resurrection of Christ (with which the opening of heaven is connected), and the final consummation of the world in the general resurrection.[4] As long as the church has existed, there has always been this hidden and glorious concurrent history, the history of heaven. The glory of the seventh day is real, though its concurrence with the perilous and painful sixth day is hidden. The eternal eighth day follows these two inter-connected days, and it will be introduced by the resurrection and judgment.[5] We might well say that in this solution, the problem of ecclesial eschatology is masterfully handled: On the one hand, Bonaventure recognizes the full heavenly glory of the souls of those who have died and have been purified; on the other hand, it remains clear that this heavenly condition is not the final state, but that it is still a part of world-history; it also stands in expectation of that which is to come. Consequently, the mystery of hope remains for Christianity; a concrete hope for a transformation of the world.[6]

b) The Scholion of the Quaracchi-edition indicates only this solution, which is faithful to tradition but which represents, nonetheless, only half of Bonaventure's theology of history.[7] In fact, it is related only to the Augustinian schema based on the number seven. This schema divides the entire history of the world from Adam to the end of time into one single series of seven parts. But we must here again emphasize what we said above; namely, that Bonaventure excludes this simple seven-part division of world history and salvation-history from his own theology of history; he favors the view which presupposes, first of all, the two-fold division of the Old and the New Testament. After the Seraphic Doctor has shown the relations based on the numbers 1 to 5, he then indicates the fittingness of a double division into seven periods

within the two-fold division of the Testaments. This he develops into his own plan for the theology of history. This
double-seven-schema must be clearly distinguished from the
simple-seven-schema found in Augustine and the ancient
Church as well as in medieval theology prior to the time of
Joachim, for a completely different understanding of time and
of history is expressed in it. We will treat this more fully
below; but the difference can be briefly summarized as follows:
For the Augustinian schema, Christ is the end of the ages;
for the Bonaventurian schema, Christ is the center of the ages.[8]
The widely-spread notion that Bonaventure places the Augustinian doctrine of the seven ages in opposition to the Joachimite doctrine of the three ages is not to the point.[9] In reality,
Bonaventure contrasts the double-seven-schema of Joachim
with the simple-seven-schema of Augustine, and decides in
favor of the former.

The axiom "septima aetas currit cum sexta" does not hold
in this double-seven-schema. Instead, this schema recognizes
a seventh period of history in its own right.[10] The connection
between the two schemata should be seen this way: The sixth
period of the continuous Augustinian structure embraces the
seven ecclesial ages of the bipartite Bonaventurian structure.

The following picture emerges:

A u g u s t i n e

1	2	3	4	5	6
Adam-Noe -	Abraham -	David	- transmigratio -	Christus -	finis
			Babylonis		mundi

Vetus testamentum   Novum testamentum

B o n a v e n t u r e

(Joachim)

```
1  ...............................................➤ 1
2  ...............................................➤ 2
3  ...............................................➤ 3
4  ...............................................➤ 4
5  ...............................................➤ 5
6  ...............................................➤ 6
7  ...............................................➤ 7¹¹
```

The Augustinian tradition remains as the broad framework; but for the actual interpretation of history, it is superseded by new ideas.

2. The basis for the preference for the number seven.

Bonaventure has given us an express account for the preference given to the seven-fold division over all the other schemata. The number seven expresses in a remarkable way the entirety of reality;[12] it does this relative to God, to man, and to the world. Rather than give a long explanation, we will simply present the schema in which the seven-fold structure of these three "worlds"—the *mundus archetypus,* the *mundus minor,* and the *mundus major*—is worked out.[13]

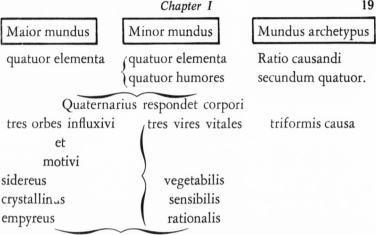

Maior mundus	Minor mundus	Mundus archetypus

quatuor elementa ⎧ quatuor elementa Ratio causandi
  ⎨ quatuor humores secundum quatuor.

Quaternarius respondet corpori

tres orbes influxivi tres vires vitales triformis causa
  et
  motivi
sidereus vegetabilis
crystallinus sensibilis
empyreus rationalis

ternarius respondet spiritui

This relationship, therefore, means more than a mere play with numbers because it makes us aware of the inner relations of reality which, for Bonaventure, are a part of the harmony that he confidently believes to be present in the universe created by God.[14]

Similarly, history is not a concatination of blind and oppressive chance happenings. Rather, it is illumined by that same divine order which is the unifying law of all reality. The schema given above presents the static relationship of these three worlds standing next to each other. To this we must add the dynamic relationship of the historical process of becoming which is involved in the affirmation of the seven-fold division of history. Here the rational structure of history is decisively affirmed.

#5. The Historical Prophecy of Bonaventure.

The real point of Bonaventure's new vision of history is not the understanding of the past, but prophecy about that which is to come, as has already been said often. But a knowledge of the past is necessary for the grasp of the future. In order to clarify further the connection between the past and the future, we will present on a special page a detailed outline of the great double-seven-schema found in *Hexaemeron* XVI 11-31 (Vol. V 405-408) so that it may be referred to easily in the following presentation.

originalia (*semina*)	figuralia (*arbores figurarum*)	Tempora — collatae gratiae … gratiosa (*fructus*)
dies lucis formatae	tempus naturae conditae ab Adam—ad Noe tria: Formatio hominis tentatio-trangressio-nudatio-eiectio	collatae gratiae a Christo et apostolis—ad Clementem I (+ca. 99, 4th Pope) Formatio Christi haeresis Ebionitarum eiectio Judaeorum
aquae divisae	purgandae culpae a Noe—ad Abraham fabricatio arcae ostensio arcus divisio linguarum	baptismi in sanguine a Clemente—ad Silvestrum (314-335) Clemens in arca decem tribulationes+pax Constantini "remansit confessio Christi in populo christiano"
terrae fecundae	gentis electae ab Abraham—ad Moysen generatio patriarcharum (12) descensio in Aegyptum afflictio populi	normae catholicae a Silvestro—ad Leonem I (440-461) semen doctorum altissimorum (12) descensio imperatoris Constantinopolim afflictio populi per haereses
lucis sidereae	legis statutae a Moyse—ad Samuelem latio legis prostratio hostium distributio hereditatum	legis iustitiae a Leone—ad Gregorium I (590-604) lex canonica, politica, monastica data hostes per Iustinianum prostrati distributio hereditatum: Gallia, Britannia, Germania conversa ad fidem (dilatatio in terra promissionis, non apud Graecos)
motivae vitae	regalis gloriae a David—ad Ezechiam deiectio superbi regis (Goliath) ampliatio cultus divini divisio decem tribuum	sublimis cathedrae a Gregorio—ad Hadrianum I (772-795) patriarcha Constantinopolitanus excommunicatus ordinatio officii divisio Graecorum ab ecclesia
humanae formae	vocis propheticae ab Ezechia—ad Zorobabel praeclaritas victoriae doctrinae vitae propheticae	clarae doctrinae ab Hadriano—ad ? victoria Caroli, pax ecclesiae inceperunt legere et philosophari cfr. the analysis in the following development.
quietis primae	quietis mediae a Zorobabel—ad Christum reaedificatio templi restauratio civitatis pax data	pacis postremae a clamore angeli (Apoc. 10,6,7) — ? reparatio divini cultus reaedificatio civitatis "tunc pax erit"

A. The promise of the seventh age.

Now that we have established the fact that the primary concern of Bonaventure's view of history is related to the future, we can determine more precisely the point around which everything is centered. This central point of interest lies in that small section of the sixth age which is yet to be realized, that is, in that mysterious border-line area which separates the perilous present time from that age of Sabbath Rest which is yet to come within the framework of this world. What is it that we are to expect before that long-awaited hour strikes and peace enters the world forever? Everything revolves around this question and is concerned with the determination of that final period of the *sexta aetas* which remains to be realized.

In contrast with this problem, the question of the seventh age is relatively simple, and will be treated immediately. Bonaventure himself clarifies what is meant by the seventh age when he says: "Then the prophecy of Ezechiel (40ff) will be fulfilled: The Holy City will come down from heaven; not, however, that city 'which is above' (Gal. 4, 26), but that one which is below, that is, the church militant. But she will be formed in the likeness of the Church triumphant in as far as this is possible in her pilgrim-state . . . And then there will be peace . . .".[1] Two things are obvious:

a) We are dealing with a thoroughly inner-worldly condition. The pilgrim-character is expressly emphasized, and the designation of the "Church militant" is emphatically held in contrast to the "Church triumphant."

b) This period of time represents a state of salvation of a completely new sort. But this does not destroy its inner-worldly, inner-historical, and therefore pre-eschatological character. It is first in this period that the great prophecies of Ezechiel and Isaias[2] will be fulfilled; it is only in this age that the state of redemption will find its full meaning.

c) Immediately a question arises. How is this seventh age of Bonaventure related to the seventh age of Joachim? We can take a stand on this question only when we have presented the opinion of Joachim himself, and when we have discovered the new form which the concept of revelation takes on in the *Hexaemeron*. This concept of revelation will follow from the Bonaventurian theology of history which we are about to develop.

For the present, we merely point out that the Seraphic Doctor had clearly and decisively rejected any crass form of the Joachimite doctrine such as had been developed by Gerard of Borgo San Donnino. Gerard considered Joachim to be the Angel of the Apocalypse 14, 6 about whom it is stated: "I saw another angel flying in mid-air with an eternal Gospel . . ."

The writings of Joachim were seen to be this eternal Gospel which was supposed to take the place of the temporary New Testament message.[3] This theory, which was expressly condemned by the Church,[4] was rejected also by Bonaventure. He writes: "No other testament will come after the New Testament; and no sacrament of the new Law can be done away with, because this is already the eternal covenant."[5] Therefore, the seventh age is expressly placed not only within this course of history, but also within the time of the New Testament. The New Testament is described as the eternal Testament; it therefore embraces all that remains of the course of history. Thus it is clearly seen that this new, transformed historical schema is still developed within the older Augustinian framework, as we have already indicated. Though it is apparent that Bonaventure rejected Gerard's view together with the notion of an *Evangelium aeternum,* it would be incorrect to equate this with the rejection of Joachim himself, as one might be tempted to do.[6] We must, rather, clearly distinguish the two so that the true situation can come to light.

B. The problem of the sixth age.

I. The course of the sixth age in general.

The allusions concerning the character of this final part of the sixth age, which is partly present and partly future, are scattered throughout the entire *Hexaemeron.* This is another indication that this problem was close to the heart of Bonaventure. But there is one primary citation concerning this question in which we find nearly all the themes of his speculation about the future; namely, *Collationes* XVI 29, vol. V. 408 a-b. We will proceed on the basis of this citation, and the other material will be brought in at the proper points along the way.

1. The texts.

In order to provide the necessary foundation for the following presentation, we will first give the texts with which we are concerned. In the left column is the basic text from which we are working; in the right column are the most important parallel texts which will help us gain a better understanding:[7]

Hoc tempore oportuit venire vitam per ordinem, qui haberet vitam propheticam (as parallel to 'praeclaritas vitae propheticae' in the OT, see Schema on p. 21)	XVI, 16, p. 405 b: Et necesse fuit, ut in hoc tempore veniret unus ordo, sc. habitus propheticus, similis ordini Jesu Christi, cuius caput esset "angelus ascendens ab ortu solis . . ." (Apoc. 7,2)

et conformis Christo.—Et dixit, quod iam venerat. Vide XXII 21 p. 440b.: Huic respondent Cherubim, hi sunt Praedicatores et Minores,+XXII 27 p. 441b: revelatio (respondet) Cherubim.
XV 28 p. 402: vide infra.

Hoc autem tempus est geminum, unde, sicut in passione Domini fuit primo lux, deinde tenebra, postea lux; sic necesse est, ut primo sit lux doctrinae et succedat Josias (4 Kg. 22; reign 638-608) Ezechiae (4 Kg. 18-20; reign 721-693), post quam facta est tribulatio Iudaeorum per capitivitatem. Necesse est enim, ut surgat unus princeps zelator ecclesiae qui vel erit vel iam fuit—et addidit. Utinam iam non fuerit—post quam fit obscuritas tribulationum.

Vide XXII 22 p. 441a: Quis autem iste ordo futurus sit vel iam sit...

Hoc tempore similiter Carolus (768-814) exaltavit ecclesiam, et ejus successores oppugnaverunt eam: tempore Henrici quarti (1056-1106) fuerunt duo papae, similiter tempore Frederici magni (1152-1190)[8] duo. Et certum est, quod aliquis inter eos voluit exterminare ecclesiam; sed "angelus ascendens ab ortu solis" clamavit quatuor angelis: "Nolite nocere terrae et mari, quousque signemus servos Dei nostri in frontibus eorum" (Apoc. 7,2).

vgl. XX 15 p. 428a: . . . consummabuntur passiones, quas modo corpus Christi patitur. Oportet enim surgere Herodem, sub quo illudatur Christus et Petrus incarceretur (presumably Frederick II. 1215-1250).[9]
XVI 16 p. 405 b, vide supra.
XXII 23 p. 441a, XXIII 3 p. 445b, XXIII 14 p. 447; De perf ev q. 2, a. 3, ad 12, V 164b; Legenda s. Franc, Prol 1,2, VIII 504b; c 4, 9 p. 515 a-b; vide infra Nr. II

Unde adhuc restat ecclesiae tribulatio.

XX 15 p. 428a, vide supra.
XXVII 28 p. 414b.

Et dictum est Angelo Philadelphiae, qui sextus est: "Haec dicit Sanctus

XX 29 p. 403b; Nota quod duodecim signationes sunt sub sexto sigillo et Verus; qui habet clavem David qui aperit et nemo claudit, claudit et nemo aperit. Scio opera tua, quia ecce, dedi coram te ostium apertum" (Apoc. 3, 7).

et sub sexto angelo . . . et sexto angelo, sc. Philadelphiae, qui interpretatur conservans hereditatem dictum est de clave David, . . . hoc est, dabo notitiam scripturarum isti sexto angelo.

Et dixit, quod intelligentia scripturae daretur, vel revelatio vel clavis David personae vel multitudini; et magis credo, quod multitudini.

XXIII 29 p. 449b: Hic est angelus sextus Philadelphiae, salvans, hereditatem. Relative to XXIV 4 p. 445b vide infra.
III 21 p. 347a and III 32 p. 348b do not belong here.

2. The prophetic schemata

This entire presentation is concerned with that final section of the great course of history which embraces 7 x 3 periods. We have already given the general schema above. Bonaventure is no longer satisfied with the comparative study of the Old Testament and the days of Creation. In order to cast some light on the darkness that envelops the events that are so imminent, he makes use of everything that can be of any assistance. So we come upon two new auxiliary schemata:

a) The series of seven from the Apocalypse are brought in. As regards their content, the seven series of seven in the Apocalypse are identical with one another according to the view of Bonaventure. Each one points to the same thing in a different way; namely, the seven-staged course of church history.[10] Consequently, the sixth figure of each series offers a new insight for the solution of the problem of the future.[11] This interpenetration of the various schemata leads to surprising results for Bonaventure, and often gives him cause to point out to his listeners the wonderful harmony of Scripture.[12] In particular, the following figures are used:

a) The sixth seal (Apoc. 6, 12-17 and c 7).[13] This is the richest citation, and it ultimately provides the real key for understanding his interpretation. It is under this seal that an event takes place, the concrete fulfillment of which can be seen with one's own eyes in the present: It is the appearance of the angel with the "Seal of the living God." This point must be treated separately and in detail later (II).

b) The angel of Philadelphia, to whom the sixth letter is addressed (Apoc. 3, 7-13).[14] The most significant and helpful clues in this text are: "clavis David" and "porta aperta." When these two are taken in connection with the sixth age of the Old Testament, which was an age of prophecy, they make it possible to predict that we may await a new insight into Scripture. This in turn makes it possible to draw conclusions which will have to be treated. It is in the same direction that the etymology of the word *Philadelphia* is worked out. This etymology is taken from the work of Haymo, and the name is understood to mean "Conservans hereditatem."[15]

c) In Apocalypse 21, 9, we read: "Then one of the seven angels who had the seven bowls full of the seven last plagues came and spoke to me: Come, I will show you the bride, the spouse of the Lamb." Concerning this, Bonaventure says that this must be the sixth of the seven angels with the bowls; but he does not make any detailed use of the vision of the bowls in his prophecy.[16]

d) Finally, the sixth trumpet is also taken into account. It is at the time of the sixth trumpet that the "opening of the book" (Apoc. 10) and the measuring and description of the city (Apoc. 11, 1 and 2; Apoc. 21, 9-22, 5) take place. This also points to a new understanding of Scripture. The vision of the new city is, indeed, already a vision of the seventh age which will be characterized by God's peace upon earth.[17]

From this, the basic lines for determining the final course of the sixth period are somewhat clear and unified. And when we see how everything falls together almost naturally for Bonaventure, then we can understand why he can close his schema with one statement which reveals unmistakably the hidden joy of a discoverer who has achieved such success: "Et sic patet, quomodo scriptura describit successiones temporum; et non sunt a casu et fortuna, sed mira lux est in eis et multae intelligentiae spirituales."[18]

b) By means of a typological explanation, the Passion of Jesus is extended from the "Head" to the "Body."[19] In the case of Jesus' own sufferings, there was first light, then darkness, then light again. Similarly, the Mystical Body must go this way of suffering; and on the sixth day of this way, it also must count on a similar alternation between darkness and light. Without a doubt, this division of the Passion is not taken directly from the Gospels. Rather, it is modeled after Bonaventure's closing Old Testament schema which we must study in greater detail. This schema itself is already a structuring of Old Testament events in accordance with the needs of Bonaventure's own interpretation of history. Therefore it is not fully clear what precisely is meant by this alternation of darkness and light relative to the historical course of the Passion. But from other notions of Bonaventure, this much is certain; he thought not only of two periods of light, but also of two periods of darkness for the Church before the final appearance of the glory of the seventh age.[20]

c) Surprisingly enough, the eschatological statements of Jesus play practically no role here. In the entire *Hexaemeron,* these statements are cited only three times; and in these cases, it is only the thought of the coming tribulation which is used; and even this thought is developed more significantly in the most important passages on the basis of other sources.[21] We may well see the reason for this in the fact that the simple and powerful eschatological message of Jesus offered practically no material for the speculations with which Bonaventure was concerned other than the idea of the great tribulation; and this was apparently almost self-evident. Actually the scriptural material may have seemed to be an obstacle, especially since it seemed to allow no room for the idea of the great peace of the seventh day.

3. Summary

Though there is a series of valuable indications in the Apocalypse which may be helpful in determining the concrete content of the near future, nonetheless the external framework of the schema is still determined by the Old Testament. This can be set up as follows:

praeclara-victoria +praeclara doctrina	— Ezechias or Ozias Manasses	— zelator ecclesiae — tribulatio	— Charlemagne —Henry IV; —angelus Frederick I. sexti sigilli *prophetia*
praeclaritas vitae propheticae	Josias	— zelator secundus[22]	— vel erit vel iam fuit
	Babylon. Exile	— tribulatio	— tribulatio, ex qua nascitur ordo futurus. (**XXII,** 23, p. 441a;
pax	Zorobabel	— ı estauratio- pax	**XX,** 15 p. 438a.) — pax, ultima revelatio.

The course of the coming historical period is presented by Bonaventure as follows. It is certain that Charlemagne was the great Zealot for the well-being of the Church corresponding to Ezechias or Ozias. In him, the Church of that period achieved a glorious victory and outstanding learning, which was clearly demanded by the Old Testament typology. Similarly, it is certain that Henry IV and Frederick I were the hostile kings corresponding to Manasses. They brought about for the Church that tribulation which had been predicted typologically. Further, the great growth of prophetism which took place in the corresponding period of travail in the Old Testament has already found a New Testament parallel in the appearance of the angel of the seals mentioned in *Apocalypse* 7 and in the prophetic movement initiated by him. We will give a detailed treatment of what is meant by this later in this work.

In any case, the course of history up to this point is clear. Indeed, up to now we are dealing with things that have already taken place. Nonetheless, this theological clarification of the past provides us with significant results for the interpretation of the future. For it becomes clear that now only two events separate us from the great peace of the seventh day. There must be a second "Charlemagne," who would correspond to Josias; he would be a second great Zealot for the Church of God. And corresponding to the Babylonian Exile of Israel, there must be a second great tribulation for the Church. Out of this time of tribulation will emerge the *ordo futurus;* the new People of God of the final age. (For this translation, see III, 1.)

Bonaventure indicates a degree of uncertainty in dating these events; but in any case they are understood to be imminent. He holds it as possible that the second Zealot of the Church is already present, and he allows for the possibility that the *novus ordo* has already begun. Yet his own viewpoint would seem to tend more to the opinion that both of these are still to come.[23] After this general clarification of the course of the coming final age, it remains for us to determine what meaning Bonaventure sees in the apocalyptic angel with the seals who has already appeared, and what he means by the *ordo futurus.* For it is here that his prophecy takes on concrete form and color for the first time.

But before we go on to this question, we would like to point out the combination of the prophetic-typological statements in the schema of the final age which we have just treated. The two-fold alternation of *zelator-tribulatio, zelator (secundus), tribulatio* is parallel to the series of Ezechias—Manasses—Josias—Babylonian Exile. This is strictly parallel to the two-fold alternation of light and darkness as Bonaventure had described it in the Passion of the Lord (*vide supra* under b.). From the first *tribulatio* onward, the apocalyptic concept of the sixth angel is joined with the Old Testament schema. The figure of the angel leads to the actual determination of the content of the last age in as far as the other apocalyptic types in the sixth position are related to it, as we indicated above. We will now treat this in greater detail.

II. The eschatological position of St. Francis.

1. Bonaventure's two-fold theology of Francis in general.[24]

As a Franciscan, Bonaventure—like the entire Order of Franciscans—saw Francis not simply as another Saint, but as a sign of the final age, as one sent by God. Francis had a very precisely determined and unexchangeable place within an exactly delimited historical line of salvation history. We can determine two tendencies in the theological understanding of Francis, which is always simultaneously a Franciscan eschatology.

a) *Francis—praeco Dei—John the Baptist—Elias.*

Francis had called himself the "Herald of a great King."[25] Taking this as a point of departure, Bonaventure sees Francis as the eschatological *praeco Dei,* as the resurrected John the Baptist. The word "Herald," which was originally used without any theological significance, easily provides a bridge to a new theological interpretation in which the word is applied to one who in fact is a "Voice crying in the desert." This one is the Herald of the Kingdom of God which has come upon us. From here, a further connection is obvious: The Lord Himself had called John the returned Elias (Mt. 11, 14; also Mk. 9, 12ff., and Lk. 1, 17). Consequently the two figures remain related to each other forever.

For this reason, when Francis has been designated as John the Baptist, it is only natural that he should be seen as Elias as well. The two names are used interchangeably to express the same idea.[26]

But this alternation of names is not without significance, for the name of Elias points more clearly to an eschatological dimension than does the name of John the Baptist. The prophecy of Malachy, which was so important in the New Testament, was connected with the name of Elias, and not with that of John. "Behold, I send you the prophet Elias, before the great and terrible day arrives . . ." (Mal. 3, 23). From this citation, it is fully clear what Bonaventure means when he says: In Francis, Elias has appeared.[27] Furthermore,

the name of Elias makes it possible to connect Francis with
the historical prophecy of Joachim of Fiore who had related
the biblical expectation of Elias (Mal. 3, 23) to the apocalyptic prediction of the two witnesses (Apoc. 11, 3ff). As a
result, he predicts the appearance of a new Elias and a new
Henoch at the beginning of the third period of history. It was
possible to see this prediction fulfilled in Francis and Dominic.
Bonaventure has these prophecies in mind when he writes:
". . . Elias must come; he will restore all things again (—he
will restore the state of the *ecclesia primitiva*); with him
Henoch also will come. But the Beast will overcome the two
witnesses."[28]

b) *Francis, the "angelus ascendens ab ortu solis."*

The understanding of St. Francis as the "Angel who ascends
from the rising of the sun" (Apoc. 7,2) became familiar to
the Order through Bonaventure, and retained its significance
for centuries.[29] The first indication of this idea in Bonven-
ture's work is found in the *Quaestiones disputatae* concerning
evangelical perfection[30] which date to the end of 1255, or in
any event, before the fifth of October, 1256. But he says
nothing about this again until his *Legenda maior*. In the Prologue to this work, he places the apocalyptic interpretation of
Francis side by side with the theological treatment of Elias.[31]
At any rate, the designation of Francis as Elias is still clearly
preferred. Ideas and terms from the theology of Elias and
John are used six times. This indicates a decided preference,
since the image of the angel is used expressly only twice.[32]
But in the *Collationes in Hexaemeron,* the relationship is
reversed. In this work we have found only one citation referring to Elias[33] in contrast to five which refer to the angel.[34]

Of these five, three must be seen as texts of basic significance for the entire work.[35] It is clear that here the theological treatment of Elias has lost some of its significance. The notion of the "angelus ascendens ab ortu solis" has become the central concept of Bonaventure's theological understanding of Francis as well as of his theology of the history of salvation. We will now treat this in detail.[36]

2. A detailed treatment of the theology of Francis in the Hexaemeron.

a) *The figure of the "angel with the seal of the living God."*

What does Bonaventure intend to say with the figure of the "angelus ascendens ab ortu solis?" In order to answer this question, we must first give a brief presentation of the content of the apocalyptic text. The citation in question is found within the first series of plagues which are let loose by the opening of the seven seals of the heavenly book. A scene is inserted after the sixth plague (= the sixth seal). Four angels stand at the four corners of the earth and create a great silence by holding back the four winds. At this moment, "another angel" ascends from the rising of the sun[37] "with the seal of the living God." He commands the plagues to cease until the servants of God have been marked with the seal of God. They are 144,000 in number.

There are two facts in the life of St. Francis which apparently occasioned the application of this citation to his person, for both of these facts seem to point immediately in this direction. First there is the fact that Francis himself was accustomed to sign all his letters with the tau-sign "T". Here there is an obvious connection with Ez. 9, 4 which says that those who were to be saved in Jerusalem were to be marked with this sign. The *Legenda* relates that Francis attributed to him-

self the historical function of the man in the linen garment,
a fact which must be evaluated as genuinely historical according to the indication of the Letter to Brother Leo.[38] Since
Ez. 9, 4 had been connected with Apoc. 7, 2 already in
antiquity, a first line of thought arises here which could lead
to such a theological interpretation of Francis. Even more
important, however, is another event — the Stigmatization —
which stood as something unique and unparalleled; it all but
cried out for an interpretation. Such an interpretation offered
itself on the basis of Apoc. 7, 2. Had not the seal of the
living God — the figure of the crucified Christ — been impressed on the body of the Saint? Does not the image of the
Apocalypse acquire here its real coloration and significance?
As for the full actuality and the moving probability of this
interpretation, this was to come in the encounter of this event
with the entirely independent prophecy of the Abbot of Fiore[39]
who had in brilliant words predicted the coming of the angel
with the seal of the living God. He had seen in this angel the
novus dux de Babylone and the *universalis pontifex sanctae
Hierusalem.* He would receive "full freedom for the renewal
of the Christian religion."[40] In view of the amazing coincidence of the particular factors, it is no longer surprising that
the identification of Francis with the angel of the Apocalypse
should have become an historico-theological axiom of practically unimpeachable certitude. Even Bonaventure could not close
himself to the suggestive power of this fact. As a result,
apocalyptic prophecy and the actualized reality of the life of
Francis are woven together for Bonaventure ever more into
an insoluble unity.[41]

b) *The community of the 144,000 sealed.*

For the general structure of the Bonaventurian theology of

history, the interpretation of the rest of the vision of *Apocalypse* 7 is no less important than the figure of the angel from the rising of the sun. In the text of Scripture, this angel bears the seal of God; and with it, he seals the 144,000 elect from the twelve tribes of Israel (Apoc. 7, 2-8). What significance can this have when it is applied to St. Francis? At this point we will present the difficult text which answers this question (*Hex.* XXIII 14, Vol. V, 447 a). We will also add the most important and most illuminating parallel texts. We will give the text first in the original and then in translation. Our translation will be as literal as possible, but we will attempt to work into it also the important ideas which are to be found in the parallel texts.

Sic anima contemplativa signatur a Deo. Unde sub sexto angelo dicitur quod apparuit angelus, "habens signum Dei vivi" (Apoc. 7,2), hoc fuit in assignatione Jerusalem ut in caelo consistentis. Huic angelo apparuit signum expressivum,

quantum ad modum vivendi consonum isti signo, quod est, quod signatur: "Ex tribu Juda duodecim milia signati" etc. (Apoc. 7, 5ff):

Relative to expressivum-expressum-impressum, *vide* XXII 23: tertius ordo correspondet Seraphim, et isti sunt propinqui Jerusalem et non habent nisi evolare . . . Et dicebat, quod illa apparitio Seraph Beato Francisco, quae fuit expressiva et impressa, ostendebat, quod iste ordo illi (=beato Francisco) respondere debeat, sed tamen pervenire ad hoc per tribulationes. *vide* XXVI 20. XXIII 16-30: Extension of the 12 tribes=the 144,000 sealed because of the basic characteristics of the anima contemplativa.

XXIII 2 p. 445 a: Si autem ducantur duodecim per duodecim, erunt centum quadraginta quatuor, numerus scilicet civitatis Jerusalem. Anima enim sic hierarchizata est civitas, in qua Deus habitat et videtur . . .

XXIII 4 p. 445 b: . . . oportet, quod in fine generetur ecclesia contemplativa. Ecclesia enim contemplativa et anima totum habet in se, quod ecclesia in multis. . .

et hoc est: qui habet hanc triplicem lucem elevantem

sc solarem — lunarem — stellarem (Deus — ecclesia militans — ascensus + descensus + reascensus animae) XXII p. 437-444; XXIII 1 p. 444-445 a.

triplicem oportet quod habeat perfectionem respondentem caritati.

triplex perfectio: Without obviously clear parallels (Poverty, chastity, obedience? Vide De perf. ev. q. 2-4: V p. 125-198).

Unde signare hoc modo est per professionem ad hoc alligare et imprimere signum, ut respondeat illi signo caritatis.

Leg maj Prol Vol. VIII 504 b: . . . officium, quod habuit (Franciscus) . . . signandi (que) thau super frontes virorum (Ez. 9, 4) Cf. *ibid* c 4, 9 VIII p. 515 a-b.

We could translate this text somewhat as follows: ". . . Thus the 'contemplative soul' is sealed by God. Therefore it is said under the sixth angel that (another) angel appeared bearing the seal of the living God. This took place in relationship to the sealing of the heavenly Jerusalem. Now to this angel (of the seal i.e. Francis), there appeared an expressive sign (the Crucified in the form of a Seraphim. It is expressive in so far as it was able to leave behind the 'impression' of the Stigmata).[42] As regards the manner of life intended here, it is synonymous with that sign concerning which it is said: From the tribe of Juda 12,000 were sealed, etc. This means: He who has the 'three-fold elevating light' (which constitutes the essence of contemplation), must also have the three-fold perfection which corresponds to love. (I.e. he must have the monastic form of life without which the state of contemplation is unthinkable.) 'To sign with this seal' (i.e. the process of sealing described in *Apoc.* 7 is now clarified) means, according to this, to oblige someone by profession (=through the vows) to this (=to the contemplative form of life) and to impress on him a seal which corresponds to the seal of love."

Here it becomes clear not only that St. Francis himself is the bearer of the seal of God by reason of the Stigmata, but also that he shares in the function of the apocalyptic angel of the seal. He is to share in the task of sealing the elect of the final age. It is his task to sign the 144,000 elect with the seal of God, and in this way to establish the community of the final age. This new and final "Order" which is to arise out of the tribulation of the final days will be a Franciscan Order; its proper form of life will be that of St. Francis.[43] With this, the one question that leaves all the other problems of our text in the background now becomes acute. To what extent can we identify the actual Order of Francis, which already exists and of which Bonaventure is the General, with the Order of the final age with its 144,000 who are the mystical expression of the *ecclesia contemplativa* in which the sixth day will be transformed into the Sabbath Rest of the seventh day? In order to answer this question and thus complete the description of the sixth age and its course, we will set aside for the present all the other questions which arise here, especially the important problem of the relation of salvation history and mysticism, which must also be decided of the basis of this group of texts.

1. The development of the question prior to Bonaventure.

Joachim of Fiore clearly expresses the idea of a new Order in which the *ecclesia contemplativa* of the final age is to find its proper and definitive form of existence.[44] In this context, the concept "Order" receives a new meaning. As Benz correctly observes, *novus ordo* can be translated as a "new order of salvation" and a "new religious social order."[45] Thus, the entire eschatological hope of the Calabrian abbot is expressed in summary form in the concept of the new Order. With this word, he attempts to set down the essential form of the new age which is yet to come. We could perhaps translate *novus ordo* as the "new People of God." It was almost necessary from the very nature of the case to see Joachim's prophecy of the "angelus ascendens ab ortu solis" fulfilled in the person of the Poverello. Even more clearly, perhaps, must the community of the Saint of Assisi have awakened the thought of the *novus ordo.* It may well be that all the various *Legenda* of St. Francis depict a theologically interpreted "Francis of faith" instead of the simple "Francis of history."[46] But we can be certain, nonetheless, that Francis himself was led by a consciousness that was strongly eschatological though lacking in apocalyptic tone.[47] By this distinction, we mean that Francis was far removed from any historico-theological speculation concerning the nature and the time of the end; but in an amazing and entirely authentic though totally unreflected way, he was filled with that primitive eschatological mood of Christianity which is expressed in the statement: "The kingdom of God is at hand" (Mk. 1, 15). In fact we can say that without this eschatological consciousness Francis and his message is no more understandable than is Christ and the message of the New Testament, the eschatological character of which is being brought out ever more clearly at the present.[48] In fact, every interpretation of Franciscanism which abstracts from its original determination with regard to the history of salvation and, more precisely, with regard to eschatology, ultimately misses the essence of Franciscanism.[49] The unsophisticated and unrealistic way in which Francis tried to make the Sermon on the Mount the rule[50] of his "new People"[51] is not understood properly if we designate it as "idealism," as W. Nigg has shown.[52] It is understandable only as the fruit of a vital consciousness that has raised itself above the question of the possible, and above the institutions and forms of this aeon; it is dominated by that eschatological confidence of the New Testament, which, as it were, puts an end to time. It believes in the Father who clothes the flowers of the field and nourishes the birds of the air, who neither sow nor reap nor gather into barns (cfr. Mt. 6, 25-32). It is at this point that we come back to our original question. Joachim had predicted that in the new and final church of the Spirit the Sermon on the Mount would be observed literally "sine glossa." This development would consist in the gradual overthrow of that *licencia* which was still allowed for the men of the second and third ages.[53] Must not this also have directed attention to the Poor Man of Assisi who, in his testament, forbade every explanation of the Rule in "strict obedience?"[54] And it was a Rule, after all, which was intended to be nothing else but an application of the unfalsified and literal Sermon on the Mount and the Gospel of Jesus Christ.[55]

This development of thought underwent another change in the light of the pseudo-Joachimite *Commentary on Jeremias,* which apparently attempted to promote a positive cooperation between the Franciscans and the Dominicans by proclaiming not one but two new Orders. From among the many images used to designate these Orders, we choose the following:

Ox — Ass
Elias — Henoch
Paul — John
Joseph — Benjamin
The two Witnesses of the Apocalypse (c. 11)[56]

No doubt, the anonymous forger could have made use of genuine texts of Joachim for his purpose; for the Abbot of Fiore had said that at the end of the sixth age God would send two Orders to the world. One would have the task of leading the spiritual People in the desert as Moses had done; the other would have the task of living in solitude far from the community of men as Elias had done.[57] But an important difference between Joachim and pseudo-Joachim appears if we compare this text from the *Concordia veteris et novi testamenti* with another from the *Enchiridion in Apocalypsin.*[58] While pseudo-Joachim apparently considers these two Orders to be final and definitive,[59] the Abbot of Fiore himself ascribes a provisional significance to them. They are to prepare for the transition from the sixth to the seventh age. They correspond to the angels of the communities of Philadelphia and Laodicea; "they are passing on to the third stage, yet they still share in the second stage." "They are more spiritual than those which have preceded them; they are less spiritual and less contemplative, however, than those which will follow them. They will still be concerned with scientific work and the pursuit of knowledge[60] whereas the spiritual men of the third age will be already in possession of the knowledge of truth and will strive only to savor heavenly things." According to Joachim himself, there will be only one final Order; but the period of transition will give rise to two temporary Orders. We will see how Bonaventure reaches back beyond pseudo-Joachim to Joachim himself and appropriates Joachim's solution as his own.

2. The solution of Bonaventure.

We must distinguish two questions. First there is the question of the nature and form of the new Order in itself; then there is the concrete, historical question of the relation of this Order to the Franciscan Order. Here the question of the present historical moment finds its most pointed formulation in the view of Bonaventure.

a) *Nature and form of the ordo ultimus.*

For Bonaventure, the basic statement concerning the new and final Order is the same as it had been for Joachim: It will be an Order of *contemplatio*.[61] But this *contemplatio* is to be a new insight into Scripture. It is here that Scripture will be fully and truly opened, so that we can speak of a new and extensive "revelation" which consists in a new understanding of the old Scriptures.[62] We will have to give a fuller treatment to this idea as well as to the concept of revelation that lies behind it (Ch. 2).

This Order is prefigured by Paul and Benjamin[63] as well as by John,[64] Joseph of Egypt,[65] Moses,[66] and Daniel.[67] But the primary types are Benjamin-Paul and John. The connection between Benjamin and Paul is ancient, and Paul himself had paved the way for it.[68] It is based on the parallel between the Apostles and the twelve Partriarchs of Israel;[69] it sees Paul as the youngest, as the one born out of time, and as the beloved of the Father. Besides this, Rachel, the mother of Benjamin is the type of the *vita contemplativa,* as we have already indicated; and Benjamin himself shares in this function. He thus contributes to the formation of the figure of Paul into the new type of the contemplative life. In the context of the typology of the Orders, it is only natural that Benjamin, the child of the *vita contemplativa,* should be the the type of that last Order which the Church brings forth on her way through history: the *ordo contemplativus.*[70] But Paul himself, by reason of his own personality, is a fitting type of this new community. He is a man who could say of himself, "We proclaim wisdom among the perfect; not the wisdom of this world, but the secret and hidden wisdom which no eye has seen, and no ear has heard, nor has it entered into the heart of man; but it has been revealed to us by the Spirit of God."[71] Such a man had no need of the mediatory figure of Benjamin in order to be able to prefigure that Order in which the long-hidden mysteries of wisdom should become a public and revealed wisdom for a new age. The text of *II Corinthians* which describes the ecstasy in which Paul was taken up into the third heaven was used to clarify this statement about the wisdom of God,[72] and it served to confirm the view that the "revelation" on which the wisdom of the "perfect" is based is a revelation arising from mystical understanding. Consequently, Paul appears as the anticipation and the sign of the final age.

Here we see that it was not only the final Order that determined the way in which Paul was understood, but the figure of Paul helped to form the concept of the final Order. Now we can develop further the clarification which we gave above. As a contemplative Order, the new Order will be also a community that enjoys the deepest and the final "revelation." It is in this Order that the wisdom which had formerly been limited to the circle of the *perfecti* will truly become "public."[73] We have already touched on the axiom that stands behind this application of the typology of Paul: the Final Age = the First Age. This axiom predicts that at the end of time there will be a full realization of all that was present for a short time in the primitive community, and which pointed toward the future.[74]

The other important type is the figure of the Apostle John. In contrast to Pseudo-Joachim's *Commentary on Jeremias,* Bonaventure sees this type to be identical with the type of Paul. That is, the two figures point not to two different Orders but to one and the same *Ordo futurus.*[75] Bonaventure, like Joachim, connects the typology of John with Jesus' statement: "Sic eum volo manere, donec veniam" (Jn.21, 22).[76] While this statement has no real meaning when it is applied simply to the individual figure of John, it begins to take on genuine significance when it is interpreted in terms of the theology of history. It proclaims that the definitive form of existence is presented in the figure of John, a form of existence which will endure after the abrogation of all that is provisional until the return of the Lord. It hardly needs to be proved that John, who was known since the Patristic Age as the "Eagle" among the Evangelists[77] because of his Gospel, is a particularly apt type of the *ordo contemplativus.*

But for the concrete, historical localization, a third figure is even more helpful than Paul or John. This is the figure of St. Francis. To the two statements: "Paulus, per quem significatur ordo futurus",[78] and "iste ordo intelligitur per Joannem",[79] Bonaventure adds a third: "iste ordo illi (= beato

Francisco) respondere debeat."[80] It is even stated that Francis belonged to this Order: "De isto (sc. ordine) videtur fuisse Franciscus."[81] It is obviously an erroneous conclusion determined by an apologetic tendency when the Scholion of the Quaracchi edition attempts to obviate this difficulty by saying that "order" is apparently used here in a broader sense so that it extends from the primitive church to the end of time; since both John and Francis are presented as members of this Order.[82] We hope to have shown clearly above that Paul and John are prophetic, anticipatory types. (Such was Joachim's viewpoint as well.) But each individual text that treats of a *futurus ordo* shows with sufficient clarity that a new, future state of salvation is intended, namely, the community of the seventh day. This community, therefore, has a very definite, delimited historical place. Furthermore, these texts show clearly that we are not concerned with a purely spiritual community of mystics which would be extended over the entire time of church history.

But it is not said that Francis is already the actual founder of this Order; nor that his "empirical Order" — the Order of Franciscans — is already this "eschatological Order" of the seventh day. But St. Francis must be placed in a different and a more immediate relation to that future Order than John and Paul simply on the basis of his place in history which we attempted to determine above. In some way, the real historical beginning of this Order is given with him.[83] And so we come back again for the last time to the question with which we began this section: How is the "empirical Order of Franciscans" related to the "eschatological *ordo futurus?*" We must give our attention to this question.

b) *The Franciscan Order and the ordo futurus.*

a) *The distinction between the two Orders.*

The decisive thesis of the Spirituals involved the full identification of the actual Franciscan Order (esp. its Spiritual branch) with the *ordo* of the final age. The proper, characteristic attitude of the Spirituals is pointedly summarized in this relationship which identifies the two Orders as promise and fulfillment. The fact that Bonaventure was clearly opposed to the Spirituals at least at the beginning of his activity as General[84] makes it probable from the start that he did not accept this full identification. But as far as this question is concerned, we do not have to be satisfied with suppositions. There is one citation in which Bonaventure clearly and expressly distinguishes the two Orders from one another. This is found in the schema in which he draws up the typological parallels between the various hierarchies — the divine, the "heavenly" (= the hierarchy of angels), and the various expressions of the ecclesiastical hierarchy. This schema, which is built on the number 3, is the most important schema of the entire *Hexaemeron* with the exception of the seven-part historical schema given above (p. 21). Because of its special importance, we present it here on a separate page (p. 47); we have omitted the less important elements.

HEX XXII 1-22, p. 437-444a

XXII 2, p. 438a: Oportet ergo, quod ecclesia militans habeat ordines correspondentes hierarchiae illustranti. Distinguentur autem tripliciter: uno modo secundum rationem processuum; alio modo secundum rationem ascensuum, tertio modo secundum rationem exercitiorum.

Processus

(ecclesia) in tempore nascitur et procedit (3)

ordines	fundamentales	—Pater (5)	
patriarchalis	(Pater in se	—Throni	—fides
prophetalis	in Filio	—Cherubim	—illuminatio +prophetia
	in SpS)	—Seraphim	—caritas
apostolicus	promoventes	—Filius (5)	
	(Filius in Patre	—Dominationes	
martyres	in se	—Virtutes	
confessores	in SpS)	—Potestates	
virgines			
	consummantes	—Spiritus Sanctus (5)	
praesidentes	(SpS in Patre	—Principatus	
magistratus	in Filio	—Archangeli	
regulares	in se)	—Angeli	

Ascensus

purgativi

ostiarii	—Angeli
lectores	—Archangeli
exorcistae	—Principatus

illuminativi

acolythi	—Potestates
subdiaconi	—Virtutes
levitae	—Dominationes

perfectivi

sacerdotes	—Throni
episcopi	—Cherubim
patriarchae	—Seraphim

"Si autem sic esset ordinatio interius sicut exterius, optima esset". Nr. 15

Exercitia (16)

vita activa—Pater (16)
ordo laicus

plebes	—Angeli
consules	—Archangeli
principes	—Principatus

permixta—Filius (16)
ordo clericalis

ministerialis	—Potestates
sacerdotalis	—Virtutes
pontificalis	—Dominationes

contemplativa—Spiritus S. (16)
ordo monasticus

supplicatorii	—Throni
	—Cherubim
	—Seraphim

"et in his consummabitur ecclesia" 22

Nr. 9: . . . oportet, quod (ecclesia) . . . compleatur per Spiritum Sanctum. Per ordinem regulantium et regulatorum comprehenditur vita monastica; et isti sunt ultimi, quia oportet mundum consummari in castitate.

Regarding the relation between the *apostoli-seraphim* with the *regulares-angeli*, see what has been said and will be said about the axiom, "Beginning = End." as well as the rest of this schema. (Compare Nr. 9 with Nr. 22 in the text.)

20-22 names the orders which are concretely intended:
Supplicatorii —the ordo monasticus sive albus sive niger; speculativi—Praedicatores et Minores; sursumactivi—the ordo ultimus.

The importance of this text is obvious at first sight. We have already rejected the notion that Bonaventure opposed the Augustinian schema of seven ages to the schema of the three ages. As we have seen, Bonaventure accepted the double-seven schema of Joachim and inserted this into the very center of his theology of history in place of the simple seven-schema of Augustine. These two schemata must be clearly distinguished. The text before us now shows that the other part of the rejected opinion is also incorrect, for here we find a trinitarian structure of history. Following the example of Joachim, this would envision three stages in history related to the Father, the Son, and the Spirit. There is an antithesis and a synthesis between Joachim and Bonaventure which is far more subtle than a quick glance at the text might indicate. It would go beyond the limits of our study if we were to work out in detail how this text implies both Yes and No to Joachim.[85] We simply point out that this schema does not contain any chance elements. In as far as it presents the three different forms of hierarchy each with its own levels, it indicates three different aspects, none of which can be bypassed without doing harm to the truth. There is, first, the aspect of ecclesiastical office;[86] here the official clerical church is and remains the highest level in the hierarchy. This aspect, which pertains more to the externals of the Church,[87] is necessary and justified; but it is not the only one. It must be supplemented by another aspect which we can call "pneumatic." (This points to the fundamental problem of Office and Pneuma which was brought to a critical state in the Spiritualist controversy.[88]) Here it is true to say: "Though the position of the prelates is at the highest point in the order of ascent, yet it is only in the center as regards the order of activ-

ity ..."[89] These two schemata, which attempt to achieve a
balance between Pneuma and Office, are finally drawn into a
historical framework by the first schema. But this historical
construct brings about a reversal of the relations. The *Regu-
lares* are historically the *novissimi;* but as regards their rank,
or more precisely because of their rank, they remain *primi.*[90]
For the present, we must bypass the other problems of this
text which offers a synthesis of history, office, and Pneuma
that is structured in terms of the Trinitarian order described
earlier.

We will now return to our question and study the relationship between the Order of Franciscans and the eschatological
Order of Francis on the basis of this citation.

In the light of the schema given above, this question is very
easy to answer. In the third column, under *vita contemplativa,*
the individual Orders are given by name and placed in the
hierarchy. The ancient monastic Orders are placed in the
lowest group, which corresponds to the choir of Thrones in
heavenly hierarchy. This includes the Cistercians, the Premonstratensians, the Carthusians, etc. The Cherubic Order, whose
proper characteristic is *speculatio,* is represented by the Franciscans and the Dominicans. The coming final Order will
correspond to the Seraphim; it will be "Seraphic." The question as to whether it has already begun or whether it is entirely
of the future is expressly left open.[91] This amounts to an
express denial of the identity between the Order of Franciscans already in existence and the Order of Francis, which is
eschatological. Here we have Bonaventure's answer to the
Spirituals; but in order to avoid a gross over-simplification,
we must be fully aware of the fact that Bonaventure is definitely of the opinion that the eschatological Order must be an

Order of Francis. This Order will see and venerate in Francis
its true beginning; and Francis himself belongs entirely to the
ordo seraphicus and not to the *ordo cherubicus.*[92] Bonaventure is also of the opinion that the concrete Order of Franciscans is only *cherubicus* and not *seraphicus.* This means that
the present Order of Franciscans is not yet the true Order of
Francis.[93] In his own person, Francis anticipates the eschatological form of life which will be the general form of life
in the future.

This realistic distinction between Francis and Franciscanism
is not a new discovery of the liberal school of Franciscan research.[94] It had already been expressed by the great Franciscan General of the thirteenth century. In it we find not only
Bonaventure's answer to the Spirituals, but also the key to
understanding his conduct as General and his own personal
manner of life as a Franciscan. Gilson has already pointed
this out in a different context and with a difference of emphasis.[95] In carrying out his office as General and in living
his own personal life, he could set aside the *sine glossa* which
he knew from the Testament of Francis to be the real will of
the Founder. He could do this because the proper historical
hour for such a form of life had not yet struck. As long as
it is still the sixth day, the time is not yet ripe for that radically Christian form of existence which Francis was able to
realize in his own person at the divine command. Without
feeling any infidelity towards the holy Founder, Bonaventure
could and had to create institutional structures for his Order,
realizing all the while that Francis had not wanted them.[96]
It is a too facile and, in the final analysis, an unlikely method
to see this as a falsification of true Franciscanism. In reality,
it was precisely the historical accomplishment of Bonaventure

that he discerned the true historical situation in the controversy between the visionaries and the laxists and that he sub-
mitted himself in humble recognition of the limits demanded
by reality. Bonaventure recognized that Francis' own eschatological form of life could not exist as an institution in this
world; it could be realized only as a break-through of grace
in the individual until such time as the God-given hour would
arrive at which the world would be transformed into its final
form of existence. Everything else is naively visionary. Bonaventure was able to give the Order a form that could be
realized in this world because he recognized this fact and had
the courage to accept it. His first concern in doing this was
to preserve whatever could be preserved of that radically
eschatological character.[97] Since the beginning of the liberal
school of research, we have become accustomed to academic
protests against what is felt to be a watering-down of Franciscanism. There is a destructive quality in these complaints,
for they lack the seriousness required in such an important
issue. Generally they do not arise from a desire for the real
renewal of the eschatological form of life. Rather, they stem
from the mere desire for criticism. The more such criticism
fails to assess the limits of possibility, the more it loses in
significance.

b) The stages of approach.

We have already stressed that Bonaventure attempted to
preserve whatever could be saved of the eschatological character and task of the Franciscans in as far as this was possible
within the limits demanded by the given historical situation.
This can be seen already in the schema given above. As we
have said, the difference between the *ordo seraphicus* and the

ordo cherubicus can be seen in their proper activity; that of
the *ordo cherubicus* is *speculatio*; that of the *ordo seraphicus*
is *sursumactio*. Both the Dominicans and the Franciscans belong to the *ordo cherubicus*, but they stand on different levels.
For the Dominicans, the primary emphasis is on *speculatio*
while *unctio* holds a secondary place. For the Franciscans,
it is just the reverse; for them, *unctio* has primacy over *speculatio*.[98] Here they clearly stand at the bridge to the final age.
In an obvious reference to the letter of St. Francis to Anthony
of Padua,[99] Bonaventure says that St. Francis was willing to
have his Brothers cultivate learning; but they must first do
that which they teach. "For of what use is it to know much
and to savor nothing?"[100] This passage is of significance also
because it indicates that Bonaventure identifies the Franciscan
and Dominican Orders with the two Orders of Joachim which
stand at the transition from the second to the third age, and
yet belong to the second age. They are very much concerned
with the *gustare*, and yet cannot do without the *studere*.[101]
Here as in many other points, the solution of Joachim is taken
over substantially.

Two other considerations are perhaps more important. We
must consider the fact that within this schema there are parallels also on the horizontal level. The Apostles are parallel
to the Seraphim; so is the *ordo ultimus*. Consequently, we
find the further parallel, *ordo ultimus — apostoli*. The apostolic life will be restored in the men of the final Order:
The end and the beginning coincide. But the primary characteristic of the apostolic life is poverty.[102] On the other
hand, Bonaventure is untiring in his efforts to inculcate poverty as the essential characteristic of the concrete Order of

Franciscans.[103] Would not this naturally involve a close relation between the two Orders?

For the second consideration, the same horizontal parallel is of importance. If the *seraphici* and the *apostoli* are parallel to each other, then the *prophetae* and the *cherubici* are as well. This parallel is worked out expressly in another passage.

OT	NT
tempus quartum illustrationis prophetarum	tempus quartum religionum multiplicationis, quod respondet . . . maxime Rechabitis . . . qui pauperes erant. [104]

From a functional viewpoint, the *revelatio* which is attributed to the *cherubici* in the hierarchic schema (p. 47) corresponds to the *vita prophetica*.[105] But in the seven-fold schema (p. 21) and elsewhere, *revelatio* is seen to be the privileged possession of the final age and of the new Order.[106] Anyone attempting to interpret this text might conclude to an identity between the Orders if it were ñot for the fact that the opposite view is expressly stated elsewhere. But perhaps we would have to reckon with the possibility that the schemata used by Bonaventure originally presupposed an identity and only later had to be reworked in another sense. This would also help to clarify a series of lesser inconsistencies.[107]

c) The theory of defection.

Many texts seem to indicate that Bonaventure believed that the Franciscan Order was originally determined to be the final, eschatological Order immediately, and was to bring about the beginning of a new era. In this case, it would have been the failure of its members that impeded the realization of this.

Now the Order would have to be purged by another final tribulation before it would be able to find its true and final form.[108] As a matter of fact, it may have been precisely this idea that provided Bonaventure with a bridge to the view that affirmed the factual separation of the two Orders without a basic rupture between them. Here at the end of our search through the Bonaventurian prophecy of history we give the primary text that seems to be closely related to this idea:." . . . He (= Bonaventure: the *Reportator* speaks) added: Give heed to your calling (1 Cor. 1,26); it is a great calling. And he said that God will judge the poor according to their tribulations (Jb. 36, 6): they "shall judge the twelve tribes of Israel" (Lk. 22,30). For such people, contemplation is in place in this life. Such contemplation, however, can be attained only through the greatest simplicity; and this simplicity is possible only together with the greatest poverty. And this will be the characteristic sign of the final Order. The intention of St. Francis is directed to perfect poverty. He (= Bonaventure) said also: We have departed far from our original state. Therefore God allows tribulation to come upon us so that we may be led back to that state which holds the Land of Promise . . ."[109]

c) *Summary.*

If we may attempt to give a brief summary of Bonaventure's view of the historical situation of his own times on the basis of what has been said up to now, we could state it as follows. In the eyes of Bonaventure, the situation of peace before the final storm indicated in *Apocalypse* 7 has begun with Francis. Francis is the apocalyptic angel of the seal from whom should come the final People of God, the 144,000 who are sealed.

This final People of God is a community of contemplative men; in this community the form of life realized in Francis will become the general form of life. It will be the lot of this People to enjoy already in this world the peace of the seventh day which is to precede the Parousia of the Lord.

Though this new People of God may rightfully be called Franciscan, and though it must be said that it is only in this new People that the real intention of the Poverello will be realized, nonetheless, this final Order is in no way identical with the present Order of Franciscans. It may be that the present Order was originally destined to inaugurate the new People immediately. But even if this had been the case, the failure of its members has frustrated this immediate determination. For the present, the Dominican and the Franciscan Orders stand together at the inauguration of a new period for which they are preparing, but which they cannot bring to actuality by themselves. When this time arrives, it will be a time of *contemplatio*, a time of the full understanding of Scripture, and in this respect, a time of the Holy Spirit who leads us into the fullness of the truth of Jesus Christ.[110]

CHAPTER II

THE CONTENT OF BONAVENTURE'S HOPE FOR SALVATION.

#6. The Graces of the Final Age: Pax and Revelatio.

From the treatment given thus far, it should be sufficiently clear that Bonaventure's theology of history culminates in his hope for an age of God-given Sabbath-Rest within history. The real content of this age is described with the word "Peace."[1] This idea offers no difficulties. Every hope of salvation in this world must view "Peace" as the first and most necessary pre-supposition of a better age. If we reflect further on the tempestuous age in which the work of Bonaventure originated,[2] on the promises of peace found in Isaias and Ezechiel on which Bonaventure relies,[3] on Joachim's renewal of these promises,[4] on the basic significance which Francis himself gave to the greeting of peace, as well as on the primary position which the message of peace held within the Order,[5] then we would hardly have to search further for an explanation.

But there is another aspect which is more difficult. The final People of God (the "New Order") is described as an *ecclesia contemplativa*.[6] The meaning of this is clearly stated elsewhere in as far as it is said that there will be a *revelatio*. What is the meaning of this? Is this a resurgence of the idea of an *evangelium aeternum* rejected by the Church? And if not, then what does it mean? This question must now be clarified.

56

#7. **Basic Considerations concerning revelatio.**

1. General limits of Bonaventure's statements on revelation.

In order to gain some insight into the difficult problem that arises here, we will first make some general observations concerning the notion of *revelatio* in the thought-structure of Bonaventure without in any way coming close to a clarification of the whole of this difficult problem. This must be reserved for a later work; what is said here is admittedly provisional.

First, it must be emphasized that Bonaventure did not know the question concerning the nature of revelation in the same sense in which it is treated by our current fundamental theology in the tract *De revelatione.* This would seem to be the clear conclusion from an exact study of the *Sentence Commentary.* the *Quaestiones disputatae,* as well as commentaries on Scripture, and those works which may be called Franciscan in a narrower sense. We could say that Bonaventure does not treat of "revelation" but of "revelations."[1] Or to express this more in line with Greek thought, Bonaventure recognizes and deals with the many individual revelations which have taken place in the course of history; but he never inquires about the one revelation which has taken place in these many revelations. It is primarily the latter which our current theology attempts to treat in the tract on revelation. In Bonaventure, we find clear and detailed analyses concerning the process of revelation;[2] but all these texts treat the individual acts of revelation which can be repeated, and which in fact are often repeated by God. In these acts, God turns toward the individual recipient of the revelation. But we do not find a treatment of that

unique revelation which stands behind all the individual, repeated instances of revelation. Naturally, however, the element of uniqueness and permanence which is essential to
Christianity is thoroughly recognized. It is expressed in such
concepts as *Christus incarnatus, scriptura, doctrina,* and *fides.*[3]
Nonetheless, there is no easily determined, systematic unity
between these two types of statements.

This means that the Bonaventurian concept of *revelatio*
(and *inspiratio, manifestatio, apertio*)[4] is not immediately
comparable with similar concepts of modern theology. It is
only with this express reservation that the following statements can be made. We deliberately avoid any attempt to
compare these notions with those of modern theology even
though such a comparison would be possible. Instead, we will
merely try to present the ideas of Bonaventure as they stand.
In the following development, when the word *revelatio* is used
side by side with the English word "revelation," it is always
done under these limitations.

2. Terminological considerations.

The basic affirmation that *revelatio* generally refers to the
individual act of revelation and not (or at least not immediately) to revelation in its totality and unity must now be
amplified by a more precise treatment of the special terminology of the *Hexaemeron.* In general, the basic meaning is
"the unveiling of the hidden."[5] This general meaning can be
specified in three directions:

a) At times in the *Hexaemeron, revelatio* means the unveiling of the future.[6]

b) More often, it is the hidden "mystical" meaning of Scripture that is referred to as the hidden mystery of *revelatio.*[7] *Revelatio,* therefore, effects a pneumatic understanding of Scripture. As will become clear, this line of thought is especially open to the acceptance of the notions of Joachim.

c) Finally, *revelatio* can also refer to that imageless unveiling of the divine reality which takes place in the mystical ascent.[8] Here the influence of the theology of Pseudo-Dionysius, the Areopagite, is especially obvious. In the following discussion, we will be concerned with the inner richness of the problem which lies hidden behind the levels of these terminological elements.

#8. The Theological Place of Bonaventure's Hope of Revelation in the Four-fold Concept of Wisdom in the "Hexaemeron."

In *Collatio II,* the *Hexaemeron* provides us with a basic text to help establish the broader theological context in which Bonaventure's hope for a new, final "revelation" stands. In this text, the inner unity and the common root for all the following statements concerning this point may be clearly seen. For this reason, we will sketch the basic lines of this text. This will provide us, at the same time, with the themes for the further development of this chapter.

In this lecture, Bonaventure presents the goal of Christian learning. The goal is: Wisdom; a wisdom which can never be attained by learning alone, but ultimately only through sanctity.[1] This wisdom has various degrees. It can be divided into:

sapientia uniformis
      multiformis
      omniformis
      nulliformis.[2]

The "uniform wisdom" flashes forth in the knowledge of the eternal rules, those basic principles of all knowledge. We do not judge about these principles; rather we are capable of judging by them. At this level of wisdom, therefore, man grasps those basic truths which are simply given and which one can contradict only "ad exterius rationem." These rules and the wisdom corresponding to them are rooted in God and lead to God; but He is not grasped immediately with them.[3] Moses is the type of this wisdom.[4] This first stage of *sapientia* may be omitted from our treatment since it obviously has to do with that wisdom proper to philosophy; that is, with a wisdom "sola ratione," if we might phrase it this way.[5]

In comparison with this first stage, the *sapientia multiformis* represents a significant step forward. Bonaventure takes this concept from the Epistle to the Ephesians, where we read: "Yes, to me, the very least of all saints, there was given this grace, to announce among the Gentiles the good tidings of the unfathomable riches of Christ, and to enlighten all men as to what is the dispensation which was hidden from eternity in God, who created all things; in order that through the Church there be made known to all the Principalities and the Powers in the heavens the manifold wisdom (*multiformis sapientia*) of God . . .(Eph. 3, 8-10).[6] Paul here acknowledges himself as the "professor" of this wisdom which consists in an understanding of the mysterious language of Holy Scripture.[7] Scripture speaks in images and parables; it is "veiled" (*velata*) for the proud and revealed (*revelata*) for the little ones and the humble. He who possesses this wisdom has the "facies revelata" about which the Apostle speaks (2 Cor. 3, 18); or in a word, this wisdom is a wisdom from revelation. Hence, as the *sapientia uniformis* is a wisdom from certain rational truths, so the *sapientia multiformis* is a wisdom that arises from divine revelation.[8] We will have to examine this more precisely in what follows.

In the third place, Bonaventure names the *sapientia omniformis*. This is that wisdom which discovers in all things the reflection of the Creator and follows His traces through all of creation. Solomon is the type of this wisdom. The Philosophers also are representatives of this wisdom although they often stand in danger of remaining with created things themselves instead of finding their way back to the Creator by seeking His traces in creatures. Thus their wisdom becomes folly.[9] This wisdom also is based on revelation; on that revelation, namely, which Paul has in mind in *Romans* when he writes: Deus enim illis revelavit (Rm. 1, 19).[10]

Till now we have found an increasing fullness of forms from the *sapientia uniformis* to the *sapientia multiformis* and to the *omniformis*. But at the high point of this movement there is a reversal to total formlessness in the *sapientia nulliformis*. Here the mystic approaches in silence to the very threshold of the mystery of the eternal God in the night of the intellect whose light is extinguished at such heights. It is true here more than on the two preceding levels: Non est cuiuslibet, nisi cui Deus revelat.[11] This is the wisdom that Paul had taught to the Perfect — Timothy and Dionysius — but had kept hidden from the ordinary faithful. For them, he was a teacher of the *sapientia multiformis* only, while the *sapientia nulliformis* remained limited above all to the

small circle of the elect, as is clearly stated in 1 Cor.:
Sapientiam loquimur inter perfectos . . . sapientiam abscon-
ditam, quam nec oculus vidit nec auris audivit nec in cor
hominis ascendit; nobis autem revelavit Deus per Spiritum
suum (1 Cor. 2, 6-10).[12] In the writings of the Areopagite
we discover who these Perfect are to whom the *nobis autem
revelavit* applies. As we have already indicated, besides Paul,
Timothy and especially Dionysius himself are meant here.
There is a double revelation, therefore, at the inception of
Christianity. The entire dynamic of Bonaventure's theology
of history arises from the separation of these two revelations
and from unification of them which is hoped for but not yet
realized. Here, for the first time, we stand at that point at
which we can clearly see the historico-theological tension
which must have arisen for Bonaventure from his unique understanding of the concept of *revelatio*. With this text as a
point of departure, we will now examine more closely the
three forms of the wisdom arising from revelation: *sapientia
multiformis* (#9 and 10), *sapientia omniformis* (#11),
sapientia nulliformis (#12).

#9. The sapientia multiformis: Revelation as the Allegorical Understanding of Scripture.

I. "Revelation" = the spiritual sense of Scripture.

As far as I can see, at no time does Bonaventure refer to the
Scriptures themselves as "revelation."[1] He speaks of *revelare*
and *facies revelata* primarily when a particular understanding
of Scripture is involved, namely that "manifold divine wisdom" which consists in grasping the three-fold spiritual sense
of Scripture — the allegorical, the anagogical and the tropo-

logical. These three are understood in analogy with the three
divine virtues of faith, hope, and love.[2] Not only in the
Hexaemeron, but just as much so in the short dogmatic treatise
known as the *Breviloquium* and in the *Reductio artium ad
theologiam,* it is expressly stated that we grasp that which we
are to believe not from the letter of Scripture, but first of all
by the use of allegory.[3] The letter by itself is merely the water
which is transformed into wine in the spiritual understanding;[4] the letter is a stone, which must be changed into bread;[5]
or as Bonaventure says together with Joachim, the letter is the
skin around the true fruit.[6] Indeed, the letter is (as we will
clarify later) the Tree of the Knowledge of Good and Evil
which became a disaster for the Jews and banned them from
the Paradise of the primitive Church; it is in the spiritual understanding that Scripture becomes the Tree of Life.[7] Consequently, it is the *Judaeus* and not the *Christianus* who corresponds to the letter regardless of whether it is a question of
the letter of the Old or of the New Testament.[8] In other
words, where there is only the letter, there we find the Old
Testament and Judaism, regardless of whether we call this
letter "New" or "Old" Testament. The mere letter is not
"New" Testament; the New Testament is truly present precisely where the letter has been surpassed by the Spirit. Consequently, that which is properly New Testament does not
consist in a new book, but in the Spirit who makes these books
full of life. Here, therefore, "revelation" is synonymous with
the spiritual understanding of Scripture; it consists in the God-
given act of understanding, and not in the objective letter
alone. Only those who understand Scripture spiritually have
a "facies revelata."[9]

II. "Revelation" and the inspiration of Scripture.

In a study of the exegetical principles of Bonaventure, P. Dempsey points out that the Seraphic Doctor uses the notions *revelatio* and *inspiratio* interchangeably and that he fails entirely to distinguish between "inspiration" and "revelation."[10] After all that has been said above, this should not be surprising. Furthermore, we must keep in mind that the definition of prophecy first given by Cassiodorus and generally accepted by Medieval theology clarifies prophecy as "inspiratio vel revelatio."[11] Here all three concepts are brought into a remarkably close relationship and remain this way for the time being. Bruno Decker has undertaken a very careful study of the matter, and more recently, Hans Urs von Balthasar has taken up the line of thought initiated by Decker. In their studies, they have clearly pointed out the relation between the individual theologians on the question of "prophetic inspiration" as revealed in the critical study of the original sources. They have succeeded in presenting an extensive, common basic structure which is involved in the opinions of these theologians.[12] Here we will give the fundamental idea on the basis of a text of Rupert of Deutz which has been emphasized by Wilhelm Kamlah;[13] for here the problem emerges with special clarity. Following Augustine,[14] Rupert distinguishes three types of vision:

The *visio corporalis — corpus,* (external, bodily process of sight)

The *visio spiritualis — spiritus* (internal power of imagination — dream: Pharao, who has a dream but does not understand its meaning)

The *visio intellectualis* — Mens Dei spiritu illuminata
(Joseph, who understands the dream in spirit
through divine illumination.)

We can speak of *revelatio* only in the case of the third *visio*.
This third spiritual vision is identical with the "third heaven"
to which Paul was taken up. Augustine already had made this
identification.[15] Furthermore, we must say that while only
Paul speaks expressly of being taken up into the third heaven,
this was not a privilege of Paul alone. Rather, it was granted
to all the Apostles and inspired writers of Scripture; for it is
identical with the process of inspiration.[16] This means that
since Scripture is born from a mystical contact of the hagio-
graphers with God, it can be understood ultimately only on a
level which must be called "mystical." It is clear that the
meaning of Scripture lies on the level of the *visio intellectualis;* anyone who approaches Scripture on the level of the *visio
corporalis* or *spiritualis* will necessarily miss its meaning.

Regardless of all the individual elements that may distinguish Bonaventure's theory of revelation from this text, the
Seraphic Doctor does have the same formal basic structure
which we find in Rupert and Augustine. He distinguishes the
three *visiones*[17] just as they do. A series of texts shows that
the process of "revelation" which takes place through "inspiration" is understood to be a *visio intellectualis, i.e.* a penetration through all the peripheral elements to the spiritual
core. Ultimately it has a mystical status.[18] Certainly it is not
unconditionally necessary to connect this with any judgment
concerning the personal sanctity of a hagiographer; Bonaventure leaves room for border-line cases of "revelation" to sinners and through sinners. As examples, we have Bileam, Saul,

and the sinful Solomon.[19] But even here, *revelatio* is understood as a penetration through the peripheral-sensible to the spiritual and the real; it is a new seeing and understanding of what is given from out of its true depth of meaning. That is, it includes a *visio intellectualis*.[20]

From this perspective, we can now understand in a new way why Bonaventure holds that the content of faith is found not in the letter of Scripture but in the spiritual meaning lying behind the letter. Furthermore, we can see why it is that for Bonaventure, Scripture simply as a written document does not constitute revelation whereas the understanding of Scripture which arises in theology can be called revelation at least indirectly.[21] We can easily understand this in view of the process of revelation itself; for in this process, "revelation" is understood to consist precisely in the understanding of the spiritual sense. But there is another reason for this prior to the fact that the "quid credendum" is to be found not in the literal but in the allegorical sense of Scripture; namely, the fact that the process of inspiration includes a penetration through the *mundus sensibilis* to the *mundus intelligibilis*. It is precisely in this penetration that inspiration lays claim to its special status as revelation (*revelatio* = unveiling!). Obviously this notion necessarily leads to what we have already said about the content of faith. For the inspired writer cannot relate his *visio intellectualis* in its naked spirituality; he must wrap it in the "swaddling clothes" of the written word.[22] This means that that which truly constitutes revelation is accessible in the word written by the hagiographer, but that it remains to a degree hidden behind the words and must be unveiled anew.

Here we could easily fall into a misunderstanding. We might well ask whether such a view would not destroy the

objectivity of revelation in favor of a subjective actualism. Such
an idea has no foundation in the intellectual world of Bonaventure. For the deep meaning of Scripture in which we truly
find the "revelation" and the content of faith is not left up to
the whim of each individual. It has already been objectified
in part in the teachings of the Fathers and in theology so that
the basic lines are accessible simply by the acceptance of the
Catholic faith,[23] which — as it is summarized in the *Symbolum*
— is a principle of exegesis.[24] Here we gain a new insight
into the identification of *sacra scriptura* and *theologia*.[24a] Only
Scripture as it is understood in faith is truly holy Scripture.
Consequently, Scripture in the full sense is theology, i.e. it is
the book *and* the understanding of the book in the faith of
the church. On the other hand, theology can be called Scripture, for it is nothing other than the understanding of Scripture; this understanding, which is theology, brings Scripture
to that full fruitfullness which corresponds to its nature as
revelation. Now we can also understand why it is that in the
programmatic introduction to the *Sentence Commentary* Bonaventure refers to the theologian as the *revelator absconditorum*
and to theology as the corresponding *revelatio absconditorum*.[24b] In the light of this, it should be obvious enough
what a difference lies between Bonaventure's view and any
actualistic misinterpretation of it. We can express this difference as follows. The understanding which elevates the Scripture to the status of "revelation" is not to be taken as an affair
of the individual reader; but is realized only in the living understanding of Scripture in the Church. In this way the objectivity of the claim of faith is affirmed without any doubt. If
we keep this in mind, we can say that without detriment to
the objectivity of the faith, the true meaning of Scripture will

be found only by reaching behind the letters. Consequently, the true understanding of revelation demands of each individual reader an attitude which goes beyond the merely "objective" recognition of what is written. In the deepest sense, this understanding can be called mystical to distinguish it from all natural knowledge. In other words, such an understanding demands the attitude of faith by which man gains entrance into the living understanding of Scripture in the Church. It is in this way that man truly receives "revelation."

With this, the historico-theological consequences begin to emerge more clearly. For it is obvious that mere faith is only the lowest level of such a mystical penetration into Scripture.[25] The stages of faith are also stages of mysticism; and in such a viewpoint, they are seen naturally as stages of *revelatio* as well. *Revelatio* refers not to the letter of Scripture, but to the understanding of the letter; and this understanding can be increased.[26] If now we were to assume a period of time in which the power of true mystical elevation were granted to all men, then — in this view of things — we could refer to such a time in an entirely new way as a time of revelation. On the other hand, we would have to admit that the real meaning of the age of the New Testament, which consists in *revelatio*, has been realized up to now in a limited degree. It is clear that Bonaventure does not view this final future revelation to consist in a new Scripture as had been the case in the primitive view of Gerard of Borgo San Donnino.[27] Instead, it will consist in a new understanding of the old and enduring Scriptures, which would be closer to the meaning of Joachim himself. For this reason, in contrast to both Gerard and Joachim, Bonaventure can emphasize the definitive character of the New Testament despite, or rather, precisely because of his hope for a new revelation. "Post novum testamentum non erit aliud, nec aliquod sacramentum novae legis subtrahi potest, quia illud testamentum aeternum est."[28]

III. The different forms of understanding the Scriptures.

It is now clear that the spiritual understanding of Scripture is understood to be "revelation." Furthermore, we have tried to show the relation between this notion and Bonaventure's concept of inspiration. After these basic statements, it remains for us to give a deeper treatment to a question already touched upon previously, namely: how does Bonaventure view this spiritual understanding of Scripture concretely? His answer to this question is not entirely consistent. It wavers between two poles; one which is more academic and scientific and the other which is more prophetic.

On the one hand, there is the statement that the *revelata facies* is the result of that speculation in which the *credibile* moves in the direction of the *intelligible*.[29] This thesis was expressed above all in *Collatio X*; and it returns again, especially in the great hierarchical schema given on p. 47 above. Here the peculiar charism of *speculatio* is attributed to the second-last level of the hierarchy, i.e. to the *ordo cherubicus,* or concretely, to the Franciscan and Dominican Orders. At the same time, the proper gift of this hierarchical level is *revelatio*;[30] consequently, "revelation" is, for the most part, identified with the speculative-scientific exegesis of Scripture. In this context, we must point out that for the Scholastics prophecy is often identified with the *gratia interpretandi*.[31] Certainly, especially in the case of Bonaventure, it is never entirely forgotten that this *speculatio* is truly a *gratia*; hence the charismatic-mystical characteristic is never completely lost.

According to the view of Bonaventure, the hope for a greater fullness in the sort of revelation described above is already realized in the Franciscan and Dominican Orders.[32] It is not difficult to understand this if we think of the tremendous upsurge of theological science and of preaching which these two Orders had brought about in the short time since their founding.[33] Bonaventure himself had been a witness as well as a partial cause of this phenomenon. Likewise, it is not difficult to understand that Bonaventure could see this not merely as a natural progress of science but as a divine sign to the Church which was drawing near to the final age. On the other hand, if we keep in mind the profound inadequacy which Bonaventure experienced in all academic science, especially toward the end of his life (Ch. 4), we will also understand why he awaited a new and purer *revelatio* which could become a reality for all practical purposes only in the *Ordo* of the final age.[34] He does not give enough indications to enable us to form a complete picture; and practically, we arrive at nothing more than assumptions. Nonetheless, two streams of thought seem to play a role here. The *revelatio* of the final age leads beyond the *sapientia multiformis* of the present time. It tends more in the direction of the *sapientia nulliformis* described above all by Pseudo-Dionysius. If Augustine is the Father of the present age and of the present state of revelation because of his character as the normative master of *allegoria*, so Dionysius is related to the future.[35] However it is not only Dionysius but Francis as well who stands as an anticipation of this new state of revelation. (How could we have expected otherwise?) That which has become visible in him is a movement beyond the discursive thinking of the present exegesis in favor of a simple, inner understanding in accordance with the statement of the Lord: "I praise you, Father, Lord of heaven and of earth, that you have hidden these things from the wise and the clever, but have revealed them to the humble" (Mt. 11, 25).[36]

This statement of the Lord plays no outstanding role in the Scripture commentaries of Bonaventure, and it does not appear at all in his *Sentence Commentary*. But it appears with greater frequency from the time of the *Quaestiones de perfectione evangelica;* and precisely in his interpretation of Francis, it plays a significant role. Francis appears over and over as the exemplary *parvulus* in whom this word of the Lord is fulfilled in a particularly noticeable way.[37] So, in accord with the view of the Seraphic Doctor, we can say that, according to the word of the Lord, there is in general an essential relationship between *humilitas* and *revelatio*. This relation is of such a sort that anyone who is entirely lacking in *humilitas* is also incapable of receiving any knowledge of revelation.[38] The degrees of *humilitas* indicate also the degrees in the understanding of revelation.[39] Thus, that age in which the humility of St. Francis shall have become the universal form of life will naturally also appear as an age of *revelatio*.[40] The revelation of the final age will be distinguished from the form of revelation already realized in the present age in the Franciscan and Dominican Orders in that it will be non-discursive and non-scholastic in character. It will be a simple, inner familiarity with the mystery of the Word of God.[41]

IV. The mediation of revelation.

In the light of what has been said, *revelatio* must always be understood as a *gratia gratis data*, and thus as the working of God on the individual.[42] Yet it would be false to conceive of this *revelatio* in purely individualistic terms somewhat in the sense of an exclusive I-Thou relation. Rather it stands in a great cosmic-hierarchical context. Not only is the divine Spirit involved in it, but in some way the entire cosmos of Intelligences takes part in it. These Intelligences stand between God and man in the order of essence. But over and above this, they have a factual mediatorial function.[43] In order to clarify this point, which is not without importance for Bonaventure, we must indicate at least briefly the broader context in which this question stands.

The problem of the part played by the angels[44] in human knowledge became acute first from a philosophical aspect. At the very beginning of High Scholasticism, a theory which was not unlike the view of the later Latin Averroism, had been developed on the basis of Avicenna. This theory has been called by Gilson "augustinisme avicennisant,"[45] for it is an attempt to synthesize the Augustinian and the Avicennan theories of knowledge. In this synthesis, the cosmic-apersonal thought of Arabian neo-Platonism is joined with the thought of Augustine in such a way that Illumination appears as a share in the cosmic spheres or Intelligences. It is significant to know that John of Rupella, who was one of the predecessors of Bonaventure on the Franciscan Chair at the University of Paris, had adopted this doctrine. His viewpoint on this question is summarized pointedly as follows: "*Intellectus agens* is God Himself for those objects of knowledge that lie *supra intellectum*, that is, for the knowledge of God; for those truths which the soul knows *juxta se* and which are related to the angel-world, the *intellectus agens* is an angel. Finally, the *intellectus agens* is a power of the soul itself in relation to all those insights which the soul achieves *intra* or *infra se.*"[46] The difficulty which this theory had attempted to solve had arisen together with the attempt to unite the Arabian-Aristotelian theory of the *intellectus agens* with the Augustinian theory of Illumination which in itself has no place for an *intellectus agens.*

In contrast with this, Bonaventure, like Aquinas, had tried to achieve a synthesis of Aristotle and Augustine on this point.[47] He had grasped the decisive point of the Augustinian Illumination theory with great sensitivity: the immediacy of the human spirit to God. He emphatically holds the immediate divine illumination of the human spirit.[48] The reduction of all degrees of certitude to the illumination of the divine light is not directed in the first place against Aristotle. Bonaventure believed himself to be at first in full agreement[49] with Aristotle and later in at least partial agreement[50] with him. Actually it is directed against the Avicennan obfuscation of Christian doctrine which had been represented by some of the *Magistri* long before the appearance of the so-called Latin Averroism.[51]

While in this way the immediacy of the human soul to God was fully assured for Bonaventure in the area of the so-called natural knowledge, the problem in the area of revelation was remarkably much more difficult for him. This was caused by the fact that on this point he had to reckon with the authority of Pseudo-Dionysius. The basic hierarchical law of Dionysius authoritatively demanded a cooperation of the angels in the process of revelation. God, angels, and man are fitted into an inflexible schema as *hierarchia supercaelestis, hierarchia caelestis, hierarchia subcaelestis.* This schema allows of no exceptions. Thus it is an inviolable law that any higher order can exercise an influence only on that order which follows it immediately. The higher order cannot reach downwards by by-passing any intervening orders. This means that only the angels of the lowest choirs can work upon the world of man; the Seraphim, Cherubim, etc. cannot do so.[52] "It is the spirits, placed in a hierarchy through glory (i.e. the angels and the blessed) who first receive the (divine) illumination, because that (divine) sun first illumines them and, through them, us. For order demands that illumination should first come to those who are nearer to and more similar to the sun."[53] "Note that the first hierarchy receives its origin and illumination from God alone; the middle hierarchy receives it from God and from the higher hierarchy; the lower hierarchy receives it from God, from the higher and from the middle hierarchy; the ecclesiastical hierarchy receives from all the above. Indeed, the ray of the eternal sun illumines first that hierarchy which lies nearest to it and sets it up in a hierarchical structure as a reflection of itself. Then the ray comes through this first hierarchy to the middle hierarchy; through both of these to the lowest; and through all of these to the ecclesiastical hier-archy . . ."[54] We are almost tempted to ask whether there is not a serious danger that the evil spirit of Averroism which had been exorcised on the philosophical level does not return in a worse form on the theological level; for here a subtle system of manifold cosmic mediations is inserted between God and the human soul. In the final analysis, this system has a pagan quality.[55] Nevertheless, the thesis of Augustine re-mains: "Inter mentem et Deum nihil cadit medium."[56] Like all his contemporaries, Bonaventure adopts the notion that the angels are involved in a mediatorial way in all revelations.[57] But they are never the cause of revelation. The only source of revelation is the divine ray of light. The light which illumines us immediately is the divine light. In the process of revelation, the angels act only *occasionaliter* like a man who opens the window and lets in the light though he himself is neither the source nor the cause of the light.[58] In this way revelation remains, on the one hand, entirely the work of God; on the other hand, it is withdrawn from all individualistic isolation and is placed in the context of the divine activity which embraces the world. In this context, every creature, as a part of the "hierarchy," is engaged in a holy work which takes its origin from God and leads back to God by way of fellow creatures.

#10. **The Historical Character of Scripture and its Revelation.**

Now let us return again to the *sapientia multiformis* of Scripture. Bonaventure believed that there was a gradual, historical, progressive development in the understanding of Scripture which was in no way closed. In order to understand his peculiar, dynamic viewpoint, we must now sketch briefly the hermeneutical situation in which this surprising notion has its place. Corresponding to the object of this study, we will limit ourselves to the more precise question: How did Bonaventure present the relation between Scripture and history? We will attempt to point out the more important lines of thought which had an influence on the Seraphic Doctor in this question.

I. The influence of the unhistorical thought of Scholasticism.

The ancient concept of history was inherited by the Middle Ages from St. Augustine. According to this view, history is a flow of individual events; that which is common or general in these events is not known. Consequently, there can be no real science of history; for science treats precisely the universal. Thus, Augustine writes in his book of *83 Questions*: "Alia sunt, quae semper creduntur et nunquam intelliguntur, sicut est omnis historia temporalia et humana gesta percurrens."[1] We must say, then, that whatever is historical can only be "believed" and cannot be "understood," because in the historical there is only a purely external reality and no inner intelligibility. Certainly in Christianity this unhistorical mode of thought necessarily had a limited applicability from the very start because of the prophetic interpretation of the Old Testament history given in Scripture. Like a light, this interpretation penetrates into the context of the historical happenings and clarifies their inner unity and significance. From the start, this fact influenced the concrete evaluation of the historical which played such an important role precisely in Augustine. But it was not able to destroy the fundamental judgment concerning the status of history cited above.[2]

Consequently the predominant impression remained that history lay outside the limits of that which is properly intelligible and thus below the proper area of concern for theology. This notion was able to assert itself even in Bonaventure's *Hexaemeron* where it appears together with the Augustinian concept of inspiration and of revelation side by side with quite different tendencies which we will treat immediately. There we read: "Nota etiam, quod quaedam sunt credibilia, non tamen intelligibilia per rationem, ut 'Abraham genuit Isaac' sive facta particularia; quaedam autem credibilia sunt intelligibilia, et quando intelliguntur, rationes solidas habent."[3]

II. The influence of symbolic thought forms.

In the *Hexaemeron,* the symbolic mode of thought is employed even more emphatically than the rational-scholastic concept of Scripture and history which we have just treated and which can be related to Augustine with a rather limited degree of justification. The symbolic approach dominates the entire concept of history in this work. Certainly it is not presented uniformly. In the context of the present question, which is not a question of the division of history as such but a question of the relation between Scripture and history, it seems to us that two principle directions are clear. On the one hand, there is the tendency of early Scholasticism to look backwards. This is especially the case in Hugo of St. Victor. This view tends toward a certain canonization and fixation of the patristic symbolism. On the other hand, there is the tendency of Joachim to look forward to the future. This tendency does not shrink back from the task of transforming and reformulating because it is convinced that in the present moment we can affirm things which were not yet known to the Fathers.[4]

1. The "Canonization" of the Fathers: Hugo of St. Victor and other early Scholastics.

We have already seen that the true meaning of Scripture is found only when it is understood spiritually. He who does not understand Scripture spiritually does not understand it at all. He is a *Judaeus.* We have attempted to uncover the roots of this thesis in Bonaventure's concept of revelation and inspiration. We must now make some important additions to this thesis. "By himself, man cannot come to this (spiritual) understanding (of Scripture). He can do this only through those

to whom God revealed it, i.e. through the writings of the
Saints such as Augustine, Jerome, and others."[5] This means
that the spiritual understanding does not arise purely and
simply as a penetration from letter to spirit which, as spirit,
would lie beyond the world of mere words and as such could
be grasped only in individual cases. Rather, it has already
found its binding rules and even its content in the writings
of the Fathers. This understanding, which cannot be reached
by man alone, was "revealed" to them once and for all. Thus,
in an entirely unforeseen way, the ground is prepared for a
concept of revelation which understands "revelation" as a unique, delimited, and objectified reality which has been given
its written fixation in the exegetical works of the Fathers.

With this fixation of the pneumatic exegesis to the writings
of the Fathers, Bonaventure opts for that concept of Sacred
Scripture which had been developed above all by Hugo of
St. Victor and by Robert of Melun, who was influenced by
Hugo as well as by Abelard and finds his place here despite,
or rather precisely because of his struggle against the unlimited
domination of the *Glossa*. In its basic lines, this view was,
indeed, common to the greatest part of early Scholasticism.
As Grabmann has expressed it, for Hugo, Scripture and the
Fathers flow together into one great *Scriptura Sacra*.[6] This
basic orientation appears even more clearly in Robert of
Melun, who distinguishes four types of *auctoritas* in the Prologue to his *Commentary on the Sentences*; there are, then,
four types of writings that have the rank of *auctoritas*:

a) Writings which have *auctoritas* by reason of their writer
   = writings of the prophets and the Apostles.
b) Writings which have *auctoritas* by reason of *acceptio* by
   posterity, e.g. the Book of Job.

c) Writings which in themselves are heretical; but by reason of later acceptance in many points have a certain degree of *auctoritas,* e.g. the writings of Origen.

d) Writings which have *auctoritas* primarily by reason of *acceptio,* secondarily by reason of the writer; e.g. the works of Augustine, Jerome, etc.[7]

If we compare the second and the fourth group with one another, it becomes clear that the concept of the canon has not yet been fixed in our sense and that the Fathers are indissolubly connected with Scripture; they stand on an equal footing with many parts of the Sacred Book, which as yet is not understood to be a unified book. Not long before this, we find an even more variegated mixture of the works of Scripture and those of the Fathers in the *Ars lectoria* written by Aimeric of Angouleme in 1086. He distinguishes four levels of *auctoritas* according to the four metals: gold, silver, tin (stagnum), and lead. As silver, he reckons, among others, the Book of Daniel, the Wisdom of Solomon, the two Books of the Maccabees, the Epistle to the Hebrews; the Letters of Cyprian, the writings of Ambrose, Jerome, Hilary, Augustine, Gregory; the Canons of the four major Councils.[8] The results are the same. There is as yet no boundary line drawn between Scripture and the Fathers. Or, in other words, because of their great respect for the Fathers, the men of the Middle Ages were confronted anew with the problem of the Canon which had been basically determined already in Christian antiquity. This new determination of the Canon which acquired decisive significance for the formation of the Catholic concept of tradition is a fact that has received little attention up to the present. For the most part, the decision on this matter had already been made when Bonaventure held his lectures on the

Hexaemeron. Essentially, the Canon was already set down for him as it stands today.[9] But the Fathers are not simply eliminated from the picture. They are the bearers of a new spiritual "revelation," without which the Scriptures simply would not be effective as revelation.[10]

Our reason for treating this problem in this context consists first of all in the fact that here a fixation of the symbolic interpretation of Scripture has taken place, it is with this type of interpretation that we are here concerned. Secondly, it should be pointed out that we have here an extension of the age of revelation far beyond the time usually ascribed to it when we see the end of the time of revelation to coincide with the death of the last Apostle. The entire concept of the Canon which we find here is thinkable only on the presupposition of a dynamic understanding of revelation which cannot be given a definitive, temporal fixation. Certainly, here there is such a fixation, but it carries within itself the seed of its own destruction. If we are aware of this situation, then the rise of Joachim will not appear so unmotivated and so unintelligible as it had generally seemed to be in previous investigations.

2. The progressive line of Joachim.

a) The new exegetical situtation created by the event of Francis.

The patristic exegetical tradition, which had seemed to be so solid up till that time, was now abruptly thrown into question by the event of St. Francis. Francis had dared to make the unheard of attempt to translate the word of the Sermon on the Mount into the living work of his own life, and to make the spirit of Jesus Christ and the immediate demand of the Gospel into the only norm for Christian living. His Rule was intended to be nothing but a summary of the Sermon on the Mount, a summary of the central elements of the Gospel.[11]

Thus, the event of Francis effectively shattered a concept of tradition which had become too canonical. Francis' own life had developed from an immediate contact with the Scriptures, which he desired to understand and to live literally *sine glossa* in an immediate encounter with the Lord Who speaks to us in the Sacred Writings.[12] An echo of this spirit can be discerned in the remark of Bonaventure: "Unde rationes, exempla et auctoritates concedenda sunt ad istam partem, ad quam sufficientissime astruendam una sola auctoritas expressa ex ore Christi consulentis dimittere omnia esset sufficientissima etiam si multa glossarum et expositorum dicta viderentur contraria."[13] All tradition is of no avail against the immediate word of the Lord; this is the bold wisdom of the word with which Bonaventure discovered the break-through to the immediate encounter with Scripture, following in the foot-steps of his master, Francis.

This new-found readiness to accept the literal meaning of Scripture certainly had to be justified in the eyes of their contemporaries, and it paved the way for a new understanding of the concept of "tradition." Till that time, the Scholastic debate had been a dispute between the Dialecticians and the anti-Dialecticians.[14] But new lines of combat were drawn up in the debate on poverty, which must be understood precisely as a struggle for the proper understanding of Scripture and tradition. Here it became a question of the meaning of Scripture itself and of the manner of its explanation. The Mendicants, and especially the Franciscans, pointed to the fact of the *vita apostolica,* which had become a reality in Francis. In this way, they sought to lend legitimacy to their understanding of Scripture, which stood in contrast with the then current theology. But when the question was raised as to whether

this really was the *vita apostolica,* it became necessary to provide a foundation adequate to confirm the Mendicants' interpretation. Such a foundation was found in the Church and in
the *sedes apostolica* which had canonized Francis and Dominic
and approved their Rules.[15] To fight against the Franciscan
form of life, therefore, is to fight against the Church itself,
and to declare the Church guilty of error. "We would have
to conclude . . . that the entire, universal Church has erred
and has fallen into a deception; and that all who have taken
on this form of life have succumbed to damnation. But the
assumption that God has thus allowed His entire holy People
to err is despicable and entirely incredible . . ."[16] The "Holy
People of God" which is the Church of the present, is here
placed side by side with the classical "Saints" of theology,
that is, with the Fathers of the Church; and the Church of the
present is understood to be a new criterion of interpretation
with equal rights. With this, the purely retrospective allegory
of early Scholasticism is limited by a principle of interpretation which shows a decidely progressive character.

Furthermore, in his polemic against the opponents of the
Mendicants, the Seraphic Doctor not only places the *populus
sanctus* of the present alongside the *sancti* of the past, but he
also brings in Francis and Dominic as witnesses in his proof
from tradition since the sanctity of both had been guaranteed
by the judgment of the Church.[17] Thus we perceive a history
of the saints themselves. Here Joachim's notion of a progressive history of the church finds some clarification almost
naturally. Already the *Quaestiones disputatae* indicate an
initial contact with the ideas of Joachim when they present
a division of the Church into *ecclesia prima, media,* and
finalis.[18] Even today the comparison of the Francis-event with

the prediction of Joachim is puzzling enough for the historian
and helps him but little in understanding the joyful amazement
of the Franciscans who saw in this identification a definite confirmation of the place of Francis' work in the history of salvation.[19] It was in this way that the progressive exegesis of
Joachim found its way into the work of Bonaventure.

b) Belief in the progressive, historical development of Scripture.

We have already described (#4 and #5) the influence of
Joachim's exegesis on Bonaventure's understanding of Scripture and the theology of history that arises from it. The key
hermeneutical concept was seen to be that of the *theoriae* with
which Bonaventure adds a new historical-typological and prophetic exegesis to the old allegorical and typological understanding. He himself attempts to clarify this with the concept
of the *rationes seminales*. Scripture is full of hidden seeds
which are developed only in the course of history and therefore constantly allow new insights which would not have been
possible for an earlier age (#2). The relation between Scripture and history can now be summarized in the two following
statements:

a) Scripture has grown in an historical way. Only he
   who knows its history knows its meaning. History is
   a structural element of Scripture's intelligible form.
   "Scripturae intelligi non possunt nec mysteria, nisi
   sciatur decursus mundi et dispositio hierarchica."[20]

b) Scripture, however, is not simply a product of a past
   history, but is simultaneously a statement about and a
   prediction of the future. Since the Scriptures were
   written, part of this future has already become past,
   while part of it still remains future.[21] This means
   that the total meaning of Scripture is not yet clear.
   Rather, the final "revelation," i.e. the time of a full

understanding of revelation, is yet to come. " . . .
Isaias: Repleta est terra scientia domini sicut aquae
maris operientis (Is.11,9) . . . Et hoc potissime refer-
tur ad tempus novi testamenti, quando scriptura mani-
festata est et maxime in fine, quando scripturae intel-
ligentur, quae modo non intelliguntur. Tunc 'erit
mons'; scilicet ecclesia contemplativa, et tunc 'non
nocebunt', quando fugient monstra haeresum sapientiae usura. Sed hodie mons Sion propter vulpes dis-
periit (*Thren.* 5,18.) i.e. propter expositores versipel-
les et foetidos."[22] Bonaventure's hope for revelation
thus arises organically out of the hermeneutical
streams of thought into which his own times had
implanted him.

#11. The sapientia omniformis: Creation and Revelation.

In the second lecture on the *Hexaemeron* Bonaventure in-
serts the *sapientia omniformis* between the two fundamental
forms of divine revelation which are expressed in *sapientia
multiformis* and *nulliformis*. It is in the *sapientia omniformis*
that the letter of creation becomes understandable and speaks
to us of the glory of the Creator. Since this *sapientia omniformis* may be reckoned as one of the essential elements of
the Franciscan understanding of the world,[1] we cannot bypass
it entirely in our presentation.

As regards this form of wisdom, Bonaventure speaks also
of a "revelation";[2] and significantly, this revelation also is
realized as an understanding of a given "letter." Like Scripture, the things of the world have a "literal" external side.
And as in the case of Scripture, here also we are threatened
with the danger of remaining with the letter and of thus over-
looking the true sign-value of things. Because of our situation

in salvation history, this danger has become particularly acute. Indeed, wisdom raises its captivating and inviting voice in all things. But "we do not find her (wisdom), just as the unlettered layman is not interested in the contents of the book that he holds in his hands. So it is with us. The language of the universe has become like Greek, Hebrew, or some barbarous language; it has become fundamentally unknown."[3]

So there is a striking parallel between the revelation of Scripture and that of creation. In both cases, the revelation is hidden behind the letters that veil it; in both cases, the unveiling of the revelation is the task of the Spirit who transcends the level of the literal in a living, existential movement which penetrates into the realm of the intellectual-spiritual. In both cases, there is also the danger of becoming imprisoned by the letters. It is from this danger that the two basic religious errors arise. As regards the understanding of creation, the philosopher who forgets or even denies the possibility of reducing things to their true meaning represents that which the Jew represents relative to Scripture.[4] It is the viewpoint of Bonaventure, which he had already developed extensively in his *Commentary on the Sentences*,[5] that the contemplative power in man has been extinguished in the present historical situation[6] so that the understanding of the book of creation will be inaugurated only with the healing and helping revelation of grace.

This conviction of the sign-character of the entire creation is the root of the Bonaventurian symbolism of creation which Gilson has beautifully described in his book on Bonaventure. The most important document giving expression to this understanding of creation is the *Itinerarium mentis in Deum*. Like the Francis of the Celano *Legenda*, this work attempts to con-

struct a "ladder" to the Creator from all the things of this
world. "He who does not allow himself to be illumined by
the glory of created things, is blind; he who does not awaken
to their call is deaf; he who does not praise God for all His
works is mute; he who does not discover the First Principle
from all these signs is a fool. Therefore, open your eyes, call
upon your spiritual ears; loosen your lips and apply your heart
so that you may see, hear, praise, love, serve, glorify, and
honor your God in all creatures, lest the entire universe raise
itself up against you. For therefore the earth will rise up to
to struggle with those who do not understand (Sap. 5,21);
but it (the earth) will be the foundation of glory for the wise
who can say with the Prophet: "For you have made me glad,
O Lord, by your works, of the deeds of your hands I joyfully
sing. How great are your deeds, O Lord. In Wisdom you
have made them all; the earth is full of your creations"
(Ps. 91,5; 103,24).[7] This text shows more clearly than any
analysis we might attempt how far Bonaventure has abandoned anything that might be called merely a Greek "physical-
theology" such as that which is often attributed to the unbibli-
cal renewal of the Catholic *theologia naturalis*.[8] Bonaventure's hymn of praise to the creator-God lives entirely from
the spirit of the psalms. He does not deny the inheritance
coming from Greece, but this heritage here enters fully into
the service of the Christian faith.

#12. The sapientia nulliformis: Mysticism and Revelation.

According to Bonaventure, the "manifold wisdom" of the
allegorical interpretation of Scripture is superseded by the
"formless wisdom" of the most interior mystical contact with

God taught by Dionysius the Areopagite.[1] Since this wisdom arises from "revelation," and since it is therefore "revelation,"[2] and since the "revelation" of the final age clearly must be conceived in terms of this form of wisdom,[3] we must now determine its place more clearly within the whole of Bonaventure's historical thinking. This will simultaneously involve a clarification of the role which Bonaventure ascribed to Pseudo-Dionysius within theology.

1. The Dionysius-Renaissance of the 13th Century.

It is one of the most well-known facts of medieval cultural history that the general intellectual picture of the thirteenth century was influenced in a decisive way by the discovery of the whole of Aristotle's works which had become accessible since the middle of the twelfth century. This was a fact that left a decisive imprint on the intellectual debates of High Scholasticism.[4] Up till the present, we have given less attention to the fact that at the very same time the discovery of Pseudo-Dionysius took place, and that the Dionysius-renaissance which arose from this fact was also of great significance for the reformulation of theology. The fact that already in the ninth century John Eriugena had produced a translation of the works of Dionysius can easily mislead us. For the most part, this translation remained ineffective like the work of the great Scot in general.[5] So at the beginning of the twelfth century, John Sarracenus was led to say in the Prologue to his new translation of Dionysius that the works of the Areopagite "prae nimia difficultate intelligendi vix legantur ab aliquo,"[6] that they had till then produced "parum aut nihil utilitatis,"[7] and that the works of Dionysius were to be found "rarius."[8] Thomas Gallus speaks in a similar vein in the pre-

face to his *compendiosa extractio.*[9] It is obvious that this is
not an exaggeration if we keep in mind the fact that apparently Abaelard and Peter Lombard knew Dionysius only from
references found in Gregory the Great.[10] As a matter of fact,
John Sarracenus and Thomas of Vercelli succeeded in opening
the doors of Latin theology to a considerable extent to Dionysius. Already the *Summa Halensis* cites Dionysius for the most
part from the translation of Sarracenus.[11] Even more so is
this the case with Bonaventure. This is a fact that escaped
the editors of his works, for the translation of Sarracenus was
apparently unknown to them.[12] Even the works of the Abbot
of Vercelli were apparently known to the Seraphic Doctor.[13]
Vercelli's text was like a Targum. It was an expansion of the
original which in itself was all too brief and unclear. For this
reason, the Vercelli text must have made a considerable contribution in making Dionysius understandable and thus in aid-
ing the spread of his ideas.[14]

These prefatory remarks concerning the literary-historical
problem were necessary to help us place in proper perspective
the general significance which Pseudo-Dionysius had for the
thirteenth century and to clarify the picture of the thirteenth
century as such in as far as it concerns us here. This confirms
again a fact which we have already treated (#9, IV), namely
that the mere opposition between Aristotelianism and Augustinianism does not suffice to explain this tumultuous century.
We will have to refer to this fact again for the general evaluation of Bonaventure.

2. The theology of Dionysius in the work of Bonaventure.

It would require a complete monograph to give a detailed
presentation of the influence of the Areopagite on Bonaven-

ture. Here we are merely concerned with pointing out the
principal areas of influence and to show how the Dionysian
theology of Bonaventure comes more and more to a head in
the concept of revelation. Originally the two had nothing to
do with each other, but in the end, the Dionysian theology
made an essential contribution to the concept of revelation.

In his *Commentary on the Sentences*, it seems that Bonaventure knew Dionysius only from the perspective of the
School-theology. That is, he knew the Areopagite primarily
as the originator of the doctrine of the hierarchy which was
developed in rather close contact with Peter Lombard.[15] At
this period one thing stands out: From the very beginning
Bonaventure's image of the world is dominated by the paired
concepts of *egressio-reductio* which remind us strikingly of the
thought-forms of the Areopagite. The same is true later of
the world-view of Thomas Aquinas.[16] At the same time, we
are not justified in concluding that Bonaventure had a personal
contact with the works of Dionysius beyond what would norm-
ally be the case at that time. It must remain an open question
as to how this pair of concepts attained such a dominant role.

This contact is perceptible as a new intellectual line for the
first time at the end of Bonaventure's activity as *Magister*, and
appears simultaneously in the *Quaestiones de perfectione
evangelica* and in the *Quaestiones de scientia Christi* and *De
mysterio trinitatis* as well as in the *Breviloquium*. While it is
only the doctrine of the hierarchy that is developed further
and made more precise in the questions on poverty,[17] two
other elements come to light in the later works. In the first
place, the Dionysian concept of "theology" acquires a new
accentuation which we cannot treat in detail at the present.[18]
Furthermore, the mysticism of Dionysius acquires an astound-

ing degree of significance. This should not be understood to mean that we can show any noteworthy change in content in the mystical theory of Bonaventure. There had always been sufficient reason for the Seraphic Doctor to agree with a doctrine which saw the highest summit in the creature's ascent to God to consist in a contact with God that would be fully free of knowledge and would therefore be super-intellectual. He was encouraged in this view not only by the often cited statement of Pseudo-Bernard that "love reaches further than the power of sight";[19] he would have been inclined in this direction already by reason of his Franciscan view which attributed a higher value to the *affectus* rather than to the *intellectus*.[20] Thus, already in his *Commentary on the Sentences* he speaks of an *ignote ascendere*,[21] of a *docta ignorantia*;[22] and even before this, in the early *Commentary on John* he speaks of a knowledge of God *in caligine* which is more a *sentire* than a *cognoscere*.[23]

But these remained merely scattered texts; they pointed in some way to a border-line area of that which was possible, but they did not seem to be of any particular importance for the actual course of events. But this begins to change from about the time of the *Quaestiones disputatae de scientia Christi.* Here to an increasing degree the dominating force is found in the idea of a knowledge of God in that area which is characterized in the following words: "Sola affectiva vigilat et silentium omnibus aliis potentiis imponit."[24] We point out again that there is not a change in content; but there is a change of emphasis within the whole. It is this new emphasis which gives a new meaning to the entire structure of Bonaventurian theology.

Another factor must be added here in order to bring out the full significance of what has been said. First in the *Itinerarium mentis in Deum* and then again with renewed emphasis in the *Hexaemeron* this mystical contact is called "revelation."[25] Before we attempt to determine more definitely the new significance which this has for the concept of revelation, we will allow ourselves to make one more short remark about the history of ideas which is in place here. Since the work of Max Scheler, it has become customary, to some extent, to speak of the primacy of love in the thought of St. Augustine just as previously it had been common to speak of the primacy of the will. Indeed, even the notion that love precedes knowledge was traced back to Augustine.[26]

Those who know Augustine himself realize that such notions have no place in his work.[27] Their true father is not Augustine but Pseudo-Dionysius. And even in Dionysius himself, I have found no citation in which he expressly speaks of the priority of love over knowledge. It seems that this formulation occurs for the first time in Thomas of Vercelli. It is a formulation which he comes upon while tracing the thought of Dionysius almost, as it were, in passing, when he says: "... per unitionem dilectionis (quae effectiva est verae cognitionis) unitur Deo intellectualiter ignoto."[28] It is in this mysticism that we find, in fact, the original and precise point of origin for the concept of a love which creates knowledge in the darkness of the intellect.

3. The synthesis of the mystical, cosmic-hierarchial and historical order in Bonaventure's concept of revelation in the
   final age.

Now we are in a position to understand the decisive synthesis from which Bonaventure builds up his hope for a final
revelation as well the concept of revelation that lies behind it.

a) The original notion of the cosmic hierarchy of Dionysius
is transformed historically in the hierarchical schema of the
Hexaemeron (*vide* p.47). That is, we have not only a static
hierarchy structured from above to below, but we have also
a hierarchical development of history which is indicated in
this schema. When this is viewed in relation to the Church,
the full form of the hierarchy of the nine choirs is not simply
given in its finished form at the beginning; rather it is the
result of an historical ascent which takes place in the course
of the time of salvation.

b) Corresponding to this historical-hierarchical development, which is a reflection of the heavenly hierarchy, there is
also a development of knowledge which reaches from the
lowest level of knowledge to the highest form of super-intellectual affective-mystical contact with God. The historical
ascent of the Church from the Patriarchs at the beginning to
the People of God of the final days is simultaneously a
growth of the revelation of God. In other words, it is not
only the hierarchical thought-pattern that is transformed in
terms of history, but mysticism as well. Mysticism is not a
grace given in isolation and independently of time; it is, rather, conditioned by the historical development of the divine
revelation.[29] The mysticism which was described by Dionysius and which was granted to the Apostles as to the "perfect"

depicts the stage of revelation of the final Church which is to be a Church of the perfect.[30] With this it becomes decisively clear that the revelation of the final age will involve neither the abolition of the revelation of Christ nor a transcendence of the New Testament. Rather, it involves the entrance into that form of knowledge which the Apostles had; and thus it will be the true fulfillment of the New Testament revelation which has been understood only imperfectly up till now.[31] And so the final age will be truly and in the full sense of the word the "New Testament."[32]

c) The concept which grounds and supports this extensive synthesis seems to me to be that of the Seraphim. The crucified Christ had appeared to St. Francis in the form of a Seraph. From the time of his own meditation on Mount Alverna, this vision had never lost its power over Bonaventure.[33] To the meditating spirit of the theologian, it must have seemed beyond doubt that the essence of the mysterious event was indicated here: the comprehension of Christ was realized here on the highest level of love, on the level of the Seraphim. Therefore, as the stigmata single out the Poverello as the *angelus cum signo Dei vivi,* so the seraphic form of the Lord who appeared to Francis points to the hierarchical position of the Saint and to his historical position. Accordingly, he must belong to the seraphic Church of the final age. Thus an extensive synthesis of hierarchical thought, mysticism, and history is revealed in the unusual double-form of that vision. It is a synthesis in which Bonaventure attempts to come to terms with the theological and religious heritage of his age.[34]

d) Finally, the hierarchical structure remains effective even in heaven and in the eternity of God. For there, men will be distributed among the various angelic choirs according to the level of their being; they will fill up the gaps which resulted from the fall of the evil spirits. And those men whose merits have not reached the requisite level will form a tenth choir with which the tenth cosmic sphere will be filled up.[35]

This theory, which was known to Scholasticism generally,[36] is here placed into a new light by reason of the new context. It now states clearly that the historical situation of the individual will in some way co-condition his place for eternity. Benz even claims that in his *Legenda* of St. Francis, Bonaventure holds the opinion that the heavenly place of the proud Lucifer was reserved for the humble Saint of Assisi. In this way the fall of the Prince of Darkness would have been repaired in Francis, and with this the history of salvation would truly have come to its goal.[37] Actually, this idea is found only in the *Speculum perfectionis* which is not a work of Bonaventure.[38] But it is certainly true that for Bonaventure the hopeful dawn of a new age had broken through in Francis, who bore the wounds of Christ's passion and thus bore the "seal of the living God" (Apoc. 7, 2). This would be that age in which "Nation would rise against nation" no longer (Jes. 2,4). Of such a time one might be able to say: "And then there will be peace."[39]

CHAPTER III

THE HISTORICAL SETTING OF BONA-VENTURE'S THEOLOGY OF HISTORY

After delineating the external structure of Bonaventure's vision of history in general and of history's approaching end in particular, we have another and no less difficult task; namely, to uncover the basic forces of this vision of history and to determine its position relative to the Christian concept of history. We cannot do this meaningfully unless we first briefly describe the pre-history of the Bonaventurian structure. The most important material for this purpose has already been gathered and examined in Dempf's *Sacrum imperium*.[1] Other important material will be found in Kamlah's *Apokalypse und Geschichtstheologie*[2] and in Hipler's *Die christliche Geschichtsauffasung*,[3] which is still a valuable book. We are not here concerned with discovering new material. Rather, our intention is to draw out the theological line of development more precisely than has previously been the case.

#13. **The Pre-Bonaventurian Development of the Medieval Theology of History.**

   I. The theology of history in the Fathers. Its reformulation in Rupert of Deutz.

We can observe two directions of thought among the Fathers concerning the orders of this world. On the one hand, there is an "imperialistic theology." As a theology of Christian world-formation, this view involves an emphatic "Yes" to the orders of the world. Since Eusebius, it has become quite common in the East; in the West, it is represented by Orosius.[1] On the other hand, there is the "pneumatic" theology which emphasizes the Christian conquest of the world understood in the New Testament sense. This view found its most important representative in Augustine.[2] While the first view transplants something of the theocratic spirit of the Old Testament into a new era, the second view preserves the eschatological heritage of the New Testament, even though with many changes. Despite the different attitudes toward the world and despite the different ways in which Christianity consequently is translated into concrete reality, nonetheless a common historical consciousness remains alive. And this consciousness affirms: Christ is the end of the ages; His birth coincides with the "end of the times."[3] On the basis of this axiom, both Chiliasm and Montanism were declared heretical and were excluded from the universal church; for they both denied this vision and awaited still another period of more definitive salvation to follow after the age of Jesus Christ. Augustine's doctrine of the six ages, which placed the coming of Christ in the final age of a *mundus senescens*,[4] was simply another expression of the viewpoint which was able to establish itself as the correct one in the wake of these debates. From Augustine, this type of historical understanding passed over to the Middle Ages where it was received as a heritage of obligatory character. The Middle Ages did not attempt to undermine this heritage, but tried instead to create from it a new and living feeling for the proximity of the end.

We can sense the first impulse toward a change in the work
of the abbot, Rupert of Deutz (1070-ca.1135).[5] He himself
stands entirely within the patristic vision on this point; in fact
he leads this formulation to a new and surprising high-point
of development.[6] At the same time, a new tendency begins
to manifest itself in his thought, even though unwillingly.
As a thinker, Rupert has received too little attention in the
past.[7] In a way that is somewhat foreign to the academic
science of his own times, he attempted to penetrate to the
spirit of Scripture by way of meditation rather than by way of
Scholastic methodology. In this respect, he is closely related
to Joachim of Fiore, another abbot who contributed much to
the decisive reformulation of the theology of history. In his
extensive work, *De sancta trinitate et operibus eius*, Rupert
takes up again the attempt which Augustine had made in his
Civitas Dei, but now with an even greater energy in his historical thinking. He treats history in its entirety from creation
to the final judgment, and attempts to give it a theological
interpretation based on Scripture. Like the Fathers, he also
constructs his historical typology on the creation-account; but
unlike the Fathers, he attributes to this account a three-fold
historical meaning instead of the two-fold meaning. First of
all, this account indicates the work of creation itself, which is
the work of the Father. It indicates further the history of salvation which was worked out in the well-known six ages
of history; this is the work of the Son. And finally, as a new
dimension, it points to the history of salvation determined by
the Holy Spirit in the world-epoch of grace opened by Christ.[8]
Thus there arises a trinitarian super-structure above the seven-
part patristic schema. The time of the Father reaches from
the first "Let there be" to the Fall; the time of the Son ex-

tends from the Fall to the completion of His saving work on the Cross. With the resurrection, the time of the Holy Spirit begins; and it reaches to the end of the world.[9] The eschatological character of the age of the Spirit is expressly maintained. It is called the time of the resurrection, following the inspiration of St. Augustine. First, there is the resurrection of souls; then follows the resurrection of bodies.[10]

The special character of this period is also preserved in another way; for it is no longer time in the proper sense. Rather, it is the fulfillment and the perfection of all that is hoped for and awaited in all the ages. Here again a series of seven arises which is naturally presented in relation to the seven gifts of the Holy Spirit. But here precisely in relation to the series of seven, it is emphasized several times that the works of the trinity cannot be separated, and that in fact there is an interpenetration of the persons of the trinity as well as of the periods of history related to them. So behind the seven days of creation stand the seven gifts of the Spirit; they are also hidden in the six (or seven) periods of Christ-history in the Old Testament.[11]

Yet there is a difference. The axiom: " . . . inseparabilis trinitas unus Deus inseparabiliter operatur" is complemented by two other principles: ". . . sola Filii persona est, quae carne induitur" and ". . . propria Spiritus Sancti persona . . . gratia est." This makes it possible to say that an *actio propria* corresponds to a *proprietas personae,* and that each of the three works — creation, salvation, sanctification — is a *proprium opus* of that person to whom it is appropriated.[12] From this it follows that there is a proper time of the Holy Spirit, and that the history of the world can be divided into three world-weeks, each of which is divided into seven parts. There is the week of creation about which the creation account speaks in the literal sense; there is the week of redemption which is spoken of in the historical division of the Fathers; and there is the week of grace which is divided according to the seven gifts of the Holy Spirit.[13]

This third week is of special interest to us here. It is worked out as follows. The spirit of wisdom is revealed in the mystery of the Passion of Jesus Christ.[14] The tearing of the veil of the Temple (Mt.27,51), was an image of the covering that was torn away from the face of Moses (*vide* Ex. 34,33,35 and 2 Cor. 3, 12-18). It was also an image of the understanding of Scripture which poured into the hearts of the Disciples because of the fact that they were filled with the spirit of understanding.[15] The spirit of divine counsel is manifest in the rejection of the Jews. In the struggle and victory of the martyrs we see the spirit of fortitude. The spirit of knowledge is recognized in the holy Fathers who followed after the period of the martyrs.[16] The spirit of piety points toward the future conversion of the Jews at the end of history.[17] And, finally, the spirit of the fear of the Lord announces the final hour of inner-worldly history: the final judgment. On the basis of this, we find the following schema of the third world-week presented in the history of the Church:

Spiritus sapientiae ....passio
    intellectus ....intellectus scripturarum apostolis datus
    consilii ....caecitas in Israel
    fortidudinis ....tempus martyrum
    scientiae ....tempus doctorum.
    pietatis ....conversio Israel
    timoris Domini ....ultimum iudicium

It is clear, on the one hand, that the eschatological character of the Church is fully preserved,[18] and, on the other hand, that something new has already begun in the Church. In itself, the number seven used to designate the gifts of the Holy Spirit is not a schema of history. It would be more exact to see this number as indicating the unfolding of the one Spirit in seven forms. Consequently this use of the number seven differs from the previous seven-fold division of history. Basically it does not divide history but emphasizes the oneness of the Spirit. In fact, it indicates that with the outpouring of the Spirit, the division of the ages is transcended and that the new era of the resurrection — the *gemina resurrectio* — has begun; an era in which there will no longer be any succession of periods but only the seven gifts of the Spirit, which, taken together, represent the one Spirit. Here again, in a new and creative way, the unity of the sixth age and its final character are brought out.[19]

On the other hand, the schema of the seven gifts acquires a more historical meaning by reason of its relationship to the creation account and to the six ages of Christ-history. While the schema, in itself, retains the seven gifts in a unity, the new historical interpretation of the gifts tends somewhat to dissolve the unity of the Spirit. It is impossible to hide the fact that the historical parallels with which the *dona Spiritus* are clarified do indeed involve a division of Church history into periods. The order in which they stand corresponds to the traditional schema of the gifts, and as yet shows no traces of the later Joachimite expectations. Their path does not lead from a primeval age of perfection through ages of imperfection to an age of perfection within history. Instead, the entire period of time from the passion of Christ to the final judgment is of the same character; it is the "time of the Spirit," a time of the greatest fulfillment. If we were to view any one of these periods as especially singled out, then it would have to be the time of the *intellectus,* that is, the time of the Apostles; for this age is seen to be normative by reason of the gift proper to it. Moreover, the periodization of history is overcome and drawn up into a unity by the fact that the interpretation of these periods is made precisely in terms of the gifts of the Spirit. For this means that these periods are only apparent periods; in reality, they are forms of the unfolding of the one Spirit. But as soon as we set aside the gifts of the Spirit or make use of another typology, as we might easily be tempted to do, then the entire interpretation is destroyed.

In place of the unity of the Spirit, we will then have a temporal sequence. Church history then becomes simply one period of time that takes its place among the other periods of history; it is no longer the final age. Instead, it is simply the second age which comes after the first age of the Old Testament history. At the same time, the unity of the time of Christ, which Rupert had maintained, is destroyed.[20]

But the path towards Joachim's solution can already be clearly seen. If we wish to preserve the schema of the three world-weeks and with it the notion of a time proper to the Spirit which is truly a time of fulfilled promises; and if we presuppose, on the other hand, a temporal periodization of the Church as the real time of Christ, then naturally the prophecy of a Spirit-church of the future arises. Thus Rupert synthesizes the theology of the past, but at the same time all the seeds of the future development are already perceptible in his work.

II. **The transformation of eschatological consciousness in Honorius of Autun and Anselm of Havelberg.**

1. Honorius of Autun.

Though we cannot determine exactly the dates of the lifetime of Honorius of Autun, he did know and respect Rupert of Deutz.[21] It was Honorius who undertook the step indicated above. Rupert's strict division of history with its subtle synthesis of trinitarian thought and patristic historical typology is left behind. Instead, history is set up perhaps for the first time as a continuous line from Adam up to the present in such a way that there are five *ordines* (*status*) before Christ and five after Christ. These can be seen as the *decem status ecclesiae*.[22] The patristic notion of the *ecclesia ab Abel*[23] now shows its inner tendency to bring about uniformity. It is brought into harmony with the eschatological notions in as far as the appearance of Jesus Christ is connected with the idea that the church, which till then had been hidden, now becomes visible.[24] There thus arises a one-lined concept of history which not only fails to take account of the understanding of the church as the end-time, but over and above this, makes the incarnation of the Logos practically meaningless for the total picture of history.[25] Certainly this presentation of history in Honorius is only a chance by-product of his allegory.[26] By and large, it does not play a great role. But the fact that this new step is made almost naturally is a sign of the intellectual character of an age in which the patristic structuring of history is now passed on only like an old garment behind which a new form has been built up almost unnoticed.

2. Anselm of Havelberg (d. 1158).

In Anselm of Havelberg[27] this new element takes on much more precise contours. Anselm proceeds from a question which must have concerned him precisely as a member of the newly-founded Order of Premonstratensians. He remarks that a question is being raised not "manifeste, sed latenter et insidiose." What are all the innovations in the church supposed to mean? What is the meaning of the new Orders which seem to threaten the unity of religion by their multiplicity. They shatter any confidence in the dependability and the truth of this religion.[28] The answer is based on the concept of the *ecclesia ab Abel.* If the church has existed already since the time of Abel and not only since the time of Christ, then it is clear that *mutatio* belongs to the essence of the church. It is no longer difficult to show "quomodo ecclesia Dei sit una in se et secundum se et quomodo sit multiformis secundum filios suos, quos, diversis modis et diversis legibus et institutis informavit et informat, a sanguine Abel iusti usque ad novissimum electum."[29]

At the very inception of this presentation, we find the affirmation of the temporal-historical growth of the church. This is illustrated by a first example according to which the Old Testament openly proclaimed the Father alone while it spoke of the Son only in a hidden way. On the other hand, the New Testament spoke openly of both the Father and the Son; but it left the Spirit in darkness. Knowledge about the Holy Spirit has developed only gradually.[30] But the *mutatio ecclesiae* is expressed above all in that the seven seals of the Apocalypse are intepreted as the seven historical periods of time after Christ.

The white horse .... Christ
The red horse .... Time of the Martyrs.
The black horse .... Time of the Heretics (Arius, Sabellius, Nestorius, Eutyches, etc.)
The pale horse .... False Christians; at the same time, the founding of Orders (present.)

The call of the Saints under the altar

earthquake .... persecution by the anti-Christ
silence .... eternal vision.[31]

We could hardly deny that there is a certain amount of dependence on Rupert of Deutz. But here something has taken place quite decisively, while it had appeared as mere chance in Honorius and as practically nothing more than a possibility in Rupert. The history of the church is depicted as a time of a developing history of salvation. This history does not find its end in Christ but enters into a new stage with Him.[32]

Thus a very significant change in the actual historical consciousness has taken place in the development of Rupert, Honorius, and Anselm under the cover of the Augustinian historical schema[33] which is retained even by Anselm. The significance of this change for the concept of tradition and revelation as well as for the notion of eschatology and salvation history has not yet been given a full evaluation in studies on the history of dogma.[34]

III. The new eschatological consciousness of Joachim of Fiore (d. 1202)

1. Joachim's influence on Bonaventure.

It cannot be determined with certainty whether Joachim of Fiore was aware of this development.[35] But it is possible or even probable that he knew the views of Anselm of Havelberg.[36] It is not necessary here to present the details of his teaching. The extensive literature on Joachim provides us with better information today than anything which could be offered here within the limits demanded.[37] Bonaventure's dependence on the Calabrian Abbot has already been pointed out as regards particular points. This dependence is related essentially to the following thoughts:

a) The acceptance of the two-fold application of the six days of creation to the Old Testament and to the history of the church. Together with this, a double-seven series is set up instead of the simple seven-schema of antiquity.

b) The acceptance of the notion of the *novus ordo* together with a series of allegorical interpretations of Scripture pertaining to this.

c) The acceptance of the expectation of a time of salvation within history which is understood to be a state of full redemption yet to be achieved within history.

But in all three cases, it would be incomplete to see Joachim as the only source. There must have been other intermediary figures between Joachim and Bonaventure who are lost to us at least in part. These may well have already accommodated this material to the contemporary situation. Above all, they would have applied these ideas to Franciscanism.[38]

The following ideas of Joachim and the pre-Bonaventurian Joachimites are rejected:

a) The limitation of the New Testament and the time of Jesus Christ to the second age. The New Testament is the *testamentum aeternum.*

b) The trinitarian division of history is accepted in a very limited way (*vide* p. 47).

With this, the notions of the Calabrian Abbot which were to be of the greatest significance for the future have already been outlined. We have yet to ask what was the decisive characteristic of his historical consciousness.

2. The historical consciousness of Joachim.

In the case of Joachim the idea of the parallel betweeen the Testaments appears in full clarity. This notion had already been present in Rupert, while in the case of Honorius and Anselm it slipped into the background again. But Joachim's development is different from that of Rupert. Joachim understands the time of the New Testament with full seriousness as a temporal, progressive history of salvation parallel to that of the Old Testament. Here something new takes place; the Old and the New Testaments appear as two halves of historical time. These halves are structured parallel to one another, and Christ appears as the turning-point of time. He is the center and the turning-point of history. With Him the course of the world begins again, as it were, on a new and higher level. For this reason, it is not entirely exact when Kamlah says that Christ is no longer the "axis of world history" in Joachim as He had been in Rupert, but rather "one dividing point among many;"[39] for the idea of viewing Christ as the axis of history was as foreign to Rupert as it was to the entire first Christian millenium.[40] For the first thousand years of Christian theology, Christ is not the turning-point of history at which a transformed and redeemed world begins, nor is He the point at which the unredeemed history prior to His appearance is terminated. Rather, Christ is the beginninng of the end. He is "salvation" in as far as in Him the "end" has already broken into history. Viewed from an historical perspective, salvation consists in this end which He inaugurates, while history will run on for a time, so to say, *per nefas* and will bring the old aeon of this world to an end. The idea of seeing Christ as the axis of world history was prepared for by Rupert, Honorius, and Anselm. But it appears clearly for the first time in Joachim; and even here it is somewhat hidden at first by the fact that the history of the world has not one but two axes, and that it is made up not of two but of three great periods. The rejection of this latter notion was effected forcibly by the triumph of orthodox dogma; but the other idea remained. Consequently Joachim became the path-finder within the church for a new understanding of history which to us today appears to be so self-evident that it seems to be *the* Christian understanding. It may be difficult for us to believe that there was a time when this was not the case. It is here that the true significance of Joachim is to be found. And in the face of this, even the indisputable significance which the later history of Joachim's thought was to have in Franciscan Joachimism recedes into the background.[41] In fact, we must say that even this later history is important above all because it brought about the acceptance of this new historical consciousness by forcing the issue to the point of a polemic that exposed a false Joachimism. It should be clear that the church and redemption are rendered historical in an entirely new way which cannot be a matter of indifference for the history of dogma nor for systematic theology.

If, therefore, Joachim attributes an historical significance to the work of Christ in an entirely new sense, it is no longer viewed as the incipient suppression of history. Instead the work of Christ is seen to be firmly rooted in history. Nevertheless a new eschatological consciousness develops here, and it is demanded precisely by the new manner in which the church as it has existed up to the present is interpreted historically. This does not mean that Honorius of Autun and Anselm of Havelberg had fully extinguished the feeling for the proximity of the end. Both of them had constructed their historical schemata in such a way that they themselves and the period in which they lived stood at the end of history. The distinction between their view and that of the patristic age is found simply in the fact that neither Honorius nor Anselm understood the end to have been ushered in with Christ. It arrives only after another lapse of time.[42] On the other hand, Joachim concludes that a truly good and redeemed history is yet to come since an unredeemed and defective history continues after Christ. But this redeemed history is now at hand, as he understands it with gratification. Indeed, it has been growing for a long time in a hidden way, and it must soon burst forth in the open.[43] It is in this imminent event that the Calabrian Abbot places his hopeful joy and his confident expectation, and this is the significant thing about it. It is really possible to look toward that future with the joyful hope that once sounded in the *Marana tha* of the first Christians who awaited the fullness of salvation with the return of the Lord. In the meantime this joy had long been disturbed by the fear of the terrible day of judgment which was to precede the dissolution of the world. No such fear lay between the present time and the coming salvation.[44] Now again a true expectation of the end was possible; an expectation which was penetrated entirely with the spirit of hope.

#14. **The Historical Consciousness of Bonaventure.**

I. **The double development of Bonaventure's historical thought in the period of his Magisterium.**

1. The recasting of the doctrine of the six ages by the concept of medietas.

Before Bonaventure came upon Joachim's theology of history,[1] he himself had already taken a path which had inclined him in this direction and had created a degree of openness for the ideas of Joachim. In his *Commentary on the Sentences* he still makes reference exclusively to the patristic understanding of history. He does this with a slight, time-conditioned nuance that still leaves untouched the peculiar character of the patristic viewpoint: Christ became man "quasi in fine temporum."[2] The affirmation of "Christ as the end of time" already undergoes its first limitation by the insertion of the word *quasi*,[3] but by and large it remains intact. The *Breviloquium*, which was written at the end of his *Magisterium*, still presents the doctrine of the six ages;[4] neither Joachim nor Bonaventure gave it up completely, for it apparently had a quasi-dogmatic value.[5] But here it is given a new tone which significantly comes entirely from Bonaventure's own world of thought and can apparently be traced to no outside influence. "That is why the coming of the Son of God marks the fullness of time: not because time ends with His coming, but because the hidden prophecies of all ages have been fulfilled. Had Christ come at the beginning of time, He would have come too soon; and had His coming been delayed until the very end, He would have come too late. It belonged to Him as the true Savior to provide a time of healing right between the time of sickness and the time of judgment; as the true Mediator, to come mid-

way, some of His elect preceding and others following Him."[6]
Almost imperceptibly something new is created here out of
the old Scholastic concepts that had served to clarify the
plenitudo. temporum.[7] This is found in the statement that
the "fullness of time" is simultaneously the "center of time."
Even the concept of Mediator, which in itself has an entirely
different meaning, is employed here to provide a basis for this
statement. The concept is here understood not simply in the
sense of mediating salvation, but in the sense of standing in
the center of time. Furthermore, this use of the concept of
mediator helps clarify the way in which the reformulation of
the understanding of history came about. Without a doubt,
it proceeds from Bonaventure's preference for the concepts
of the center and the mediator. Both Guardini and Silic have
studied the significance of these notions in Bonaventure's
work.[8] It is precisely the figure of Jesus Christ, the middle
person in the Trinity as well as the mediator and middle between God and man,[9] who gradually becomes the synthesis
of everything that is expressed for Bonaventure in the concept
of center. Christ becomes the center.[10] And as a consequence
of this general interpretation of Christ from the notion of
center, He becomes also the "center of time." It is quite apparent that this idea, which was originally Bonaventure's own,
must have created almost naturally a certain openness to Joachim's double-seven schema. With the elimination of an independent time of the Spirit, this schema offered a vivid description of Christ's central position in time.

2. **The development of a living consciousness of the end in
the controversy about poverty.**

Hand in hand with this development, which seems at first to
promote the de-eschatologizing (M. Werner) of Christianity,

there is another line of development. At the very same time, that is, toward the end of Bonaventure's university career, there appeared a very strong consciousness of the end-time which had been unnoticeable only shortly before in the writing of the *Commentary on the Sentences.* At any rate, the doctrine on the last things had been treated there in a strictly academic way; and Bonaventure had made no remarks which would betray a feeling that the end was very near.[11]

A basic change sets in with the beginning of the controversy on poverty in which William of St. Amour first sounded the eschatological theme. William's view stood in sharp contrast with that of Joachim and the notion of the *Evangelium aeternum,* the condemnation of which he had helped to bring about.[12] He emphasized the fact that we live in the *sexta et ultima aetas.* The proximity of the end arises naturally from this: ". . . ista aetas iam plus duravit quam aliae; quae currunt per millenarium annorum, quia ista duravit 1255 annos; verisimile ergo est, quod nos sumus prope finem mundi."[13] So he could say that the *finalis ecclesia,* the Church of the final age, is drawing near.[14] In the case of William, this proof of the eschatological character of his own era served the cause of his polemic against the mendicant Orders. With it he proved that the dangers which burdened the Mendicants belonged to the *pericula novissimorum temporum*; they should, therefore, be combatted with special vigor.[15] Naturally we can ask to what degree a truly serious eschatological expectation is involved here, and to what degree it is a question of a polemic style. Dempf is of the opinion that the controversy was "in no way intended to be eschatologically serious."[16] Bierbaum holds a similar though less incisive view.[17] A more precise judgment is now possible on the basis of a text edited by Faral. This is the text of William's self-defense before a commission of Cardinals.[18] William's proclamation of the anti-Christ had provoked the dissatisfaction of the ecclesiastical authorities. In the text of his self-defense, William admitted expressly that it is not yet the final age. He justified the eschatological tone of his proclamation in the following way. "Sic ergo patet, quod pericula praedicta, contra quae praeparanda est ecclesia et modo sunt praedicanda et semper a tempore apostoli fuerunt instanter praedicanda."[19] This means that eschatological preaching is justified because, in the Church, the *fines saeculorum* has arrived.[20] Consequently, since the days of the Apostles themselves, it is always well to be vigilant because the anti-Christ threatens the Church at all times. Here the eschatological attitude is seen as the common Christian disposition. In no way need it necessarily include the expectation that the end is near in a temporal sense. Therefore, when William treats the notion of the temporal proximity of the end in his *Liber de antichristo et eius ministris,* it is possible to understand this only as a polemic style.[21] It is in a similar sense that we should understand the eschatological references in the answer of St. Thomas found in the *Contra impugnantes Dei cultum et religionem.*[22] Thomas makes use of such remarks less frequently by far than does his opponent.[23]

William's view can be seen as a polemic with an eschatological character conditioned by the times. But it evokes a genuine eschatological consciousness in Bonaventure; it brings out into the open the consciousness of the proximity of the end which lay at the roots of the original Franciscan experience. So, for the first time, in the *Quaestiones de perfectione evangelica* a type of historical thought appears which clearly betrays the traces of the Joachimite-eschatological interpretation of the Order of Francis.[24] To the objection that it is better to follow the example of approved men of earlier ages than to assume a new form of life[25] Bonaventure answers that the wisdom of God has willed an order of things that involves a temporal succession. Accordingly in the Church there first arose men who were powerful in working wonders and signs. In the "central time" of the Church, men of great learning followed. In the final age, God has sent men who freely chose to be beggars and to be poor in earthly possessions. These men have been sent against that spirit of covetousness which was to achieve its greatest force at the end of the world. Furthermore, poverty arose at the very beginning of the Church (in the community of Jerusalem); it now blossoms again at the end of the Church. So Jerome's statement is shown to be true: "Omega revolvit ad alpha." In the end, the circle closes itself on its beginning.[26] Shortly thereafter, the Dominicans and the Franciscans were designated as the two last Orders sent into the world by God.[27] This is apparently based on the ideas of Joachim. The task of these two Orders is to sign the servants of God on the forehead with the seal of the living God.[28] This is clearly a beginning of the apocalyptic interpretation of Francis which develops from this point onward until it finds its way into the very center of Bonaventure's thought in the *Collationes in Hexaemeron.*[29]

On the basis of the texts, therefore, there can be no doubt that for Bonaventure there is a genuine eschatological consciousness which appears already in the *Quaestiones de perfectione evangelica.* Already at this point, he has been impressed by that mysterious "soon" with which the *Apocalypse* closes (22,20.) This means that at one and the same time in his life, the concept of Christ as the center of time was ripening from the logic of his own thought; the older concept of Christ as the end of time was done away with; and Bonaventure's own consciousness that "the end is really at hand now" arises in contrast to the usual academic indifference relative to the actual temporal fixation of the end. It should be clear by now that these two lines of development are only apparently contradictory. For the reality of an eschatological expectation can increase anew in urgency precisely in that moment in which one overcomes the lack of clarity which arises when one refers to the entire Christian history as the final age. Nonetheless, this form of eschatological thought is not identical with that of the New Testament. It may be just as far removed from that of the New Testament as is that of William of St. Amour and Thomas Aquinas. For in a certain sense, a new, second end is set up next to Christ. Even though Christ as the center is the one who supports and bears all things, still He is no longer simply the *telos* in whom all things flow together and in whom the world is ended and overcome.[30]

II. **The historical consciousness of the "Hexaemeron" and that of Thomas Aquinas.**

In the foregoing, the basic evaluation of the historical consciousness that lies at the basis of the *Hexaemeron* has already been worked out. But a further clarification can be found if we study this vision in contrast to that of Thomas Aquinas. This procedure may be seen to be justified in as far as Ernst Benz, in a series of articles dealing with the problem of Joachim, has devoted a special, detailed study to Thomas' critique of Joachim.[31] He arrives at the surprising conclusion that it is precisely in this critique that the victory of juridical thought over the original eschatological attitude of Christianity becomes apparent, and with it the Church's capitulation to the spirit of the anti-Christ. This betrayal is supposed to have been carried out in the course of the ecclesiastical rejection of the "Franciscan reformation."[32] On the basis of what has already been said above, two objections can be raised against this explanation. First, it should be adequately clear that we cannot equate the eschatological notions of Joachim with the eschatological attitude of Christianity itself. Consequently, the rejection of Joachim's view may not at all involve the rejection of the eschatological attitude of Christianity. Furthermore, we have already seen that within the Catholic Church we find not only Aquinas' answer to Joachim, but Bonaventure's answer as well.

And Bonaventure's answer takes up the basic themes of Joachim and relates them to the thought of the Church without any loss of the living eschatological tension. Here we merely want to indicate the theological point of departure from which Thomas' critique proceeds. It is found in one citation which Benz has bypassed in his extensive study. The notion that appears here will permit us to draw a final characterization of the theology of history found in the *Hexaemeron*. This also is missing in Benz's treatment.[33]

1. The central point of Aquinas' critique of Joachim.

Strange to say, Thomas entered into the theological controversy with Joachim earlier than did Bonaventure. In his *Commentary on the Sentences* Bonaventure never mentions the problem raised by Joachim's prophecies. On the other hand, Thomas devotes an entire *quaestiuncula* to the problem and deals with it in some detail.[34] The question of the time of the resurrection was usually handled in the doctrinal treatment of the last things. Within the framework of this question Thomas introduces his treatment of the problem with the objection: "Videtur, quod tempus illud non sit occultum."[35] One of the reasons for this objection is: "Status novi testamenti praefiguratus fuit in veteri testamento . . . Sed scimus determinate tempus, in quo vetus testamentum statum habuit. Ergo. . ."[36] To this Aquinas answers that the way in which the New Testament is prefigured in the Old Testament should not be understood as though any particular element of the Old Testament pointed toward a particular aspect of the New Testament, but rather in the sense that the entire Old Testament points to Christ "in whom all the types of the Old Testament are fulfilled." With full justification, Thomas refers to Augustine's *Civitas Dei* which had rejected the application of the plagues of Egypt to the Christian persecutions. This is, in fact, a rejection of that form of exegesis which is basic to the entire Joachimite theology of history.[37] Concerning Joachim himself, Aquinas says that his work must be judged in the light of the fact that some of his predictions are true, but that in other matters he had deceived himself.[38] But the central point of the critique lies in the rejection of the historical-allegorical exegesis which Joachim applied to the Old Testament. The signs and the periods of the Old Testament do not point to a similar course of events in the New Testament, for such a view would necessarily involve the suppression of the New Testament by the Old Testament. Instead, the signs and periods of the Old Testament point to Christ who is the fulfillment and the fullness of the Old Testament. In Him and in Him alone do we find the whole of the New Testament. Therefore it is in Him alone that prophetic power of the Old Testament is fulfilled. Is this thesis unchristian or anti-Christian? If it is, then the same is true of the exegesis of Augustine and of the ancient church, and even of the exegesis of St. Paul himself. The truth of the matter is that Thomas Aquinas does not set up an opposition between the eschatological view of Joachim and the juridical thinking of a church which is assumed to have been untrue to her mission. Rather he places the Christo-centric view of Scripture and of the Fathers in opposition to the historical speculation of the Calabrian Abbot. His solution to the problem is simply "Christ." In Him and in Him alone is the Old Testament fulfilled.

2. The central point of Bonaventure's critique of Joachim.

In contrast with Aquinas, Bonaventure expressly recognized Joachim's Old Testament exegesis and adopted it as his own, as we have already seen. In this case, therefore (and not only in this case), Thomas is more an Augustinian than is Bonaventure.[39] In contrast with Aquinas' clear and decisive critique of Joachim, that of Bonaventure seems at first to touch only peripheral points. It seems to involve nuances that are hardly noticeable, and which would seem to have developed quite naturally with the mere passing of time.[40] But the difference that separates Bonaventure from Joachim is greater than it may seem at first. Basically he is in agreement with the Thomistic critique, for he also affirms a Christo-centrism. Bonaventure does not accept the notion of an age of the Holy Spirit which destroyed the central position of Christ in the Joachimite view. Certainly the two final *ordines* are orders of the Spirit; and the Spirit certainly achieves a particular power in the final age; but this age, as such, is an age of Christ. It remains the *septima aetas* of the New Testament Christ-time which endures up to the end.[41] It is precisely in the *Hexaemeron* that the notion of "Christ as the center of all" reaches its highest development.[42] If it is justified to say that for Joachim, Christ is merely one point of division among others,[43] it is no less justified to say that for Bonaventure, Christ is the "axis of world history," the center of time. Even though Bonaventure accepts and affirms the parallel structure of the ages which had been rejected by Thomas, he is led in this by a completely different tendency than that which led Joachim to his structuring of time. If Joachim was above all concerned with bringing out the movement of the second age to the third,[44] Bonaventure's purpose is to show, on the basis of the parallel between the two ages, that Christ is the true center and the turning-point of history.[45] Christ is the center of all. This is the basic concept of Bonaventure's historical schema, and it involves a decisive rejection of Joachim. In the final analysis, he is closer to Thomas than to Joachim.

CHAPTER IV

ARISTOTELIANISM AND THE THEOLOGY OF HISTORY.

The philosophical position of Bonaventure's theology of history.

In the foregoing, we have attempted to present the background from which Bonaventure's theology of history grew. In order to achieve a full understanding and a balanced evaluation, we must look also at the antithesis of this view; for Bonaventure's own approach is reflected in a new way precisely in his rejection of the antithetical view. Here we are confronted with the problem of Aristotelianism and Bonaventure's position relative to it. As we will see, his rejection of Aristotle is not primarily metaphysical nor epistemological; rather, it involves first and foremost the question of the theology of history. Since the question of Bonaventure's anti-Aristotelianism has become one of the principal points of dispute in the modern study of Bonaventure, we will first present the development of this controversy and its present state at least briefly in its basic lines. Finally, on the basis of the texts themselves, we will attempt to develop the problem anew and to give an answer from a new perspective.

#15. **The Modern Controversy concerning Bonaventure's anti-Aristotelianism.**

1. **The thesis of Gilson and his followers: Bonaventure, the Augustinian.**

It is to the credit of Jules d'Albi[1] that he was the first to have pointed out clearly the anti-Aristotelian and anti-Thomistic tone of Bonaventure. Somewhat later, Gilson undertook the task of interpreting the entire work of Bonaventure from the aspect of his anti-Aristotelianism. He attempted to follow the traces of this anti-Aristotelian tone, and has demonstrated a masterful command of the texts down to the most subtle ramifications of Bonaventure's thought.[2] Naturally even Gilson could not overlook the fact that there is no noticeable anti-Aristotelianism in the works of Bonaventure's *Magisterium.* These works may be called "scholastic" in the stricter sense. It has been pointed out that in the first period of Bonaventure's scientific activity, which lasted until 1257, there are over four-hundred citations in which Aristotle is treated expressly in a friendly manner;[3] and we have found no text which would indicate the opposite. During this period, Aristotle is the Philosopher for Bonaventure just as he would always be for Thomas.[3a] Thus, Gilson speaks of a "certain moderation" with which Bonaventure treats Aristotle in the peaceful time of the *Commentary on the Sentences.*[4] He speaks of the "obvious forebearance" which is apparent in this work relative to Aristotle while a far less benign attitude is extended to Plato.[5] Nonetheless, the same basic viewpoint which is present in the later *Collationes in Hexaemeron* is found already in the *Commentary on the Sentences.* "In the year 1273 Bonaventure was better informed about the persons and their responsibility. He no longer saw a praiseworthy consistency in the position of Aristotle; it now appears to be a blind obduracy in error. On the other hand, he praises Plato as the first to have taught the creation of the world in time. There is no change in Bonaventure's thought at the basis of this new evaluation of the persons. The *Hexaemeron* simply applies a judgment which had been made long ago in the *Sentence Commentary.*"[6] The reverse side of this thesis, which sees Bonaventure simply as the great adversary of Aristotle in the Middle Ages, can be summarized briefly in the formula: Bonaventure, the Augustinian. It is supposed that Bonaventure's work is the great mediaeval synthesis of Augustinianism; that it breathes the spirit of Augustine. It is assumed that the work of Bonaventure lives as totally from the work of Augustine as the work of Thomas lives from that of Aristotle. Briefly, this thesis holds that the clear Augustinian tone of the Seraphic Doctor is the genuine and authentic basis of his anti-Aristotelianism.[7]

In this way, a new image of Bonaventure was created. For the thesis of Gilson, which saw Bonaventure as *the* Augustinian, is basically different from that of Ehrle,[8] even though Ehrle's thesis may sound very similar on the surface, and even though Gilson's thesis would have been unthinkable without that of Ehrle. For Gilson, Bonaventure is not an Augustinian in the sense that he belonged to a traditional Augustinian tendency and developed this direction of thought more fully. This had been the case in Ehrle's thesis.[9] Instead, he is now seen to be an Augustinian in the sense that he created an integral anti-Aristotelian Augustinianism as a new synthesis directed against the threat to Christian thought represented by Aristotle. To put it in other words, according to Gilson, it was not only the one great synthesist, Thomas Aquinas, who offers an answer to Aristotle in the cultural milieu of the thirteenth century. Actually, there were two great answers given to Aristotle at the same time; that of Thomas Aquinas and that of Bonaventure. This means, according to Gilson, that the work of Bonaventure would be an answer to Aristotle in the same sense as is the work of Aquinas. Just as we must take the work of the great Dominican as a whole and understand it as a painstaking and fundamental discussion with the Stagirite, we should understand the work of Bonaventure in the same way. Or to put it in yet another way, in the confrontation with Aristotle, the Christian spirit brought forth not only the one synthesis of Thomas, but two syntheses of equal stature. Certainly they differ from one another. The one is pro-Aristotelian in as far as this is possible for a responsible Christian thinker; the other is just as clearly anti-Aristotelian, and it forms a different system which makes use of certain Platonic structural elements which had already been refashioned in a Christian way by Augustine.[10] According to this viewpoint, Thomas Aquinas and Bonaventure stand as two high-points in Scholasticism and enjoy equal rights.[11] In as far as this presentation corresponds to the facts, all the force was taken out of the argument of those who held that the Augustinianism of Bonaventure, which must be acknowledged to some degree, is to be traced to an ignorance of Aristotle's work, and that for this reason, Bonaventure could be rejected as antiquarian.[12]

It is clear that a thesis which had been presented with so much spirit and warmth together with such an extensive knowledge of the sources could not die away unheard. P. Robert speaks of a *concert de louanges* that was evoked by Gilson's book.[13] In Germany, the agreement with this thesis was even more unanimous and undivided than in France where P. Mandonnet objected sharply to Gilson. But Mandonnet's *polémique célèbre*[14] gained scant attention in Germany. Gilson's image of Bonaventure gained something of a classic stature. It found approval by research scholars such as Longpré,[15] Squandrani,[16] Thonnard.[17] G. H. Tavard,[18] Rosenmoeller,[19] Auer,[20] and Dempf[21] among others. P. Robert[22] and L. Veuthey[23] also stand on Gilson's side, though with some reservation. Also, B. Geyer,[24] H. Meyer,[25] and J. Hirschberger[26] adopted the position of Gilson in their works on the history of philosophy.

On the other hand, as might be expected, the School of Louvain did not concede the point without a fight. This School had never been able to warm up to the concept of a medieval "Augustinianism," and preferred to speak of an "aristotélisme éclectique,"[27] or as Smeets expresses it in his article on Bonaventure in the *Dictionnaire de theologie Catholique,* of "péripatétisme nuancé d'augustinisme."[28] But after the unsuccessful objection of Mandonnet, the real counterattack was relatively slow in coming. It was brought forward clearly for the first time in 1942 in the second volume of F. Van Steenberghen's *Siger de Brabant,*[29] and was developed further in his study *Aristote en Occident.*[30] In the thirteenth volume of Fliche-Martin's church history, Van Steenberghen has taken over the treatment of the thirteenth century. There he again gives a detailed presentation of his notion concerning the development of Aristotelianism and Augustinianism in the High Middle Ages.[31] As far as I can see, the discussion of his viewpoint has hardly begun in Germany.[32] Consequently, we will present his thesis in some detail.

2. The thesis of Van Steenberghen: Bonaventure, the Augustinizing Aristotelian.

Van Steenberghen places the problem of Bonaventure in the total context of the intellectual development of the twelfth and thirteenth centuries. The strength of his thesis lies in this fact. In this way, he overcomes the illusion of the historians of philosophy which has recently been criticized sharply by Gilson;[33] an illusion that would like to establish one consistent line of philosophical thought in the Middle Ages. It overlooks the fact that in the Middle Ages, there is only the one Christian wisdom of the Scriptures and of positive theology respectively; from this, gradually an independent philosophy was able to disengage itself.[34] "First of all at the beginning of the thirteenth century in Paris there are no definite philosophical lines of thought. There was a movement of logical studies which were based primarily on the *Organon* of Aristotle. There was also a movement of theological studies which was nourished from varied sources in as far as it made use of the speculative method at all. These sources were above all Augustine, Aristotle, and Pseudo-Dionysius. But at this time, neither Augustinianism nor Aristotelianism exist as philosophical systems or even as distinct doctrinal tendencies."[35] It is clear that at this time there could be no conflict between philosophical tendencies nor any real conflict between the philosophical and the theological faculties. At most there would have been a lack of unanimity on the question as to how far dialectics should enter into theology.[36] But from about the year 1200, the influence of Aristotle increased constantly. Already for Simon of Tournai, the *doctrina aristotelica* is synonymous with *philosophia*.[37] The number of citations from Aristotle increases from author to author.[38]

The early Franciscan Masters, Alexander of Hales and John of Rupella,[39] fit into this line of development. " . . . having been educated in the Arts Faculty, their minds were trained in Aristotle's logic and they had absorbed many metaphysical doctrines at the same time as this logic; psychological and moral doctrines had been taught to them while they were studying the *Ethics* of Aristotle; these philosophical studies had aroused their curiosity and they completed their training by the personal reading of Aristotle. . . Here we stand before a more or less developed form of eclectic Aristotelianism. Its nuances and inner coherence differ from case to case."[40] As we can see, it is at this point that the term *aristotélisme éclectique* enters into the picture. And we can hardly deny that the logic of the historical argument that leads to the formulation of this term is convincing in this context. As an almost natural conclusion from this line of thought, Van Steenberghen adds that "the notion of a conflict between an 'Augustinian philosophy' and an 'Aristotelian philosophy' is absolutely foreign to these theologians (absolument étrangère). For them, philosophy meant the knowledge passed on by Aristotle and the other pagan philosophers. This knowledge was now taught by the Faculty of the Arts. If they envisioned any possibility of a conflict . . . it would be between this philosophy with its pagan origin and the Christian wisdom of the Fathers which had been developed further by the theologians . . .".[41] And so the situation remains: "On the philosophical level during the first half of the thirteenth century, Augustinianism is nonexistent."[42] Taking philosophy and theology together, we can say: "On the whole, the general philosophical-theological direction of thought (le mouvement philosophico-théologique) before 1250 was neither traditionally nor essentially

Augustinian. This movement began around 1225 under the influence of the new literature. It was a question of a neo-Platonizing Aristotelianism which lacked homogeneity. The theologians joined this with the traditional doctrines of Latin theology for which Augustine was the main source. Briefly, that which we generally refer to as pre-Thomistic Augustinianism is the doctrinal form of the theological faculty as it was built up under the influence of philosophy around the year 1230."[43]

According to Van Steenberghen, Bonaventure remains basically within the neo-Platonizing Aristotelianism adopted by his Franciscan Masters and develops it further. Consequently, as far as his work is concerned, we must reject not only the designation "Augustinianism," but also the notion of "Aristotelianizing Augustinianism." Somewhat more precise would be the designation "Augustinizing Aristotelianism." But the most precise formulation would seem to be "aristotélisme éclectique néoplatonisant et surtout augustinisant."[44] "The philosophy of Bonaventure and that of Thomas do not stand opposed to one another as an Augustinian system against an Aristotelian system, but rather as two forms of neo-Platonizing Aristotelianism which have not been equally developed. It remained more eclectic in the case of the Franciscan master, while in the case of St. Thomas, it has acquired the form of a strong, seamless synthesis."[45] The synthesis of the Dominican master found no recognition among the disciples of Bonaventure, for they believed that they had to retain the characteristic theses of eclectic Aristotelianism at any price. To them, this appeared to be the traditional doctrine of the Church, while the Thomistic synthesis looked like a dangerous peace-overture toward the heretical Aristotelianism taught by the

Faculty of the Arts.[46] In order to give their system greater
unity and cogency, these theologians call upon Augustine as
the primary witness. And thus the so-called medieval "Augustinianism" arises from the opposition between a less developed
form of neo-Platonizing Aristotelianism and the more highly
developed Thomistic form. "Before the year 1270 there is no
Augustinianism in the strict sense of the word, and there is no
Augustinian school" — this is the simple conclusion which Van
Steenberghen draws from his presentation.[47]

In view of this, the Belgian philosopher holds it correct to
speak not of Augustinianism but of neo-Augustinianism. He
suggests this in order to emphasize two essential characteristics
of this movement. "On the one hand, this stream of thought
deliberately adopts Augustine and Augustinian doctrines
which had already won the right of domicile in Western theology; . . . but on the other hand, it is obviously a neo-
Augustinianism, for this philosophy adopts a considerable
number of elements which have no historical connection with
the original Augustinianism including Aristotelian doctrines as
well as concepts of Jewish (Avicebron) or of Arab (Avicenna) origin."[48] In this connection, Van Steenberghen differs
radically from the view of Gilson[49] and P. Thonnard,[50] and
agrees with the position of M. de Wulf: "The essential
theories of philosophical Augustinianism are foreign to the
spirit of Augustine."

And so the question remains: What position does Bonaventure himself take relative to this neo-Augustinianism which
had developed in the controversy with Thomas and which
Bonaventure himself had experienced? According to the studies of d'Albi and Gilson, there can no longer be any doubt
that, at least in his later development, Bonaventure had taken

a position against the Aristotelianism of Thomas. Van Steenberghen does not deny this. Bonaventure was in fact the first
to raise his voice against the threat of a radical Aristotelianism. "It seems to be beyond doubt that the doctrinal innovations of Thomas Aquinas seemed dangerous to him, and that
Bonaventure encouraged Peckham and his party in their opposition to Thomism. In this sense, he can be seen as the inspiration of neo-Augustinianism. But he is not its founder in the
strict sense of the word; for his intervention in the scientific
debates in the year 1270 was on the religious level, and his
much different preoccupation at that time did not permit him
to enter the discussion immediately on the philosophical level.
John Peckham is the true founder of the Augustinian school
. . . "[51] This school shows a considerable inconsistency in its
doctrines, many of which seem to have been antiquated already
at the beginning of the school. It lasted hardly thirty years,
only to be superseded by Scotism.[52] While the thesis "Bonaventure, the Augustinian" is still respected here in a certain
sense, it has taken on a completely different meaning than it
had in the case of Gilson. Now it means that at the end of
his life Bonaventure provided the impulse that led to the formation of neo-Augustinianism, which actually was not much
more than an inconsistent anti-Thomism.

3. A provisional position relative to these two views.

This presentation did not go unchallenged. Certainly Van
Steenberghen had brought to light some indisputable facts.
But the followers of Gilson's Augustinian interpretation
attempt to give a different interpretation to the facts. It must
be conceded to Van Steenberghen that there is much Aristotelian material in Bonaventure. But Van Steenberghen's oppon-

ents argue that the spirit of the entire work of Bonaventure is Augustinian. The Swiss Conventual friar, L. Veuthey, for example, accuses the Belgian philosopher of looking only at the formulae and not at the spirit.[53] P. Alszeghy says that Van Steenberghen has given too much emphasis to the analysis of the sources and too little to the *modus philosophandi* and to the *modus realitatem explicandi*.[54] Furthermore, even in the analysis of the sources, he says, Van Steenberghen has based himself too one-sidedly on the *Commentary on the Sentences*.[55] Da Vinca makes a similar evaluation. According to him, Bonaventure's philosophy can be called Aristotelian *aliquo modo* if we consider it *materialiter*. But as soon as we approach it *formaliter*, we would have to call it radically anti-Aristotelian.[56] We may certainly be tempted to ask whether it is allowed to place so little value on the problem of the sources, and whether the question of Augustinianism is not in fact a question of the sources to a very great extent. As far as this question is concerned, we cannot limit ourselves to a consideration only of Aristotelianism, which had already become so influential. We cannot allow ourselves to be deceived any more concerning the multiplicity of influences from which medieval Platonism was formed. In this process, Augustine was merely one source among many.[57]

Let us by-pass this objection for the moment in order to ask another question. In what would the formal Augustinian element consist which would make it necessary to speak of Augustinianism despite the Aristotelian material? There are two principal answers to this question. Thonnard,[58] Veuthey and Alszeghy see the essence of Augustinianism in the theocentric approach and in exemplarism. Van Steenberghen answers this justifiably by affirming that these are basic tendencies which are to be found in all creationist systems and which are objectively rooted in any creationism. Historically they may be traced to two sources. There is a religious source, which is the Judaeo-Christian Revelation; and there is a philosophical source, which is found in Platonism. All the great Arab, Jewish and Christian thinkers, including Augustine, are dependent on these two sources.[59] "What all these authors (Veuthey, etc.) understand by the 'Augustinian spirit' is none other than the Christian spirit, which emphasizes the superiority of divine Revelation to reason, of Christian doctrine to that of philosophy, and of sacred to human sciences. This is found in Thomas just as well as in St. Bonaventure. It is not specifically Augustinian."[60] The second answer, represented especially by Gilson and Brounts, is a more significant answer. According to them, the decisive point is that Bonaventure rejected the autonomy of reason including the relative autonomy of Thomistic Aristotelianism. He demanded a philosophy that would be radically Christian, that is, a philosophy centered on Christ and worked out from Christian Revelation.[61] Van Steenberghen's answer to this suffers from rather obvious weaknesses. He says that a philosophy is present potentially in Bonaventure's theological works; and if we were to disengage it, it would be simply "a collection of purely rational doctrines, which, as such, are foreign to the properly Christian spirit."[62] Even Van Steenberghen himself has to admit that such a construct would be completely artificial; it would be a body without a soul.[63] But does this not mean, in the final analysis, that in the case of Bonaventure, philosophy is united with theology as the body with the soul and that we may not legitimately separate them and disengage the philosophy; whereas in the case of Thomas Aquinas, it is fundamentally possible and justified to disengage a relatively independent philosophy from the whole, even though this philosophy must be drawn from his theological works to a great extent?

Actually, it seems to me that Van Steenberghen is somewhat inconsistent with the results of his own studies when he defines Gilson's concept of "Christian philosophy" and when he expressly affirms the fundamental possibility of separating philosophy and theology in Bonaventure;[64] for his own presentation of the history of philosophy indicates that the so-called Augustinianism arises from the problem of the relation of philosophy and theology and that it is the result of a process of development in which this philosophy is actually being formed. It is his own presentation of the history of this period which indicates that the real question in the great disputes of the thirteenth century was not simply a philosophical fight within an already existing philosophy. Rather it was a question of Christian philosophy and Christian wisdom as such.

This becomes clear, for example, in the evaluation of the decree in which Stephen Tempier expressed the ecclesiastical condemnation of Aristotelianism. "Since the studies of Ehrle this has often been called a reaction of Augustinianism against Aristotelianism. But this would involve a judgment of the question from a secondary aspect. Actually, this was a momentous decision . . . in a crisis for the Christian intellect which had been brought about by the massive influx of pagan science. Its symptoms had already been noticeable as early as 1210."[65] If we view the matter from this perspective, then the problem of Augustinianism and Aristotelianism is not a purely philosophical problem. It cannot be treated at all if we abstract from theology, and every presentation that attempts to do so overlooks the decisive point at issue.

This understanding of the historical line of development seems to be well established by an impressive number of facts.[66] If we accept this thesis, then Bonaventure's work must be seen to have its place in the controversy concerning the unity of Christian wisdom and the duality of philosophy and theology. This controversy had not yet been brought to its conclusion at the time of Bonaventure. Furthermore, it means that the so-called Augustinianism (and neo-Augustinianism) is a decision against the Thomistic solution to the problem and naturally against the solution of Siger of Brabant. It then becomes understandable that the anti-Aristotelianism of Bonaventure is directed not primarily against the content of Aristotle's statements but rather against the attempt to make philosophy independent. This effort arises from the Aristotelian influence. Because of the fact that the lines had not been drawn up in this way until the year 1267 (*vide* #16,A), there was no real anti-Aristotelianism in Bonaventure before that time. The question remains: Can we see Bonaventure's thought as an "Augustinianism" in opposition to the "Aristotelianism" of St. Thomas by reason of the fact that he rejected the Thomistic separation of philosophy and theology which had been worked out from an Aristotelian background? Certainly we cannot and should not speak of an Augustinian philosophy in opposition to an Aristotelian philosophy, for this would mean that we would miss the heart of the question. On the other hand, the notion of the undivided unity of Christian wisdom is a genuinely Augustinian concern and not simply a Platonic idea. It was this notion that Bonaventure defended against the new Aristotelian understanding of the Christian mode of thought. Nonetheless, it would seem to me to be an over-simplification if we should want to designate the entire structure of Bonaventurian thought as an "Augustinianism" on this basis alone. This would involve a failure to recognize the multiple intellectual influences that enter in here as well as the basic intellectual point of departure which is not precisely "Augustinian" but rather medieval; it belongs to the peculiar situation of the thirteenth century.

Consequently, in the final analysis, we must admit that Van Steenberghen is correct to a great extent as regards the question of Bonaventurian Augustinianism.[67] But the anti-Aristotelianism of the Seraphic Doctor has much deeper roots than the Belgian philosopher is willing to admit; and this anti-Aristotelianism is connected very closely with an Augustinian concern, as we have indicated above. In Van Steenberghen's work, there is one point that is not clarified. How does it come about that Bonaventure, the Aristotelian eclectic, becomes the inspiration of an anti-Aristotelian neo-Augustinianism? This must remain inexplicable for him for two reasons. First, in his one-sided evaluation of Gilson's view, he attributes to the Seraphic Doctor an understanding of the relation between philosophy and theology which is conceived too much along Thomistic lines. Here he fails to recognize the basic concern of Bonaventure's concept of wisdom. Secondly, we must recognize (more than Gilson has done) that the elaboration of this ideal of wisdom in Bonaventure is not at all self-evident. In the *Quaestiones disputatae* of his period as *Magister,* his thought had taken a path which would have led him in a direction similar to that of Thomas if he had developed it consistently to the end.[68] The fact that he took up the Augustinian ideal represents a decision which cannot be convincingly shown to have arisen only from the Scholastic work of Bonaventure. It is very closely connected with the historico-theological thought of the Seraphic Doctor, and this historical concern also contributes much to the characteristic quality of Bonaventure's anti-Aristotelianism. We will now develop these points.

#16. The Historico-Theological Significance of Bonaventure's anti-Aristotelianism.

A. The development of anti-Aristotelianism in Bonaventure's work.

Bonaventure's anti-Aristotelianism appears in the *Collationes de decem praeceptis* which he held in Paris during Lent of 1267. Here he rejects two theses: the eternity of the world, and the doctrine of the unity of the intellect in all men.[1] From this point onward, the polemic against Aristotelianism becomes a recurring theme in his sermons and lectures.[2] One year later, Bonaventure presents a finished canon of anti-Aristotelianism. In the *Collationes de donis Spiritus Sancti,* he extends the number of errors from the two of the previous year to three: the eternity of the world, the necessity of fate, and the unity of the intellect in all men. Corresponding to the current tendency to systematization, he treats this triad of errors systematically. There is a violation of the *causa essendi* in the doctrine of the *aeternitas mundi*; there is a violation against the *ratio intellegendi* in the thesis of the *unitas intellectus*; finally, there is a violation against the *ordo vivendi* in the affirmation of the *necessitas fatalis.*[3] Thus, the triad of errors violates the three basic forms of truth to which the three primary philosophical disciplines—physics, logic, and ethics—are ordered.[4]

The rejection of Aristotelianism, therefore, has already acquired something of a logical, systematic form. The apparently deliberate construct which Bonaventure sets up here in order to uncover Aristotelianism as the enemy of the basic truths of human life would already reveal something of Bonaventure's apocalyptic convictions, even though he himself had not expressed them immediately in this context.[5] The point of the systematization of his polemic was to bring out the eschatological character of the attacks being made at the present moment against the decisive elements of Christianity and against the whole of Christianity. While the professors of Paris had spoken shortly before this of the "pericula novissimorum temporum" in relation to the question of the Mendicant Orders, now Bonaventure, as the Franciscan General, points clearly to the real source of these dangers. They are dangers which should characterize the final age of history, and they are evident precisely at the University of Paris which was persecuted by the devil in a special way because it was a source of genuine learning.[6] To the end, Bonaventure firmly maintained the canon of anti-Aristotelianism which he had formulated. Five years later, in the *Collationes in Hexaemeron,* he speaks again in the very same terms of the "triplex caecitas, scilicet de aeternitate mundi, de unitate intellectus, de poena et gloria."[7] Certainly this canon is developed further in as far as these three errors are traced to an antecedent error which consists in the denial of the *exemplaritas divina.* The rejection of the doctrine of the Ideas, again, involves a three-fold error, namely the neglect of the *exemplaritas,* of the *divina providentia,* and of the *dispositio mundana.*[8] This extension of the anti-Aristotelian canon is connected with the development of new systematic motifs in Bonaventure's work. In the *Collationes in Hexaemeron,* the concept of the center achieves its most extensive development. Christ is now understood as the center of all things in the most radical sense. Naturally, therefore, the final assault of the powers of darkness is understood as an assault against the "Center," that is, against Christ who, as the "middle person" of the Trinity, appears as the one who bears the *divina exemplaritas mundi.*[9]

If we are to understand the true character of Bonaventure's anti-Aristotelianism, we must see clearly the limits of his view which we have sketched here in its broader dimensions. First we must realize that Bonaventure's polemic is directed not primarily against Aristotle but against the Aristotelians of his age.[10] The Seraphic Doctor always maintained a certain reserve in evaluating the historical Aristotle. This is apparently rooted in the fact that he knew Aristotle not from his own readings, but only from the Scholastic tradition.[11] But above all, the concrete eschatological threat for Christianity arises not from Aristotle, but from the apparently Christian Aristotelians. We could perhaps say that Aristotle would be related to them as Paul and John are related to the eschatological *ordo futurus.* This statement is not found expressly in Bonaventure. But we will see that the parallel construction set up between the philosophical *Unheilsgeschichte* and the ecclesiastical *Heilsgeschichte* readily leads to such an interpretation.

There is another factor which is perhaps more important. None of the main ideas of Bonaventure's anti-Aristotelianism can be called expressly anti-Thomist;[11a] not even the attack against the doctrine of the eternity of the world. Bonaventure expressly admits Thomas' distinction between the philosophical and the theological orders when he says: De aeternitate mundi excusari posset, quod intellexit hoc ut philosophus, loquens ut naturalis . . ."[12] Above all, the doctrine of illumination is entirely absent in the canon of anti-Aristotelianism. This doctrine is often seen to be the central difference between

Augustinianism and Aristotelianism. It is not mentioned at all in the entire controversy. As a matter of fact, for Bonaventure it was not a decisive question in the matter of Aristotle and Augustine. Two things are clear from the *Commentary on the Sentences* and the *Quaestiones disputatae*. First, Bonaventure sees Aristotle also as a witness for the doctrine of illumination; second, the Seraphic Doctor sees the epistemological theory of Aquinas to be a form of illumination. It is a form which Bonaventure himself rejects, but which nonetheless remains within the framework of theological possibilities.[13] In this matter, Bonaventure sees an inner-scientific point and not a religious question like the problem that was raised by the heretical Aristotelianism and the radical threat to Christianity which it brought with it. The fact that this problem is passed over in silence in all the later discussions is a sure sign that Bonaventure never changed his viewpoint on this question.

Would we then say that there really is no serious anti-Thomism in the work of Bonaventure? No. There certainly is, but it is situated differently than we had accustomed ourselves to think of it. In the *Hexaemeron*, Bonaventure expressly criticizes three theses of St. Thomas: the doctrine of the non-composition of *substantiae separatae*; the affirmation of the real distinction between the soul and its faculties; and, finally, the thesis that the *potestas intellectiva* is the primary seat of beatitude.[14] None of these points is taken up in the actual controversy about Aristotelianism. But Bonaventure does see a connection with Aristotle. In his rejection of the Thomist viewpoint concerning the relation of the soul and its faculties, he adds the unmistakable side-remark: "licet philosophus dicat."[15] The point of this remark is obviously that Thomas should be warned against too close a bondage to

Aristotle. But the tone of the entire section is without a doubt symptomatic of Bonaventure's general attitude relative to Thomas Aquinas. He does not include Aquinas himself among the Aristotelians with whom he differed. No text can be found to provide any serious support for the opposite view.

However, Bonaventure does see in Thomas the danger of putting too much confidence in Aristotle, and he feels seriously obliged to issue a warning against this. In his eyes, every concession in such a matter would be dangerous because it does not recognize the seriousness of the danger and it favors the opponent. It is because of his viewpoint concerning the final age that Bonaventure speaks out against the opposition with such an uncompromising sharpness. Because of this background, even the concession which Aquinas makes to Aristotle on such a decisive question as the eternity of the world could seem highly suspicious to Bonaventure. Finally, he must have heard the warning of Pseudo-Joachim: "Verum caveat sibi ordo postremus (= Franciscans), ne persequatur ab alio (= Dominicans) et occurrant sibi cum exercitu magistrorum confidentium in armis disputationum Aristotelis et subvertat eum in filiis datis sibi."[16]

B. The two main forms of Bonaventure's anti-Aristotelianism.

I. Anti-Aristotelianism in the struggle for a Christian understanding of time.

In his anti-Aristotelian canon, Bonaventure set up a certain hierarchy of errors, if we might use the term in this context. This permits us a better insight into his own position. According to this hierarchy, the rejection of the doctrine of Ideas is the first cause of the following errors. These, in turn, stand in a certain casual relation to one another in such a way that the doctrine of the eternity of the world necessarily gives rise to all the other erroneous doctrines. Already in his *Commentary on the Sentences,* Bonaventure had upheld the thesis that the affirmation of an eternal world brings along with it a whole host of errors. It is therefore the real objective point of departure for an anti-Aristotelianism which could develop as soon as this doctrine was traced to Aristotle with certainty.[17] This means that the point of departure for Bonaventure's critique of Aristotle is to be found in the notion of the temporal character of the world; it is related, therefore, to the question of the philosophy or the theology of history.

This is most clearly expressed in one of Bonaventure's arguments which Gilson had already emphasized and which gives us the best insight into Bonaventure's concept of time. At the same time, it clearly delineates the way in which Bonaventure stands apart from both Aristotle and from Thomas Aquinas. Here Bonaventure affirms that it would be impossible to give order to the infinite. But if there were not a first movement at the beginning of the world, then the world and its movements would be infinite.[18] Practically, this is an allusion to the rejection of the *regressus in infinitum* found both in antiquity and in Scholasticism. But as Bonaventure well knows, Aristotle and Thomas see no contradiction in an infinite series of movements in the heavenly bodies, even though they also hold the impossibility of an infinite regress. Their argument runs as follows. The *regressus in infinitum* is impossible only in the *ordo causalitatis* but not on the level of objects of like rank whose sequence is merely accidental. St. Thomas clarifies this with the following example. It is impossible that a stone be lifted by a stick, that the stick be lifted by a hand, and that such a causal series be continued infinitely. In such a case, there must be a first cause. But it is possible that a sculptor whose hammer breaks could throw away one hammer after the other, so that finally he uses an infinite number of hammers. Here the unity of the cause is preserved in such a way that the *regressus in infinitum* is broken off. A mere accidental infinity of such instrumental causes following one another does not constitute a *regressus in infinitum*.[19] When applied to the question at hand, this means that the rejection of an infinite regress demands a first only in the order of causes on the vertical level running from above downward. Here we must accept a *primus movens* in which the series terminates. But on the horizontal level of causality among created things we have only an accidental order of causes. In such a case, we may easily hold an infinite series; for the unity of cause is already fully maintained with the affirmation of the highest *primus movens*. But this series of infinite duration is actually "finite" in the sense demanded here simply by reason of the vertical order of causes. We can see this clearly in the following diagram.

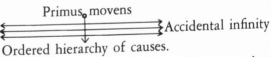

Primus movens

Accidental infinity

Ordered hierarchy of causes.

If we apply this to the problem of history, it means that history takes place on the level of accidentally ordered causes and pertains to the realm of accidental infinity. Consequently, it is not really a part of the genuinely ordered cosmos of causes; for this causality lies in a different direction. This notion conforms accurately with the concept of history which we find in antiquity and to a degree also in Scholasticism. History is the realm of chance. It cannot be treated in a truly scientific manner not only because of the mystery of human freedom that is at work in history, but because history as such belongs to the realm of accidently ordered causality found in created things. With keen perception, Bonaventure sees that this concept of history is incompatible with the Christian view. He demands an ordering of causality also on the horizontal level of world events and their temporal sequence.[20] He must make this demand because he sees an entirely different form of world-history. For him, the history of the world is ordered in an *egressus* and a *regressus*; in the center of these stands Christ.[21]

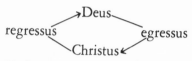

Any form of "infinity" in this closed and ordered movement is unthinkable from the very start. In this context, we can understand Bonaventure's own concept of time. For Aristotle and Thomas, time was the neutral measure of duration, "an accident of movement."[22] For Bonaventure, it is not merely a neutral measure of change. Together with the *caelum empyreum,* the *angelica natura*, and the *materia*, time is included among the four realities which were the first to be created. These are the four structural elements from which the entire world is built. Time especially had to be created in the first place "quia non tantum dicit mensuram durationis, sed etiam egressionis."[23] It is not only the measure of inner-wordly processes; but it is above all the "time of creation," which measures the ordered emergence of things from the creative power of God. In as far as it is ordered to *egressio*, it is integrated right from the start into the great Bonaventurian vision of the world; for wherever we speak of *egressio*, we affirm a *regressio* together with it. Time, therefore, is understood right from the start to be saving time. The neutrality of a mere *mensura durationis* is removed from the very beginning, and the thought of an infinite duration of time is nonsensical in this context. On this point Gilson's judgment is correct: "The root of the matter is that St. Bonaventure's Christian universe differs from the pagan universe of Aristotle in that it has a history."[24]

In this framework, we can understand in a new way the very different positions taken by Bonaventure and Thomas relative to the problem of the theology of history in Joachim of Fiore. As we have seen, Thomas rejects the speculation of the Calabrian Abbot for theological reasons; and he draws his grounds from the *Civitas Dei* of Augustine and from Holy Scripture. But he has already taken a position prior to this in the realm of philosophy which is perhaps no less important for his view. Thomas clearly emphasizes that we have no revelation concerning the time of the end of the world. But he adds that we cannot figure out the time of the end *naturali ratione* because the movement of the world and the measure of that movement, which is time, "secundum naturam suam possit in perpetuum durare."[25] Here is an indication that it was not only Augustine and the Scriptures that led Aquinas to reject Joachim's orderly systematic view of history, but Aristotle as well, even prior to the others. Such a system of history is impossible for him because of the notion of the accidental ordering of historical events. In contrast with this, Bonaventure's own very different concept of history makes it understandable that he should take a more positive attitude toward the theology of Joachim. For Bonaventure, history consists of two corresponding movements from the very beginning— *egressus* and *regressus*. Christ stands as the turning point of these movements and as the center who both divides and unites. Would not the theology of Joachim with its parallel structure of the two Testaments have seemed the ideal representation and concretization of that schema which Bonaventure himself had always had before his eyes? Here was the twofold division into seven ages with Christ standing in the middle. Obviously a very surprising agreement actually arose when the age of the Spirit was struck out precisely as an age of the Spirit and was integrated into the seventh period of the time of Christ. In this way an inner unity appears between Bonaventure's late work and his earliest sketches.

Excursus: The circular and linear concept of time in Bonaventure.

We have accustomed ourselves to see the circle as the characteristic symbol of the pagan understanding of time, and the line as the appropriate symbol of the Christian notion.[26] I have no intention of questioning the correctness of this symbolism. We will see that Bonaventure himself had similar notions. Nonetheless, we should not forget that this is only a question of symbols that express a reality which may be separated from this particular symbolic manner of expression and can possibly be expressed in other images. The basic fact consists in this, that the Christian concept of time involves limitation at both ends; what happens in history is done but once and cannot be repeated. For the pagan, on the other hand, time is a circular movement; it is a continuous repetition of the same; there are no clear limits as regards the beginning or the necessity of an end. In trying to make a judgment on the position of any individual thinker, we must always return to this basic fact.

We have already seen that, in a certain sense, Bonaventure sees Aristotle's concept of time to be linear; it is an infinite line without inner ordering. In contrast with this, Bonaventure holds a type of circular movement as the image of the Christian understanding of time; the double movement of *egressus* and *regressus*. Here the two symbols seem to be directly reversed when compared with our customary understanding. But the real, objective difference is preserved. For the characteristic of Christian time is the unrepeatable character of that which takes place, while the characteristic of the pagan notion is that of an unordered infinity. We must now clarify more precisely this notion of time as one unrepeatable, orderly circular motion which we have provisionally extracted from Bonaventure's general division of time into *egressus* and *regressus*.

1. God as the sphaera intelligibilis.

The circular concept of Bonaventure is rooted first of all in his concept of God. Basing himself on the Pseudo-Hermetic book of the 24 Masters[27] and the *Regulae theologiae* of Alan of Lille,[28] Bonaventure defines God as "sphaera intelligibilis, cuius centrum est ubique et circumferentia nusquam."[29] Or in another place, on the basis of Pseudo-Dionysius, he calls the divine love a "cyclus aeternus, ex optimo, per optimum et in optimum."[30] For Bonaventure, the first definition is far more than a mere play on words. It is a fitting expression of the real, good infinity of God which stands in opposition to the orderless infinity which Aristotle ascribes to the world and to which we may easily be tempted to apply Hegel's concept of a "bad infinity." Bonaventure emphasizes that we have not yet properly expressed the essence of eternity simply with the concept of *interminabilitas*. Certainly the lack of limitation belongs to eternity. This is expressed in the circumference of the circle which has neither a beginning nor an end. But the mere lack of limitations would be a "bad infinity" (to retain this expression) and not genuine eternity. *Interminabilitas* in itself does not constitute eternity as such; *simultas* is involved here also. *Simultas* refers to the inner concentration and unity. It is expressed in as far as God is referred to simultaneously as the *centrum,* that is, the center of the circle in which the radical, inner unity of the circle is expressed. This clarification of the circle-motif by means of the concept of the center must be kept in mind especially when this motif is transferred to creation.

2. The circle of time: From God, through Christ, to God.

With great consistency, Bonaventure transfers the notion of the *circulus intelligibilis* from God first of all to man, the image of God. ". . . vita aeterna haec sola est, ut spiritus rationalis, qui manat a beatissima trinitate et est imago trinitatis, per modum cuiusdam circuli intelligibilis redeat per memoriam, intelligentiam, per deiformitatem gloriae in beatis· simam trinitatem."[31] Here the dynamic of the individual spirit is described as a circular movement from God back to God. But like the Fathers, Bonaventure recognizes the typological correspondence between the individual man and the whole of mankind.[32] Therefore it is a very natural step to transfer the circular concept of the individual to a circular concept of the history of the world. This is already hinted at elsewhere when he says that it is through man and through the grace that sanctifies man that the world must be drawn back into the *circulus aeternitatis*.[33] In two places, namely in the *Breviloquim* and in the *De reductione artium ad theologiam,* he states clearly that the duality of *egressus* and *regressus* makes the history of the world into a great circular movement which proceeds from God and returns again to God. "Et ideo ibi completus est circulus, completus est senarius et propterea status."[34]

In the light of this, another citation which is peculiar to the *Hexaemeron* becomes clear. There Christ is presented as the center of all things. He is, therefore, also the center of all the sciences in as far as we must go on beyond the "literal sense" of the individual sciences to the hidden, deeper meaning much as we see it worked out in the *De reductione artium ad theologiam.*[35] In this vision, it is true to say that Christ, among other things, is the *medium distantiae*; that is, He is that center that is the concern of the mathematician, and He is this *medium* precisely in His crucifixion. Here we can bypass Bonaventure's detailed treatment of this theme. It can be easily understood from what has already been said. We are concerned only with the curious conclusion of this section: "Medium enim, cum amissum est in circulo, inveniri non potest nisi per duas lineas se orthogonaliter insectantes."[36] The lost middle of the circle is found again by means of two lines that intersect at right angles, that is, by a cross. This means that by His cross, Christ has definitively solved the geometry-problem of world history. With His cross He has uncovered the lost center of the circle of the world so as to give the true direction and meaning to the movement of the individual life and to the history of mankind as such.

There is still another transformation of the circular concept of salvation history to be found in the *Hexaemeron.* The typological interpretation of the creation-account which leads to a division of history into two parallel parts apparently rests on the notion that the pattern typified in the creation-account is to be repeated twice, each time on a higher level. Furthermore, several times the idea emerges that the end involves a certain return to the beginning.[37] As a result, we could be tempted to speak of three circles. But this manner of expression would not be true to the facts if it were to evoke the notion of a two-fold circular return of the same. Actually, it is not a question of a returning movement, but of a unified, progressive, ascending movement. But the ascent of this movement is realized in such a way that the basic structural law of the earlier level is repeated on the higher level. So we might be justified in speaking of a spiral, and here we would find an indication of the connection between the idea of a circle with the idea of a progressive line. Bonaventure always remains conscious of the unique and unrepeatable character of that which takes place in history.

3. The false doctrine of the philosophers concerning the eternal circle.

What we have just said about Bonaventure's understanding of the unrepeatable character of history is confirmed by the fact that he himself saw the principle error of the philosophers to consist in the doctrine of the eternal circle. He even describes this doctrine with apocalyptic terminology; it is the sign of the Beast. The errors we have already pointed out, namely, the eternity of the world, the necessity of fate, and the unity of the intellect, "are indicated in the *Apocalypse* in the number of the Beast." According to this book, the number of this name is 666. It is a cyclic number. Here Bonaventure makes a free application of the concept of the cyclic number with which the School of his time designated square-numbers in relation to a base.[38] As regards the work of creation, the number six has the meaning of a circle that is perfectly closed. The number 666 appears when the number six reaches its highest intensity. It is thus a cyclic number in a very special sense.[39] The three-fold cyclic number expresses the three-fold heretical doctrine of the cycle which is the sum of all heresies: the affirmation of the eternal world is based on the notion of the cyclic movement of time; the thesis of the necessity of fate is based on the cyclic movement of the celestial bodies; and the third doctrine is based on the concept of a common (cosmic) Intelligence that migrates from body to body. This clearly recalls what we said earlier concerning the fact that the last two errors proceed from the first.[40] It is clear that the theory of the cycle of time is exposed as the primordial heresy and as the very essence of the apocalyptic monster.

II. Prophetic-eschatological anti-Aristotelianism.

1. A comparison of two lines of Bonaventure's anti-Aristotelianism.

These last remarks have brought us back again to our real theme, that is, the question of Bonaventure's anti-Aristotelianism. We must now state that there are two distinct lines of anti-Aristotelianism in Bonaventure. Recent research has not given sufficient attention to this fact, and consequently there is considerable confusion on the point. We have already worked out the first line of thought, which has to do with the objective-metaphysical opposition separating Bonaventure from Aristotle from the very start. This consists in the firm rejection of the doctrine of the eternity of the world. The development in Bonaventure's thought can be clarified as follows. In the beginning he wavered somewhat in attributing this doctrine to Aristotle; for the concept of the eternity of the world seemed to be absurd, and he saw Aristotle as a great man who was to be respected. But from the year 1267, that is, from the beginning of Latin Averroism, he could no longer have any serious doubt. His fundamental conviction on this point however, did not actually change.

Nonetheless, the new understanding gained in the year 1267 is neither meaningless nor extrinsic to the question. In its wake, a new, second line of anti-Aristotelianism begins to develop in Bonaventure. This second line remains quite distinct from the first even though the first does not die out. I would like to call it the prophetic-eschatological line; or, following a suggestion of G. Soehngen, the line of apocalyptic anti-Aristotelianism. The first line involves an objective difference of viewpoint which was present from the start. The second line consists simply in the fact that after the rise of Latin Averroism, Bonaventure saw an eschatological phenomenon in Aristotle, or in heretical Aristotelianism. Here was the Beast that was to rise from the abyss (*vide supra*). As such, it was the negative sign that stood in opposition to the positive sign of St. Francis. But nothing had been said about this in the *Commentary on the Sentences*. It represents a new line of thought, and it develops gradually along with the development of his theology of history, both of which reach a highpoint in the *Collationes in Hexaemeron*. The two lines must be clearly distinguished from one another, for the first involves an objective contradiction while the second soon breaks through the limits of a mere anti-Aristotelianism and becomes an affirmation of far greater significance.

2. The individual motifs of apocalyptic anti-Aristotelianism.

In Bonaventure's later sermons and lectures (from 1267) and particularly in the *Hexaemeron,* philosophy and the exercise of reason in general are presented in a series of images which seem to approach a total condemnation of both. We will study these images individually so as to find their basic significance.

a) The image of Pharao's magicians.

Traditional exegesis had explained the failure of Pharao's magicians on the occasion of the third plague (Ex. 8, 14f) as an allegorical indication of the failure of the philosophers and natural reason to come to the mystery of the Trinity.[41] Bonaventure also sees the magicians of the Pharao as a type of the philosophers, but he changes the explanation of their failure to some extent. The two things which *Exodus* attributes to them, writes Bonaventure, refer to the knowledge of God from the "book written within and without," that is, from spiritual and material creation. The book which is used here as a type is that of *Apocalypse* 5, 1; as a type it is used with extraordinary variability. The third element which was lacking to them was the knowledge of God from Scripture.[42] Consequently, they were lacking in the most important thing; and despite all the light which they may have succeeded in enkindling, they still remained in darkness. They were not capable of discerning the three decisive facts of human life: "animam ordinare in finem"; "rectificare affectus animae"; "sanare morbidos."[43] Above all, this third and final task escaped them completely, for they knew nothing of man's sickness and its cause; even less did they know the Physician or the cure.[44] Thus, on the basis of a brilliant passage from Joachim's *Concordia*, Bonaventure formulates the significant statement: "Fides ergo sola divisit lucem a tenebris."[45]

Bonaventure gives a typological interpretation to the failure of the magicians at the tenth plague as well (Ex. 11, 29-36).

It indicates that the philosophers "were able to give us the nine sciences. But they could not give the tenth, which is no longer science but wisdom. In as far as it is wisdom, it is ultimately beatitude."[46] This holy wisdom which transcends the powers of the philosophers is that *sapientia nulliformis* in which the intellect is silenced and darkened by the mystical power of the divine mystery. Only love is awake and comes immediately into contact with the heart of the eternal God. In this context, the image changes again. The intellect itself is the Pharao's magician who is forced to step back in silence and who is not able to touch the finger of God.[47]

If we overlook this last image for the time being, we can see a very important conclusion emerging from our study. The statements in question are in no way decisively anti-Aristotelian; they are simply anti-philosophical. The statement, "fides ergo sola divisit . . ." points to the fact that every philosophy is inadequate. It is a question of showing that even the *philosophi nobiles,* who did not share in the errors of Aristotle, remained in darkness and did not find that light which faith alone can give. This notion is applied in a more general way in the final citation where the intellect itself is identified as the Pharao's magician. Here we have a simple anti-intellectualism which is convinced that it must raise a warning voice against the tendency to place too much confidence in the intellect as such.[48]

b) Philosophy as the lignum scientiae boni et mali.

Though the anti-philosophical polemic just sketched moves within rather moderate limits, it clearly becomes much more pointed in the designation of philosophy as the *lignum scientiae boni et mali.* "He who is concerned only with knowledge eats of the tree of the knowledge of good and evil."[49] We can assume from the start that a particular understanding of history is involved in this application of the image of the tree. This becomes fully certain when we compare the statements of a sermon held in Advent, 1267, with the corresponding citation from the great schema of history in the *Hexaemeron*. There it is stated that in the early church there were two trees, just as there had been in Paradise; the tree of life, and the tree of the knowledge of good and evil. The tree of life is Christ Himself.[50] This tree becomes accessible in the spiritual understanding of Scripture. But he who understands the Scriptures only in the literal sense eats of the tree of knowledge.[51] This application of the images of the trees to the two understandings of Scripture is the exegesis which Bonaventure had originally applied to the two trees. In no place is it ever revoked. Apparently Bonaventure was not the first to come upon this exegesis,[52] but his understanding of history allows him to take it a step further. First, the events of Paradise are repeated on a higher level in the history of the early Church. The Judaizers could not bring themselves to give up the literal exegesis of Scripture. For this reason, they ate of the tree of knowledge (see Rm. 7,7). The fact that they were driven from the Paradise of salvation in Christ was the necessary consequence. Thus the heresy of the Ebionites arose.[53] And this event is now repeated again in the final age, but on a higher level. "It is written that Adam ate from the tree of the knowledge of good and evil and was driven from Paradise. Today this is fulfilled in our teachers. The spiritual understanding is the tree of life; the literal understanding is the tree of the knowledge of good and evil . . ." He who loves Scripture, loves philosophy as well; for with it he can strengthen his faith. But philosophy is the tree of knowledge of good and evil since truth and falsehood are mixed together in it. If, however, you are a fanatic for philosophy, then you say: How can Aristotle be mistaken? Then you do not love Scripture and you necessarily fall from the faith."[54] The vision of history that lies at the root of this is clear. Just as there was a decision and a division because of the two trees in Paradise and in the early Church, so there is now in the Church of the final age. For Bonaventure, the eschatological process of division had already begun with the events which were taking place at the University of Paris. If anyone gives philosophy final and definitive validity and does not use it simply as a means, he eats of the tree of knowledge and he "falls from the faith."

It is obvious that this is not precisely a question of anti-Aristotelianism, but a limitation on the claim of philosophy as such. The fact that Aristotle may be named expressly does not change this fact. It simply indicates that at this time Bonaventure saw Aristotle to be *the* Philosopher. When he criticizes Aristotle, he does not do so with the intention of recommending Plato or some form of "Augustinian" philosophy; such notions would have been foreign to him. Rather, his concern is to criticize philosophy as such. But it remains true that "He who loves Scripture, loves philosophy as well . . ." even Aristotle. This anti-philosophical attitude, which is identical with anti-Aristotelianism, is limited and not total. It is directed against a philosophy which fails to recognize its true function; which makes itself self-sufficient and thereby becomes an eschatological sign of perdition. Obviously this development in Bonaventure would be unintelligible to anyone who presupposes an already existing form of Christian philosophizing, whether this is seen to be Aristotelian or Augustinian in tone. This is not a problem within an already existing philosophy, but a problem of the rise of a philosophy. It is on this level that Bonaventure takes his stand. For the Christian, he rejects any phiolosophy that is not ready to be integrated into the orderly structure of Christian wisdom.[55]

c) Philosophy, the Beast from the Abyss.

From this perspective, we can now understand the exact meaning of those texts which interpret the radical Aristotelianism of the University of Paris as the fulfillment of the apocalyptic prophecies of disaster. We have already pointed out the citation in which this heretical Aristotelianism is identified with the Beast of Apocalypse 13, 11-18; its number is 666.[56] In the *Hexaemeron,* Bonaventure uses another citation from the *Apocalypse.* The abyss which had been opened by the fifth angel and which emitted smoke and darkness still stands open (Apoc. 9, 1ff). The heretical Aristotelianism is the smoke from this abyss; it is the Egyptian darkness.[57] The relation between the different series of images involved here indicates that it is not a question of an exact historico-typological exegesis as we had in the great historical schema of *Hexaemeron* XVI. It is far more a question of fluctuating pictorial images which single out one appropriate element from the whole. The actual significance of these images apparently does not differ from what we have presented above. Again, here it is not a question of anti-Aristotelianism, but of that form of anti-philosophical attitude which we attempted to describe earlier.

d) Reason, the Harlot, and similar images.

Only if we keep all this in mind can we correctly understand the most pointed anti-philosophical statements of Bonaventure.

The image of reason as a harlot was later to become famous. For Bonaventure it signifies a self-sufficient philosophy, a philosophy that attempts to draw us from the hands of the royal bride that is Christian wisdom. "The Jews would not hear wisdom from the mouth of Wisdom. But we have Christ in us and still do not desire to hear His wisdom. It is a frightful abomination that the fairest daughter of the king should be offered to us as our bride; but we prefer a despicable servant girl as our wife, and we prefer to prostitute ourselves with her. We would rather return to the miserable flesh-pots of Egypt than allow ourselves to be refreshed with heavenly food."[58] "You should not love the prostitute and dismiss your bride for her sake."[59] If we keep in mind that formulations of this type were quite common in the traditional language of theologians,[60] though not perhaps of such prophetic sharpness, it looses a bit of its impact. We should also keep in mind the parallel already cited between Judaism and Aristotelianism which is centered around the image of the two trees of Paradise. In this way the deep historico-theological conviction behind these images becomes clear. It is a vision which sees the heretical Aristotelianism of the Faculty of the Arts as a phenomenon of the eschatological fall from the faith; but it does not intend to condemn a philosophy which is used properly. In particular, it does not intend to condemn the proper use of Aristotle. The image of the return to the flesh-pots of Egypt[61] and the designation of the philosophers as *luciferiani*[62] must be judged in the same way.

e) The prophecy of the end of rational theology.

A genuinely new aspect becomes clear at the end of a lecture in which Bonaventure treats of the exegesis of Scripture and particularly of the fruitfulness of Scripture for the intellect. Here he says: "Believe me, a time will come when the 'gold and silver vessels' (Ex. 3, 22; 12, 36) i.e. rational arguments, will no longer be of value. There will no longer be any justification of faith by reason, but only by *auctoritas*. As an indication of this, in His temptations the Redeemer defended Himself not with rational arguments but with arguments from authority, even though He certainly must have known the arguments of reason well. In this way He predicted what would take place in His Mystical Body in the coming trial."[63] Here he not only questions the justification of any "separate philosophy," but he predicts the end of all rational theology; that is, the end of that speculative-philosophical thought which recognizes its true function and is integrated into theology. A time will come in which the division proceeding from the *lignum scientiae* and the *lignum vitae* will reach its extreme point. Then there will be no more possibility of a pact between reason and faith. *Ratio* and *auctoritas* will stand apart, cleanly separated and in opposition to one another. Naturally, this vision of the future overshadows Bonaventure's general attitude toward reason. Without a doubt it is one of the reasons for the amazingly sharp language which he frequently uses.

Regarding our question, this prophecy of Bonaventure is significant in several ways. First of all, it again confirms the fact that for Bonaventure the whole question is not simply a matter of an opposition to Aristotle, for this would make it practically an inner-philosophical question. It is precisely that vanishing-point toward which his historico-theological line of thought is tending which proves anew that far more is intended here. It shows that we are dealing primarily with a limited anti-philosophical attitude which ultimately develops into an anti-dialectical and anti-scholastic mentality. This, of course, is not yet suitable for the present situation, but it will become necessary in the future.[64] This is in close agreement with Bonaventure's statement that the present Order of Franciscans is related to the Cherubim. Because the present Order is only a temporary state of affairs, speculative science is still allowed for it. But the eschatological Order of Francis is related to the Seraphim, and it will be taken up completely with contemplative love.[65] Bonaventure admits often that his scholastic-scientific Franciscanism has nothing definitive about it. It is only in the Church of the final age that St. Francis' manner of life will triumph. As the *simplex* and *idiota,* Francis knew more about God than all the learned men of his time—because he loved Him more.[66]

The recognition of this context is significant because it allows us an insight into the problem of the sources of this citation and of the entire line of thought which finds its climax in this text. Apparently the development from an anti-intellectual attitude to a general anti-Scholastic mentality in Bonaventure is conditioned by a growing insight into the primitive Franciscan ideal which would seem to involve almost necessarily a certain anti-intellectual element.[67] Bonaventure's Franciscan anti-intellectualism acquires its concrete form from the historico-prophetic anti-intellectualism of Joachim and Pseudo-Joachim.[68] And finally, a third source is the influence of the anti-intellectual mysticism of Pseudo-Dionysius. We have already eveluted the significance of this in detail in relation to Bonaventure's concept of revelation. Augustine, the witness of Christian science and Christian intellectual life, plays no role here. Bonaventure himself knew this clearly. At one time, he set up a sort of short salvation-history of theology in which he related Augustine to *doctrina* and Gregory the Great to the preachers; but Dionysius he saw as the patron of the *ecclesia contemplativa,* the Church of the final age.[69] Bonaventure had never set out to be an "Augustinian." His intention had been merely to give that place to Augustine which he deserved just as he wished to give to Aristotle the place he deserved. In the great hierarchical structure of Christian wisdom, it is not only Aristotle who has a subordinate and ministerial position, but Augustine as well. Certainly Augustine stands above Aristotle; but he must be satisfied with the second place. He stands far too close to the philosophers to succeed in arriving at the first place. Already in his *Commentary on the Sentences,*[70] Bonaventure had made this accusation. In fact, in this work we find that Bonaventure is quite capable of very critical observations about Augustine.[71] Consequently, it is not surprising that even Augustine becomes "dangerous" as soon as he departs from his proper place. In such a case, the difference between Augustine and Aristotle would consist in the fact that Augustine would be aware of the danger and would warn us: "When you give up Scripture and study the books of Augustine instead, he (Augustine, himself) says that this is not good."[72]

Let us now return to our point of departure, that is, to Bonaventure's prophecy of the end of rational theology. The thought which leads him on, and which we have attempted to develop here, is summarized in a classical manner in the following citation from the *Hexaemeron.* "Note this about St. Francis, who preached to the Sultan. The Sultan told him that he should dispute with his priests. But Francis responded that it was not possible to dispute about the faith by means of reason because faith was above reason. Nor was it possible to dispute with them by means of Scripture, because they did not recognize Scripture. But he requested that a fire be started; he and they would walk into it. One should not, therefore, pour too much philosophical water into the wine of Sacred Scripture lest the wine be changed into water. This would certainly be a very evil miracle, for we read that Christ changed the water into wine and not the reverse. From this it is clear that all those who believe shall derive the proofs of their faith not from reason but from Scripture and miracles. In the primitive Church, they burned the books of the philosophers (Apoc. 19, 19). Indeed, one should not change bread into stones."[73] This fact from the history of the primitive Church is a prophetic type of that which is to be realized in the final Church inaugurated with Francis. The end of rational theology is coming.

III. Summary.

On the basis of the material we have studied, we are now in a position to define the general picture of Bonaventure's anti-Aristotelianism more precisely than Gilson and Van Steenberghen have done. In the light of what has been said, we can distinguish three levels of anti-Aristotelianism of quite distinct significance.

1. From the beginning, Bonaventure differs with Aristotle objectively by reason of an entirely different concept of time which allows the Seraphic Doctor to deny the eternity of the world emphatically. But this objective difference does not keep Bonaventure from holding Aristotle in high regard nor from granting a basic recognition to the Aristotelian philosophy.[74]

2. The historico-theological anti-Aristotelianism which develops after 1267 must be clearly distinguished from this

objective anti-Aristotelianism. This second development is directed not primarily against the historical Aristotle but against the contemporary form of Aristotelianism. It is a battle against a self-sufficient philosophy standing over against the faith. Thus, his anti-Aristotelianism develops here into a general anti-philosophical attitude. In this case, the rejection of Aristotle is the rejection of a self-sufficient philosophy. This does not, however, exclude the recognition of philosophy and of Aristotle in their proper place. Philosophy must be integrated into the truth coming from Revelation.

The codification of anti-Aristotelianism found in the presentation of the three basic errors is, in a sense, a development of the objective anti-Aristotelianism which had been present already in the *Commentary on the Sentences*. But, as we have seen, it develops in an historico-theological direction and is basically a protest against a self-sufficient philosophy. Here the necessary errors of such a philosophy can be seen. In this way it is not only anti-Aristotelian, but anti-philosophical in the sense indicated. But we must emphasize again that the rejection of philosophy and of Aristotle is directed only against a philosophy separated from theology. It is not, therefore, anti-philosophical in an absolute sense. Rather, it allows for philosophical thought in as far as philosophy is integrated into and is subordinate to theology.

3. Finally, in the *Hexaemeron* we find the final development of this anti-philosophical attitude which here becomes a prophetic anti-Scholasticism in which Franciscan, Joachimite, and Dionysian themes merge. Rational theology is seen to be merely provisional. For the final age which is to come he predicts a theology based only on authority. Here an historical dimension is inserted into the anti-philosophical mentality.

For the present, speculative thought—philosophical and theological—is justified. But in the higher state that is to come, this will be transcended and will become superfluous.

From this, the meaning and the extent of Bonaventure's anti-Aristotelianism should be clear. We cannot, therefore, agree with Gilson who interprets the entire work of Bonaventure as anti-Aristotelian on the basis of certain texts in the *Hexaemeron* and the late sermons. Nor can we agree entirely with Van Steenberghen and Robert, who work from the *Commentary on the Sentences* and the *Quaestiones disputatae* and see the *Hexaemeron* to represent a new rhetoric but not a new position.[75] Actually something new has happened in the *Hexaemeron* and in the sermons dating from 1267. But neither would I like to take my stand with Veuthey, who holds that Bonaventure changed from Aristotelianism in the *Commentary on the Sentences* to neo-Platonism in the *Hexaemeron*.[76] Such a viewpoint can be justifiably rejected, for it misses the point.[77] Actually in the case of the later Bonaventure, practically nothing has changed as regards the inner understanding of the philosophical and theological problems. In as far as he philosophizes and theologizes, he does so with the same materials and the same methods as he had used earlier.[78] But there is a new element involved which may be called extra-philosophical, or extra-theological if we understand theology in the restricted sense of speculative-Scholastic, systematic theology. This new element allows us to gain a new perspective and to see anew the historical orientation of the whole question. We could also say that the change does not take place within the Scholastic, systematic framework. Rather, with his roots in the ground of Franciscanism, Bonaventure sees the entire phenomenon of Scholasticism and of scientific thought in a new and different way. He does not cease to recognize its great value for the present time; he himself does not cease pursuing it and loving it; he does not give up his concern for its correctness. But at the same time, he sees that it is not final in itself. One day the form of life of St. Francis will become the universal form of the Church—the *simplex et idiota* will triumph over the greatest scholars, and the Church of the final age will breath the spirit of his spirit.[79]

CONCLUSION

Like so many other masterpieces of scholarship, Bonaventure's interpretation of the creation-account has remained incomplete. Neither he nor Aquinas were permitted to finish the real *Summa* of their lives. And so a saddened disciple of the Master had to write in regret at the end of the unfinished course of the collations: "Sed heu! heu! heu! superveniente statu excelsiori et vitae excessu domini et magistri huius operis, prosecutionem prosecuturi, non acceperunt."[1] Nonetheless, it does form a unified whole, and the basic lines intended by Bonaventure are unmistakable. At the vanishing-point of his theology of history we find the very same word which Augustine had used at the close of his *City of God,* which in itself is so different from the work of Bonaventure. That word is peace: "And then there will be peace." But for Bonaventure, this peace has come closer to earth. It is not that peace in the eternity of God which will never end and which will follow the dissolution of this world. It is a peace which God Himself will establish in this world which has seen so much blood and tears, as if at least at the end of time, God would show how things could have been and should have been in accordance with His plan.[2] Here the breath of a new

age is blowing; an age in which the desire for the glory of
the other world is shaped by a deep love of this earth on which
we live. But despite the difference that may separate the work
of these two great Christian theologians, still there is a basic
unity; both Augustine and Bonaventure know that the Church
which hopes for peace in the future is, nonetheless, obliged
to love in the present; and they both realize that the kingdom
of eternal peace is growing in the hearts of those who fulfill
Christ's law of love in their own particular age. Both see
themselves subject to the word of the Apostle: "So there
remain faith, hope, and love, these three. But the greatest
of these is love" (1 Cor. 13,13).

NOTES

Notes to Introduction

1. Cfr. the survey of the development of the philosophy of history in K. Löwith, *Weltgeschichte und Heilsgeschehen*, Stuttgart, 1953². Also informative is H. Ott, *Neuere Publikationem zum Problem von Geschichte und Geschichtlichkeit*, in: *Theol. Rundschau* 21 (1953) 62-96. Cfr. also the statement of H. J. Marrou, who introduced his paper "La théologie de l'histoire" at the international Congress on Augustine in 1954 with the remark: Aurait on consacré a ce sujet une séance de discussion dans un des Congrés Augustininens tenus en 1930? . . . Il faut certainement mettre ce renouveau en rapport avec l'aggravation de la crise ôu se débat la civilisation occidentale . . ." (Printed in: *Augustinus Magister*, Paris, 1954, Vol. III, p.193.)

2. There is a vast literature on the *Civitas Dei.* Cfr. Altaner, *Patrology*, 1958 (English trans.) p.487f; *Augustinus Magister* III, p.193-204; as well as the bibliographies in: *Revue des Etudes Augustiniennes*, Paris, and *Augustiniana*, Héverlé—Louvain. There is also an excellent bibliography in the edition of the *Civitas Dei* of the series: *Corpus Christianorum*, Series Lat. Vol. 47 IX-XX, Turnhout, 1955 (Text according to Dombart-Kalb.)

3. A survey of the efforts to penetrate history from a philosophical or a theological perspective from the time of Augustine to the High Middle Ages can be found in A. Dempf, *Sacrum Imperium* (Darmstadt, 1954²) p.133-284. Material on the New Testament understanding of history can be found in O. Cullmann, *Christ and Time*, Philadelphia, 1964 (English trans.); H. Conzelmann, *The Theology of St. Luke*, N.Y., 1960. Especially important is F. Holmström, *Das eschatologische Denken der Gegenwart* (German by H. Kruska) Gütersloh, 1936, together with the critical survey on this work by F. M. Braun, *Neues Licht auf die Kirche*, Einsiedeln, 1946, p.103-132. Cfr. also W. Kamlah, *Christentum und Geschichtlichkeit*, Stuttgart, 1951.

4. For details on this, see Ch. 1 and 3. Pioneering work in the rediscovery of Joachim is found in the works of Denifle (*Das Evangelium aeternum* . . . in: ALKG I (1885) p.49-142. Other available material is found in Ehrle's article, *Joachim von Floris*, in: Wetzer und Weltes *Kirchenlexikon*² VI 1471-1480; and especially in the studies of Grundmann, Bondatti, Buonaiuti, Dempf, Benz, Huck, Tondelli (Cfr. Literature). A unique attempt to renew Joachimite thought for the present is offered by A. Rosenberg's: Joachim von Fiore, *Das Reich des hlg. Geistes*, ed. A. Rosenberg, Munich, 1955. Here a selection of texts from Joachim is given in German.

5. These notions, which may seem to be truly remarkable at times, are presented by E. Benz, *Ecclesia spiritualis*, Stuttgart, 1934, esp. 3-174. (Even the titles are significant; Part I Die Verheissung, Die prophetische Verkündigung des Abtes Joachim de Fiore; Part II and III Die Erfüllung). Cfr. also Dempf, *Sacrum Imperium*, p.269-334.

6. For the basis of this thesis, confer what is said in #1.

Notes to Chapter I

1. Regarding the dating, confer the Prolegomera of the *Opera Omnia*, Vol. X, c VI #1, XXXVIb — XXXVIIa; Delorme, *S. Bonaventurae Collationes . . .*, Praefatio, XIVf; P. Glorieux, *La date des Collationes de S. Bonaventure*, in: *Arch. Franc. Hist.* 1929, p.257-272. Here on page 270-272 there is a valuable table for the dating of the various "Collationes" and some of the sermons of Bonaventure.

2. Confer note 6 for the chronology of Bonaventure's life. Regarding the resignation of John of Parma confer the *Catalogus Ministorum generalium ordinis fratrum minorum* of Bernhard of Bessa, ed. by Ehrle in: *Zk Th* 7 (1883) p.338-352; John is treated especially on p. 342-344. On page 343 we find an interesting version of John's resignation from the Chronicle of the XXIV Generals (Here a report of Peregrinus of Bologna): "Fr. tamen Peregrinus de Bononia in sua Chronica dicit: quod hic Generalis, postquam de legatione Graeciae fuit reversus, aemulis ipsius, qui multi erant, accusantibus eum Domino Papae Alexandro, idem Papa sibi (i.e. ei — inserted by Ehrle) praecepit in secreto, quod renuntiaret officio et quod nullo modo assentiret, si ministri eum vellent in officio retinere. Et ego, inquit, in Capitulo fui mediator inter ipsum et ministros et hoc habeo ex ore eius."

3. Cfr. the presentation and the edition of the report of Anagni given by Denifle in ALKG I (1885) p.49-142. The strict measures which Bonaventure took against his predecessor are known. In 1262, John was summoned before an ecclesiastical court to answer the charge of Joachimism. He was found guilty and spent most of what remained of his life in a hermitage at Greccio. Cfr. J. Cambell, in LThK V 1068-1069: E. Gilson, *Bonaventue* p. 18f. Obviously this way of handling things drew down the wrath of the Spirituals on Bonaventure. Cfr. Angelo Clareno, *Historia septem tribulationum*, ed. by Ehrle in: ALKG II, p. 127-155 and p. 256-327, esp. p. 284-286. Even the moderate Fioretti render a somewhat harsh judgment in this matter. Cfr. the vision of James of Massa, ed. Sabatier, c.48, 194-200, esp. 197f.: Prae omnibus autem, qui erant in arbore, lucebat et splendebat frater Johannes . . . Qui dum sibi ipsi totus vigil attenderet, fratri Bonaventurae, qui ascenderat locum, unde

ipse descenderat . . . datae sunt ungues ferreae acutae ut nova-cularum acies radentium pilos. Qui movens se de loco suo cum impetu irruere volebat in fratrem Johannem. Quod frater Johannes videns clamavit ad Dominum et Christus ad clamorem fratris Johannis vocavit sanctum Franciscum . . . Et venit sanctus Franciscus et succidit ungues ferreas fratris Bonaventurae. Et sic frater Johannes stetit in loco suo fulgens ut sol. Translation by Schönhöffer, c. 47, p. 123-126. Cfr. also R. Brown, *The Little Flowers of St. Francis*, New York, 1958, p. 151f. and p. 342. Concerning Olivi's stand relative to Bonaventure, confer Gilson, *op. cit.* p. 489.

4. Cfr. W. Nigg, *Das Geheimnis der Mönche*, Zürich-Stuttgart, 1953, p. 249-285; K. Balthasar, *Geschichte des Armutstreites im Franziskanerorden*, 1911. The *Speculum perfectionis* takes a sharp stand against an assimilation to the older Orders. Cfr. esp. C III (IV) c 41 ed. Sabatier, 105 Nr. 3 and c 68, 194-198.

5. In the Prologue to the *Itinerarium* Bonaventure refers to himself as the "septimus in generali fratrum ministerio." (*Itin.* prol. 2 Vol. V 295a.) This may have some allegorical meaning. According to other reckonings, he appears as the ninth or even as the tenth Minister General of the Order, Cfr. *De vita ser. doct.* c 3, 1 Vol. X of the *Opera Omnia*, 47 b and note 1; also, 46f for the account of the election to office.

6. The original agreement concerning the chronology of the life of Bonaventure which placed his entrance into the Order in 1238 was first questioned by F. Pelster, *Literargeschichtliche Probleme im Anschluss an die - Bonaventura-Ausgabe von Quaracchi* in: ZkTh 48 (1924) p. 500-532. As new dates, Pelster suggested: 1244 for the entrance into the Order, 1251 for Bonaventure's time as *Sententiarius*, 1254 *Magister*, 1255 for his departure from the University, return already in 1256. Further research has led to the following chronology which is quite generally accepted. (In the *Arch. Franc. Hist.* 26 [1933], p. 268 Glorieux calls it "solidement établie") : 1243 entrance into the Order, 1248 Baccalaureus biblicus, 1250 Baccalaureus sententiarius, 1253 Magister, February 2, 1257 General. Cfr. G. Abate, *Per la storia e la cronologia di san Bonaventura O. Min.* (c. 1217-1274) ; E. Longpré, Art. Bonaventure, in: *Dict. d'hist. et de géogr. eccl.* IX (Paris, 1937) p. 745f; P. Glorieux *Essai sur la chronologie de saint Bonaventure*, in: *Arch. Franc. Hist.* 19 (1926) p. 145-168; Glorieux, *D'Alexandre de Hâles à Pierre Auriol. La suite des Maîtres franciscains de Paris au XIII siècle*, in: *Arch. Franc. Hist.* 26 (1933) p. 257-281, esp. p. 268. Also A. Tectaert, *Le répertoire des maîtres en théologie de Paris. Quelques remarques et corrections*, in: *Eph. Theol. Lov.* 10 (1934) p. 617/24; C. A. Callebaut, *L'entrée de S. Bonaventure dans l'Ordre des Frères Mineurs en 1234*, in: *La France Franciscaine* V (1921) p. 41-51. An untenable position is held

by O. Righi, *S. Bonaventura entro nell' Ordine franciscano in Parigi o nella Provincia Romana?* in *Misc. Franc.* 36 (1936) p. 505-511. Righi's view is based on a local legendary tradition; he attempts to prove that Bonaventure did not enter the Order in Paris but in Bagnorea. There are no serious historical grounds to support such a view.

7. Prooem in II *Sent.* 1a and 2a, and II *Sent.* d.23, a.2, q.3, ad 7 p. 547; Cfr. Pelster, *op. cit.*, p. 532. As far as the disputed question of the authenticity of the Prooem. is concerned, we may consider this to be definitively decided in the affirmative by F. Henquinet, *Trois petits écrits théologiques de saint Bonaventure à la lumière d'un quatrième inédit,* in: *Mélanges Auguste Pelzer,* Louvain 1947, p. 195-216. The text which is erroneously called the Praelocutio in II Sent. is actually to be seen as an Epilogus to the I Sent. which Bonaventure had later removed and replaced with a text which is in the *cod. Ass.* 183 f 273v. Henquinet has brought this text to light. At the same time, he has shown the authenticity of the disputed Epil. in I Sent. Cfr. J. Friederich, *Zum "Vorwort des hl. Bonaventure"* (Opera om. 11 1/3) in: *Franz. Studien* 29 (1942) p. 78-89.

8. Cfr. the excellent treatment of Gilson, *Bonaventure,* p. 40f. Esp. p. 72: "But for all that, he could love God in his own way and that way was the way of the learned. All happened as though ecstasy, conceded gratuitously by God to the perfection of certain simple souls, had remained for the illustrious Doctor an ideal only to be reached by the long and winding paths of learning." p. 74: "The absence of asceticism is not sufficiently explained by his physical weakness. St. Bernard or St. Francis, emaciated and almost destroyed by macerations, yet found means to impose new sufferings upon themselves, thus showing by their example that there always remains enough strength to become an ascetic when a man's mind is truly set upon it." There is a charm about that which Gilson writes concerning Bonaventure's attitude toward lending books. On page 55 we read that he composed a *determinatio* "which to this day constitutes a perfect *summa* of the reasons against lending books."

9. As an example, cfr. Gilson, p. 56. After the presentation of the *determinatio* on books, Gilson adds: "All this is perfectly true and admirably analyzed. Yet we cannot forget that St. Francis had another manner of loving books, that when one day he found a gospel he distributed its pages among his companions so that they might all at once enjoy it."

10. It is significant that in the treatment of Eschatology in his *Commentary on the Sentences* Bonaventure makes no mention of the problem of Joachim. Far different was the case of Thomas Aquinas. Concerning the different attitudes taken by Thomas and Bonaventure toward the work of Joachim confer #14, II.

11. Cfr. *Itin.,* prol. 2, Vol. V, 295a-b.

12. W. Nigg, *Grosse Heilige*, Zürich⁴ 1952. Francis of Assisi is treated on p. 35-102. Cfr. also W. Nigg, *Vom Geheimnis der Mönche*, Zürich-Stuttgart, 1953, p. 249-285.
13. For the dating of this work see W. Götz, *Die Quellen zur Geschichte des heiligen Franz von Assisi*, Gotha, 1904, p. 248. According to Götz, the *Vita* would have been finished in 1260, presented to and approved by the General Chapter in 1263, and established finally to replace the others in 1266.
14. See the compilation given by Guardini, *Die Lehre des hlg. Bonaventura von der Erlösung*, p. 7f. (*Opera Omnia*, Vol. VIII).
15. Cfr. the compilation of texts pertaining to this question in Jules d'Albi, *Les luttes doctrinales* . . p. 203-227.
16. Concerning the question of authenticity, cfr.: *Opera Omnia*, Vol. V, Prol. c 6 ##1 and 2, XXXVIff.
17. The concept "deutscher Symbolismus" has been coined by Dempf in: *Sacrum imperium*, Ch. 6, p. 229ff. See esp. p. 231: "As an exegesis of Scripture and the world in accordance with the categories of cause and finality, Scholasticism is a scientific metaphysics that arises from indirectly religious motives. What we call symbolic (Symbolik) is an immediate spiritual-religious attitude; it becomes symbolism (Symbolismus) when the intention to penetrate to the one and only meaning of the world enters into the picture so that one interprets the world exclusively in a symbolic manner." For the efforts of Bonaventure, cfr. p. 292f; p. 368f. Leclerq has presented his thesis concerning the two views of the Middle Ages in: *Bulletin thomiste* VII (1943-46) p. 59-67, esp. p. 62.
18. Jules d'Albi, *Saint Bonaventure et les luttes doctrinales de 1267-1277*, Paris, 1923, p. 53.
19. *Ibid.*, p. 222.
20. *Metaphysik des Mittelalters*, p. 119.
21. *Sacrum imperium*, p. 292f.
22. J. Tinivella, *De impossibili sapientiae adeptione*. in: *Antonianum* 11 (1936) p. 33-43. Cfr. Guardini, *Erlösungslehre*, p. 5: "The *Collationes* are replete with deep thoughts. Certainly the construction of the whole is very complex, and many sections are puzzling." Tinivella attempts to bring some aid to this unfortunate situation. Actually he goes no farther than a presentation of the philosophy of the *Hexaemeron*, so that the real problems are not treated. Consequently, he has placed himself among those who "e via tantum . . . flosculos . . . collegerunt, at . . . praeterierunt." We find that Dempf goes too far when he says that the *Illuminationes ecclesiae* (=*Hexaemeron*) are quite unjustly considered to be unclear. (*Metaphysik des Mittelalters*, p. 119.) But we must add that Dempf's *Sacrum imperium* has actually contributed much important material for the clarification of the *Hexaemeron*.

23. Cfr. *Opera Omnia*, Vol. V. prol. c 6 #1, XXXVIb. Following this, Dempf regularly refers to the work as the *Illuminationes ecclesiae*. I will make use of the ordinary title used in the editions of this work. This title also correctly emphasizes the basic schema of the work which is an explanation of the Hexaemeron. But even more so, this title indicates that the work belongs to the genus of historico-theological explanations of the Hexaemeron.

24. F. Delorme, *S. Bonaventurae Collationes in Hexaemeron et Bonaventuriana quaedam selecta*, BFSchMA, VIII, *Quaracchi*, 1934.

25. Cfr. the Additamentum in Delorme, p. 275; *Op. Omnia*, V, XXXVIIa and 450 a-b.

26. Cfr. the treatment of the center of the circle, *Princ Coll*, I,#3, 24,p.11; concerning the syllogism, *ibid.*, #4,25,p.12f; the use of the Dismas-Gesmas legend, *ibid*, 26, p.13 and many other points.

27. For further material concerning the relation of the texts, confer: Tinivella, *op. cit.*, 33-43; Delorme, Praefatio, XIV — XVI. Delorme summarizes his viewpoint in the following way: "Si autem A (= Delorme) consideretur separatim, ex epilogo reportatoris, ex examine operis interno et ex parvo codicum numero concluditur quod fuerit labor individuus et privatus, si vero B (= Opera omnia) attendatur, libenter suspicabitur quis quod sit illa reportatio quam "alii duo socii" notabant, quam postea redegerint insimul, usi notis propriis et aliis reportatoris A, quamque, viso codicum numero maiori et ejus forma meliori, viso etiam additamento, de quo fuit quaestio, S. Bonaventura ipse sua auctoritate recognoverit et authenticaverit. Haec dicta sint non absolute sententiando. Cuicumque tamen grati erimus, qui ex dictis sumens occasionem novi studii, propius ad veritatem · accesserit."

Notes to Chapter 1, #2

1. XXII, 3,p.438a: . . . in tempore nascitur et procedit (sc. ecclesia militans), non sicut angeli, qui subito creati sunt et simul firmati. Cfr. XIV, 5.6, p.393f; II 17, p.339a: Scripturae intelligi non possunt, nisi sciatur decursus mundi et dispositio hierarchica.

2. II *Sent*, 13-17, p.338b-339a; *Hex*, XIII 2+11-33, Vol. V, p.388a+ 389ff; *Brev.*, prol. #4, Vol. V, p. 205-206; *De red.*, 5, p. 321b. For the earlier history of this theory confer: E. Dobschütz, *Vom vierfachen Schriftsinn*, Harnack-Ehrung, 1921, p.1-13; Grundmann, *Joachim I*, p.27f; also important is: H. de Lubac, *"Typologie" et "Allegorisme,"* in: *Rech. th. anc. med.* 34 (1947) p.180-226, esp. p.217-218; M. D. Chénu, *Théologie symbolique et exégèse scolastique au XII-XIII siècle*, in: *Mélanges J. de Ghellinck S.J.*, 1951, p.509-526. We cannot and should not relate this to the extensive modern discussion of the spiritual meaning of Scripture.

3. XIII,2,p.388a for the program; coll. XIV and XV, p.392-402 for the execution of the program.

4. XIII,2, p.388a. For the concept of the *Theoriae* see also: Gilson, *Bonaventure*, p.212f. Here, of course, it is not treated fully; nor is its significance for the theology of history pointed out.
5. XV, 10, p.400a: Intelligentiae enim principales et figurae in quodam numero certo sunt, sed theoriae quasi infinitae.
6. Cfr. II, 17, p.339a; XV, p.400a: . . . et qui tempora ignorat istas scire non potest . . . Unde cognito futurorum dependet ex cognitione praeteritorum.
7. Cfr. Grundmann, *Joachim* I, p.40-53; Dempf, *Sacrum imperium*, p.275ff., esp. p.278.
8. XIII, 2, p.388a; XV, 10, p.400a.
9. XV, 12,p.400a: Hae sunt rationes seminales ad cognoscendum scripturas (Delorme, Vis.III c III #1,12, p.173: Et hae fuerunt rationes seminales ad cognoscendum scripturas). This notion of Bonaventure need not be seen as entirely new. There was a work called *De semine scripturarum* which, according to B. Hirsch-Reich, does not go back to Joachim of Fiore as Tondelli had believed, but was written already in 1204 by an anonymous monk from Bamberg. Cfr. *Rech. th. anc. med.* 21 (1954) p:147: Unfortunately I was not able to find this work.
10. In a number of instances, Bonaventure leaves the question open as to whether something is already past or is still to come. E.g. XVI, 29, p.400b: Necesse est enim, ut surgat unus princeps zelator ecclesiae, qui vel erit vel iam fuit et addidit: Utinam iam non fuerit . . .; XXII, 22, p.441a: Quis autem ordo iste futurus sit vel iam sit, non est facile scire.

Notes to Chapter 1, #3

1. This had been correctly seen already by H. Scholz, *Glaube und Unglaube in der Weltgeschichte*, Leipzig, 1911, esp. p.162.
2. XIV, 17, p.396a. Confer also the structure of XIV and XV, 1 — 9.
3. For the difference between the two concepts, see Grundmann, *Joachim*, I, p.36f.; also the article of Lubac mentioned above, #2, note 2.
4. Augustine's work is subsumed under the *figurae sacramentales* in: XIV, 17 p.396a. Consequently it is necessarily excluded from the *theoriae multiformes* which are developed from XV onward.
5. XV, 12-18, p.400a-b. For the related teaching in Augustine's *Civitas Dei* cfr.: H. Scholz, *Glaube und Unglaube* . . . p.154-155. Concerning the extent of this idea in Augustine, cfr.: H. Rondet, *Le thème des deux cités*, in: *Études augustiniennes*, publ. by H. Rondet, Paris, 1954.
6. *In Evang. I hom.* 19,1 PL 76,1054.
7. XV, 19, p.400f. On this point, Bonaventure expressly appeals to "others" (Cfr. p. 400b); a division into five is found, for example, in Honorius of Autun, cfr. Ch. 3, #13.
8. XV,20, p.401a.
9. XV, 21, p.401a.

10. *De civitate Dei*, XVIII, 52, CC 48, p.650 ff. (PL 41,614f.); cfr. #14 II,1. The entirely different position of Bonaventure is clear in XV,11, p.400a; 12 — 18, p.400; 22, p.401; cfr. also the great schema in XVI.

11. XV,22,p.401b.

12. XV, 23, p.401b. Cfr. the following.

13. XV, 23, 401b. Cfr. XVI, 3, p.403b. Since this is a question of traditional materials, we can already find many parallels in *Sent.* We would like to call attention to the beautiful text of II *Sent.* d.14,p.2, dub.4 r, p.369b, where the relation synagoga — tenebrae ecclesia — lumen is given a liturgical interpretation.

14. XV, 24, p.401b.

15. *Ibid.* Cfr. Delorme, Vis. III, c III, #2,24-25, p.177,: Et sequitur: Non levabit gens contra gentem gladium. Sed contra hoc dicunt Judaei "Si haec prophetia per Christi nativitatem est impleta ..., quare ergo non est modo pax in ecclesia talis?" Ad hoc respondendum quod ita esse deberet secundum evangelii doctrinam; vel dicendum quod intelligitur prophetia de tempore post mortem Antichristi et post vocationem ultimam Judaeorum. According to Benz, *Ecclesia spiritualis*, p. 234, the imperial theologians of the Hohenstaufen party related the text of Is. 2,4 to the time of Frederick II.

16. XV,26, p.402a — b. This tri-partite schema is probably involved in II,14,p.338b, where we read of the *ecclesia prima, media, et ultima;* cfr. also *De perf ev.*, q.2,a.2,ad 20, p.147f., *ibid.*, p.150a. The Lea-Rachel typology plays a big role in the writings of Joachim and in the Pseudo-Joachim literature. Cfr. *Conc.* V, 16f,68r; c 18f,69v: Natis enim sex filiis Liae quasi in sex temporibus, mox circa finem editus est Joseph, qui praefuit suis. c 20f,70r . . . Rachelis et Liae, quarum alteram terrenam et corpoream vitam, alteram spiritualem et caelestem vitam designat. Ps.-Joachim, *In Jeremiam*, Praef. (f not numbered): . . . Beniamin . . . qui religionem et vitam extremi ordinis significat in proximo revelandi et nascendi Racheli, i.e. ecclesiae generali. Examples could be multiplied; cfr. #12 and #16, II,2,e.

17. XV,28, p.402.

Notes to Chapter 1, #4

1. Cfr. A. Wikenhauser, *Offenbarung des Johannes*, Regensburg, 1949 (Regensburger NT, Vol.9) p.128f.; P. Volz, *Die Eschatologie der jüdischen Gemeinde im neutestamentlichen Zeitalter*[2], 1934, p.143f. Interesting material pertaining to this may be found in M. Werner, *Die Entstehung des christlichen Dogmas* (Bern-Tübingen, 1941) p.83-88. At first, the death of Jesus was placed in the year 6000, for this was understood to be the time for the end of the world. Afterwards, it was drawn further and further back so as to preserve the schema of the 6000 years which had been

drawn from the Hexaemeron and is found expressly for the first time in the Epistle of Barnabas.

2. There appears to be no clear harmonization of the two schemata in Augustine.

3. *Hex.* XV, 18, p.400b; also, XV,12,p.400a and XVI, 2, p.403b. Also *Brev.* prol. #2, Vol.V, 203b; Cfr. Rupert of Deutz, *De trin. et op. eius*, p.2 in vol 4 evang. c 29 PL 167,1568: Septima mundi aetas non pro tempore vel temporum ordine aetas dicitur aut septima nuncupatur. Neque enim quomodo quinta quartae, quomodo sexta quintae, sic illa huic sextae temporaliter succedit, sed coniuncta velut ex latere usque ad finem saeculi, usque ad universalis diem resurrectionis cum ea currit. Hipler, *Die christliche Geschichtsaufassung* (Cologne, 1884) p.39 indicates that this concept is found already in John Scotus Eriugena.

4. Cfr. the texts given in the note above.

5. *Hex*, XV, 12 and 18, p.400a and b.

6. Naturally, the acceptance of this schema does not yet involve a decision concerning the status of the souls of the deceased in the heavenly Church of the seventh age. It does not yet determine whether we should attribute to them the full *visio* or a provisional state of beatitude. The development of this question does not immediately touch on the form of the historical schemata. The two points must be distinguished clearly. Cfr. H. X. Le Bachelet, *Benoit XII, Constitution Benedictus Deus*, in: DThC, II, 657-696, esp. 677ff.

7. Nr. 4, p.453b.

8. On the basis of studies such as Cullmann's *Christ and Time* and Conzelmann's *Theology of St. Luke* (cfr. Literature) we may well ask whether the NT itself already understood the time of Christ as the "center." But despite the untenability of many individual aspects of M. Werner's work (*Die Entstehung des christlichen Dogmas*), he has succeeded in showing in a clear and decisive way that early Christianity never understood the Christ-Event as the 'center' of time but rather as the 'fullness' of time; that is, as the fundamental 'End' of the ages. In #13 and 14 we will trace the gradual development of the concept of the center. If, nonetheless, one still wishes to work in SS and in the Fathers with the notion of a central period of time, then this can mean at most a time which is outstanding and normative; it cannot be understood as the beginning of a new age, for this notion did not yet exist. For this reason, it would be better to give up the concept of the center if we wish to give a clear presentation of the historical understanding of the NT and the Fathers.

9. Cfr. Grabmann, *Die Lehre des heiligen Thomas von Aquin von der Kirche als Gotteswerk*, Regensburg, 1903, p.160. Grabmann's judgment is taken over by H. Berresheim, *Christus als Haupt der Kirche nach dem heiligen Bonaventura*, Bonn, 1939, note 151,

p.197-199. Cfr. p.327 where the author proves the distance separating Bonaventure from Joachim by the fact that the Seraphic
Doctor rejected Joachim's doctrine of the Trinity in I *Sent.* d.5,
dub.4 r p.121a! Gilson comes to a similar judgment in *Bonaventure*, p.18: "Later on, when he in his turn took up the problems
of the philosophy of history raised by the Abbot of Flora, he
answered them in a totally different sense, returning to the divisions of history made by St. Augustine." More cautious is G.
Bondatti, *Gioachinismo e Francescanesimo nel Dugento*, Porzi-
uncola, 1924, p.137: Negli scritti polemici di S. Bonaventura in-
contriamo espressioni che a prima vista sembrano avere una certa
affinità e forse l'hanno, colle speculazioni di Gioacchino, cioè at-
tandole o riducendole a forme ortodosse . . . p.138: È vero, che
presso di lui troviamo immagini ed espressioni che sono proprie
de Gioacchino, ma Bonaventura se ne serve in senso giusto e
generalmente intelligible. — Not even Bondatti is free of un-
justified attempts to tone down the influence of Joachim. As far
as I can see, the actual influence of Joachim on Bonaventure is
recognized only in: Dempf, *Sacrum imperium*, esp. c.7 and 10,
and in L. Tondelli, *Il libro delle figure dell' abate Gioachino da
Fiore* I (Torino o.J. 1939), p.21-224. We could do well to compare
the judgment of Tondelli (p.215) with the views of Grabmann
and Gilson given above: Nello stesso tempo però il Dottore Sera-
fico si studia di conservare dell' opera di Gioachino quanto sia
utilizzabile nella ortodossia della fede. Questi contatti sono nor-
malmente sfuggitti agli studiosi: tanto che uno studioso pro-
fondo di Gioachino e dei suoi influssi storici quale il Buonaiuti
può pensare ancora che S. Bonaventura fosse del tutto impervio
al pensiero ed alle attese di lui. Against Gilson, Tondelli says
with justification (p.224) : Certamente: nulla che non sia orto-
dosso nelle dottrine del Santo. Egli non accetta un Vangelo nuovo,
l'evangelo eterno: ma non si è troppo lontano dal vero quando si
afferma che l'escatologia bonaventuriana non ha nulla di com-
mune con Gioachino da Fiore? Cfr. also #13,III.

10. XVI, 11-13, p.405a and XVI, 30, p.408b. Tondelli also is inexact
on this point. He overlooks the difference between the double-
seven schema and the simple-seven schema. As for the axiom:
"septima aetas currit cum sexta," he sees this as the Joachimite
influence in the work of Bonaventure (p.216.) Actually this axiom belongs to the Augustinian elements, whereas the Joachimite influence is seen in the fact that Bonaventure develops the
notion of a seventh period within history. For the relation between the two lines of influence, confer the schema given in the
text. Furthermore, Joachim never totally discards the Augustinian doctrine of the ages of history. He presents it in his
Concordia V, c.24-30 (f 72 f) as the seventh or the fourth
explanation of the Hexaemeron. (c.30.) While the division of
history into three periods is related to the Persons of the Trini-

ty, the simple reckoning of time is related to the *una deitas.*
"Haec de intellectu generali, qui pertinet ad unitatem deitatis
eo quod tempora trium statuum comprehendat sub uno . . ."
c 30 f 73 r. A similar idea occurs even before this in V 18 f
69v: Quamvis autem universa aetas ista, quae vocatur sexta,
sub qua continentur septem tempora ista . . . On the other
hand, Joachim knows a continuous numbering also with Christ
in the center between the third and the fourth periods: Tondelli,
op. cit., II (edition of text of *Liber figurarum*), tav.XVIII. But
this seems to be an exceptional case; the construction of the
Concordia given above seems to be the dominant one.
11. Cfr. the schema on p. 21 for the content of the periods in the
double-seven division. For a summary treatment of Joachim's
historical schemata, confer: M. Reeves-B. Hirsch-Reich, *The Sev-
en Seals in the Writings of Joachim of Fiore*, in: *Rech. th. anc.
med.*, 21 (1954) p.211-247.
12. XVI, 7, p.404a: Septenarius secundum Gregorium est numerus
universalitatis. Cfr. also IV *Sent.* d.40, dub.r,p.853a: . . . in
septenario universitas totius vitae concluditur. Note 6 indicates
much related patristic material. Cfr. also *Comm. in Eccle.*, c 39,
Vol.VI,32b: Septenarium, qui est universitas temporis. Another
idea is expressed in *Comm. in Luc.*, c.1,8 (to V 5) Vol.VII, 14a:
. . . quia per octo novum testamentum intelligitur, sicut per
septem vetus.
13. XVI, 7 — 10, p.404a-405a. Cfr. also *Itin*: 2,2-4, Vol. V, 300.
14. Concerning the theme of the cosmic harmony see: I *Sent*, d. 44,
a.1, q.3, c p.786b: . . . universum est tamquam pulcherrimum
carmen, quod decurrit secundum optimas consonantias, aliis partibus succedentibus aliis, quousque res perfecte odinentur in
finem; II *Sent.* d.13, a.1, q.2, ad 2, p.316a: Divinae autem dis-
positioni placuit, mundum quasi carmen pulcherrimum quodam
decursu temporum venustare.

Notes to Chapter 1, #5

1. XVI, 30, p.408b. Delorme V III c IV, III 30, p.193: Istius enim
visionis decensus est finalis conformatio ecclesiae militantis cum
ecclesia triumphante, scilicet quando militans ita triumphanti
conformatur quod ab ea dicitur descendere. In line with the general tendency of the Delorme text to tone certain things down,
we find that in this case it weakens the Joachimite tone consider-
ably in comparison with the text of the *Opera omnia.*
2. Cfr. XV 24 and 25, p.401f.; also note 15, #3 above:
3. The most important of Gerard's statements are available in the
protocol of the commission in Anagni, ed. Denifle in ALKG I 99-
142. Cfr. p.99f. (Nr:91a): Quod liber Concordiarum vel Con-
cordie veritatis apellaretur primus liber evangelii eterni . . .
Quod liber iste, qui dicitur Apocalipsis nova, appellaretur secun-

dus liber eiusdem evangelii . . . Similiter quod liber, qui dicitur
Psalterium decem cordarum, sit tercius liber eiusdem evangelii
. . . comparat vetus testamentum primo celo, evangelium Christi secundo celo, evangelium eternum tercio celo. Et expressius
XXV capitulo, ubi comparat vetus testamentum claritati stel-
larum, novum testamentum claritati lune, evangelium eternum
sivi spiritus sancti claritati solis. Item XXVII capitulo comparat
vetus testamentum atrio, novum sancto, aeternum sancto sanc-
torum. Item XXX g. comparat vetus testamentum cortici, novum
teste, evangelium eternum nucleo. In his study, *Das Evangelium
aeternum und die Commision zu Anagni*, ALKG I 64, Denifle
has shown that this doctrine does not agree with the intention of
Joachim nor with that of the Joachimites who followed Joachim
rather than Gerard. Cfr. also Grundmann, *Joachim*, I, 17. I cannot endorse the view of Dempf, who opposes Denifle on this point
in his *Sacrum Imperium* 304ff. As interesting as his theory may
seem to be, we find no concrete indications of the followers of
Gerard. Against Dempf we can say the same thing that Denifle
said to Reuter: "What is the situation with the followers of
Gerard? Were there any? Did Gerard have a following, a group
of disciples? I believe there were hardly more than two . . .
What Gerard did should not be attributed to the Joachimites."
(*Op. cit.* 64.)

4. Cfr. Denifle, *op. cit.*, 88ff.
5. *Hex.* XVI, 2, p.403b.
6. Thus Gilson, *Bonaventure*, p.18f; Hipler, *Die christliche Geschichtsauffassung*, p.56 (see esp. 53-56). In treating this matter,
the Scholion of the Quaracchi edition refers to Hipler, *Hex.* p.453b.
7. The parallel text of XVI, p.406a should also be compared. It offers nothing essentially new.
8. Frederick I is expressly distinguished from Frederick II in the
text of Delorme, V III c IV, III 29, p.192: Nam tempore Henrici
quarti fuerunt diu duo papae et tempori Frederici magni. Similiter et iste ultimus Fredericus, si potuisset, omnino exterminas-
set ecclesiam, sed angelus domini clamavit ne noceret etc. The
strong position against the German emperor is understandable
if we recall that, at least for a time, Joachim saw in the Ger-
mans the new Babylon which was rising up against the new
.Jerusalem, i.e. Rome: See Grundmann, *Joachim*, II p.54-57.
Even if we assume that Bonaventure was friendlier toward the
German emperor (Cfr. Tondelli, op. cit. I,223), nonetheless Joachim's view may well reflect a feeling in ecclesiastical circles from
which Bonaventure was not entirely free.
9. Related to this is the Franciscan view of the anti-Christ which
would quite definitely see Frederick II as the anti-Christ. See
Benz, *Ecclesia spiritualis*, p.205-234; Dempf, *Sacrum imperium*,
p.317-334. Also E. Kantorowicz, *Fredrich II, Berlin*[2], 1931. William of St. Amour also judges Frederick severely when he writes

in his *Liber de antichristo* . . . P I c 3, 2 (ed. Martène-Durand Sp.1238 E) : . . . Romanorum (sc. regnum) . . . usque ad Frederici quondam Romani imperatoris condemnationem se extendit, in quo Romanum cessasse videtur imperium . . .

10. *Hex.* XVI, 20, p.406.

11. For this reason, in XVI,29,p.408b, it is expressly emphasized that the angel of Philadelphia is the sixth of the entire series. Similarly, the number six itself is emphasized each time it appears.

12. XVI,31,p.408b: Et sic patet, quomodo scriptura describit succesiones temporum; et non sunt a casu et fortuna, sed mira lux est in eis et multae intelligentiae spirituales. XVI, 16,p.405b: Et frequentissime inculcabat, quod non sunt a casu et a fortuna ista et consimilia posita in scriptura, sed maxime ratione et maximo mysterio; sed qui non considerat nihil intelligit.

13. See the parallel texts given above.

14. Cfr. p. 25. above.

15. XX,29,p.430b: here note 7 indicates the source: Haymo,I. *Expositio in Apoc.*,3,7. Regarding the question of Haymo, cfr.: W. Kamlah, *Apokalypse und Geschichtstheologie*, Berlin, 1935. Also, compare the evaluation of this statement and the combination with the Joseph-typology in XXIII,29, p.449. As regards the concrete opinion of Bonaventure, XXIII, 26, p.448f. is very helpful.

16. XXIII,4,p.445b.

17. XX, 29, p.430b. The fact that the *ostensio civitatis* already points to the seventh age is pointed out in XVI, 30,p.408b. To me it seems beyond doubt that the Ezechiel-vision of the new Jerusalem (Ez.40ff.) is combined with the corresponding Apocalypse-vision (c.21 f). Cfr. XVI 19 where *Apoc.* 10,6-7 is expressly related to the beginning of the seventh age.

18. XVI, 31, p.408b.

19. For the application of the ancient hermeneutic rule concerning the transfer from Head to Body, see XVI, 21, p.406b. Compare XVI, 17, p.396a. The text which we treat in the following is found in XVI, 29, p.408a: confer p. 25 above.

20. Greater clarity is found in the Delorme text V III C IV, III 29, p.192: Alternationes istae in ecclesia quantum ad pacem et tribulationem elegantissime significantur per hoc quod, Christo in cruce pendente, primo fuit lux sive dies, deinde tenebrae in universa terra et iterum adhuc eo pendente lux rediit. Even here one can hardly avoid the impression that this is artificial. There seems to be a clear dependence on Joachim: *Conc.* l III p 2,c 6 f 41 v: Verum tempus sextum duplex esse praediximus, liquet, quod inter duas illas tribulationes futurum est. Haud diutinum spatium quantulaecumque pacis, ut qui poterint temporis pertransire supplicia, queant resumptis viribus tolerare sequentem.

21. IX, 8, p.374a; XV, 28, p.402b; XVI, 19, p.406a. In the primary text, XVI, 29, p.498b, the notion of the *ultima tribulatio* is developed exclusively from the Apocalypse.

178   *Theology of History in St. Bonaventure*

22. Naturally, this refers to a new zealot for the cause of the Church rather than to a major persecutor of the Church as Dempf erroneously understands it; *Sacrum Imperium,* p.370. In his book, *The Spirit of Medieval Philosophy,* Gilson translates this correctly as a defender of the Church (p.398). Cfr. also Tondelli, *Il libro delle figure,* I, 223. Both Gilson and Tondelli are imprecise in the more pointed determination of this figure.

23. XXII, 22, p.441a: Quis autem ordo iste futurus sit vel iam sit, non est facile scire. The Quaracchi Scholion simplifies the problem by simply stating: Quis autem, ait, iste futurus sit, non est facile scire (p.453b).

24. Here it should be pointed out that there is a theological treatment of Francis only in the later works of Bonaventure. In the *Sentence Commentary,* Francis is mentioned only once (III, d 28 a un q l c p.622b; II d 44 a 3 q 2 p.1014b speaks of the regula beati Francisci and not of Francis himself.) And even in the one instance in which Francis is mentioned, it is in a sense that is theologically neutral. This fact is not without importance. Just as we cannot derive an understanding of Bonaventure's treatment of Francis only from the *Sentence Commentary,* so we cannot determine his relation to Joachim only on the basis of the first judgment made in this work.

25. Bonaventure, *Legenda maior* 2,5. Vol. VIII, 509a; Praeco sum, inquiens, magni regis. For the source-value of the *Legenda,* see: W. Goetz, *Die Quellen zur Geschichte des hlg. Franziskus von Assisi,* p.248; "Almost as much as nine-tenths of Bonaventure's artistic mosaic is derived from these four sources — Vita prima (i.e. of Celano), Julian (of Speyer), Vita secunda (Celano) and Tractatus (de miraculis of Celano)." I will give the parallel texts from the other *Legenda* only in as far as it is necessary for the development of the historico-theological understanding of Francis. Unfortunately the Quaracchi edition does not provide a clear indication of the sources of the *Legenda,* just as it does not clearly show the relation of the *Hexaemeron* to Joachim.

26. *Legenda,* Prol. 1, p.504 a-b; c 4, 5, p.514a; c 11, 6, p.537a (Eliseus); c 11, 14, p.538b (curru igneo); 12, 2, p.539b; 12, 7, p.540b (ignis ardens); c 12, 12, p.542a-b; *Legenda minor,* Lec 1, p.565a makes use of Francis' original name, John, in this way. Cfr. II Celano, c 1, 3 ed. Alencon, p. 169f: Joannis proinde nomen ad opus ministerii pertinet quod suscepit, Francisci vero ad dilatationem famae suae, quae de ipso, iam plene ad Deum converso, ubique cito pervenit. The Elias-theology is also in I Celano, c. 10, 23, ed. Alencon, p.26: Erat verbum eius velut ignis ardens. See also c 18, p.49-53 which treats of the vision of the fiery chariot. I could find no indications of these ideas in the *Speculum perfectionis.*

27. This places a limit on the tendency to draw too strict a parallel between Francis and Christ which appeared at times. The final

results of such a tendency is the *Liber de conformitate vitae beati Francisci ad vitam domini Jesu* of Bartholomew of Pisa. Cfr. Dempf, *Sacrum imperium*, p.316, and Dempf, *Ecclesia spiritualis oder Schwarmgeisterei?*, in: *Hochland*, XXXII 2 (1935) p.172. Dempf here takes a stand relative to the tendentious view of Benz concerning the book. In Bonaventure, the Christ-Francis parallel is used with great moderation. Cfr. S III De s. Patre nostro Franc., Vol. IX, p.584a: Item, beatus Franciscus fuit creatus ad similitudinem humanitatis Christi, videlicet quantum ad tria, quantum ad vitam, quantum ad passionem et quantum ad resurrectionem.

28. XV, 28, p.402b. See also Joachim, *Concordia* l IV c 36 f 57v: Igitur, prout ego arbitror, in tempore, quo venturi sunt, sicut tenet ecclesia, Enoch et Helias, eligendi sunt duodecim, viri similes patriarcharum et ad praedicandum Judaeis. (See also the Fioretti where emphasis is placed on the fact that the original Franciscan community consisted of twelve. For the question of the conversion of the Jews in Bonaventure, see *Hex* XV 24, p.401b). Elias plays a significant role in the *Liber figurarum*. Of significance is *Tav* XIV, back-side col 3a (ed. Tondelli): Unus enim Helias premissus est a Domino, et tamen duo venturi erant, quorum singulus dicebatur Helias. Also *Tav* II and *Tav* IV col 3 *TAV* VII. In Ps. Joachim, *Super Esaiam* p 6 f 58v, we read: In tertio, cuius initia iam tenemus angelo amicto nube dabitur liber apertus, sc. patefactio scripturarum. Duo alii ac si testes, quos in Henoch et Heliam, sed et melius in Moyse et Helia . . . praedicabunt labentis orbis pericula . . . There is a different significance given to the type of Elias in Joachim, *Concordia* V 15 f 67v: Elias and Eliseus had divided the OT as the *ordo heremiticus* and *virgineus* divide the NT. Ps. Joachim, *In Jeremiam* developed this schema most consistently (Benz, *Eccl. spiritualis*, 182f.) It is remarkable that we do not find the pair Elias-Henoch in this book, contrary to Dempf, *Sacr. imp.* p.334, who attributes this pair to the *Jeremias-commentary*. I could not find this pair anywhere in the book.

29. Cfr. Wadding, *Annales* . . . I Praef #2, IV, p. 15, Nr. 14: Praeclarum est illud Joannis Apostoli de Francisco vaticinium, dum sub sexto sigillo ait se "vidisse alterum angelum ascendentem ab ortu solis, habentem signum Dei vivi." (Apoc. 7, 2). Subiungo huius visionis ex Bonaventura expositionem. Nr. 15, p. 16: Nihil autem mirum, si Seraphicus Doctor ita intelligendum esse hunc locum indubitabili fide se colligere dicat, dum, ut refert Pisanus, id per revelationem sibi factam in aedicula Portiunculae . . . concepit. Nec sibi soli, verum et aliis hoc certo revelatum esse testatus est in Comitiis generalibus Fratrum Parisiis, si Bernardino Senensi credamus. Later it is said: . . . asseruit, se certissime scire per revelationes indubitabiles et solemnes factas talibus personis, quae de hoc non poterant dubitare, quod B. Franciscus

erat singulariter Angelus sexti signaculi . . . Cfr. Benz, *Eccl. spir.* p. 318. According to Dempf, *Sacrum imperium*, p. 291f. and 303, John of Parma had already made this exegesis into a common teaching in the Order. Yet we do not find this interpretation of Francis in the letter of John of Parma and Humbert of Romans which dates from the year 1255, and to which Dempf makes reference (Wadding, *Annales* II, Lyon, 1628, p. 108-110.) See also: G. Bondatti, *Gioachinismo e Francescanesimo nel Dugento*, 1924, p. 139 A 4. For the present, it seems that the oldest literary witnesses for this interpretation are Bonaventure and the *Liber introductorius* of Gerard of Borgo San Donnino.

30. q 2 a 3 ad 12, Vol. V, p. 164b. For the dating of this work see the Prolegomena of the Quaracchi edition c II #2, p. VIIb-VIIIa.

31. Prol. 1 and 2, Vol. VIII, p. 504b; c 13, 10, p. 545b. Also the parallels in the *Legenda minor*, De transitu 1, p. 577b, 1, 8, p. 579b. The citation is used with relative frequency (six times) in sermons which cannot be dated exactly. Earlier stages in *It.* prol 2 Vol. V, 295b and De sex alis Ser c 1, 4, Vol. VIII, p. 133.

32. Cfr. note 26 above.

33. XV, 28, p. 402b. See note 28 above.

34. Cfr. texts on p. 25.

35. Less important is XV, 16, p. 405b. XXII, 23, p. 441a gives only an indirect reference.

36. We mention only in passing that there is another line of theological interpretation of Francis to be found in Bonaventure; this one also is related to Joachim. Bonaventure sees in Francis "another Job" (*Leg. maior*, 14, 2, p. 546a.) Cfr. Joachim, *Conc.* V 86f 114r: Quod autem completa tentatione restituta sunt omnia quae possederat: significat reformari statum ecclesiae in eum gradum et similitudinem in quo fuit tempore apostolorum. See also, Dempf, *op. cit.*, p. 279. Naturally there are other comparisons that are used at times. For example, Francis is compared with Moses. But these are not applied with frequency, and they do not acquire an independent meaning. The Job-typology is found in S II de s. P. nostro Franc. I Vol. IX, p. 576b. See also: Benz, *Eccl. spir.*, p. 28.

37. Apparently Dante has taken up the idea of the "ap' anatoles" of the text in the Apocalypse. *Div. Com.*, *Paradiso*, Canto XI 52ff: Però chi d'esso loco fa parole/Non dica Ascesi, chè direbbe corto/Ma Oriente, se proprio dir vuole. For the relation between Dante and Bonaventure, see: Leone Cicchitto, *L'escatologia di Dante e il francescanesimo*, in: *Misc. Franc.* 47 (1947) p. 217-231; L, Cicchitto, *Postille bonaventuriano-dantesche*, 1940. An important source for the relation between the Franciscan (Joachimite) theology of history and that of Dante is: L. Tondelli, *Il libro delle figure dell' abate Gioachino da Fiore*, I. Introduzione e commento. Le sue rivelazione dantesche. Torino (1939). It would seem that some relation between Dante and Joachim can

hardly be denied. Cfr. Grundmann, *Joachim* II. Gilson, *Dante und die Philosophie* (*Frieburg*, 1953) throws new light on the problem. Gilson calls attention to two apparently paradoxical pairs. The relation between Bonaventure and Joachim is parallel to that between Thomas and Siger of Brabant. In both cases it would seem that a great teacher of the Church appears with his own heterodox shadow. For Gilson, the relation of Thomas with Siger would have been solved if the texts of Siger which were discovered by Grabmann and edited by Van Steenberghen had been genuine. But this has been contested by Mandonnet. The solution to the Bonaventure-Joachim problem is especially difficult for Gilson, since he is firmly convinced that Bonaventure remained to the end a radical opponent of Joachim in all points. In the light of the present studies, I believe it is impossible to hold such a view. It would seem that Bonaventure accepted Joachim in as far as this was possible. If any of the great Scholastics should form a heavenly pair with Joachim, this would be, without a doubt, Bonaventure. If Dante seems to be well informed on the matter, then this can throw some light on the question of the other pair, Thomas-Siger. This can hardly be called arbitrary. Furthermore it confirms, to a degree, the image of Siger drawn up by Van Steenberghen.

38. Cfr. the text of the "Cartula" and the remarks of Brother Leo in: H. Böhmer, *Analekten zur Geschichte des Franciscus von Assisi*, Tübingen-Leipzig, 1904, Nr. 17, p. 71, and the introduction, p. XIII. Also, Hardick-Esser, *Die Schriften des hl. Franziskus von Assissi*, p. 129ff. and p. 17. p. 130: "Unter dem Ziechen ist mit Tinte eine heute nahezu unkenntliche Zeichnung (ein Kopf?) angebracht. Bruder Leo schreibt zu diesem Zeichen: Ebenso zeichnete er dieses Zeichen Tau mit dem Kopf eigenhändig." (Simili modo fecit istud signum tau cum capite manu sua: Böhmer, *loc. cit.*) Hardick-Esser (p. 131) relates this immediately to *Apoc.* 7,3; but I believe that we should see it in relation to *Ez.* 9, 4. Significantly, Hardick-Esser states: "We may well draw the conclusion that St. Francis saw this sign as the coat of arms for the Friars Minor on the basis of: Thomas of Celano, *Tractatus de miraculis S. Francisci*, nr. 3; Bonaventure, *Legenda maior*, tr de miraculis, #10, nr. 7 . . ." Cfr. also *Leg. mai.*, 4, 9, Vol. VIII, 515a-b, Prol. 2, p. 504b. Interesting in this context is Joachim, *Concordia*, I c l f lv: The text of *Ez.* 9, 4 — et signa Thau in frontibus virorum gementium et dolentium super cunctis abhominationibus — is related to the coming tribulations.

39. This amazing coincidence of promise and fulfillment is impressively treated by Benz, *Ecclesia spiritualis*.

40. *Concordia*, IV 31 f 56r: In qua igitur generatione (= in the 42.) peracta prius tribulatione generali et purgato diligenter tritico ab universis zizaniis ascendet quasi novus dux de Babylone, universalis scilicet pontifex novae Hierusalem, i.e. sanctae matris

ecclesiae. In cuius typo scriptum est in apocalypsi: vidi angelum ascendentem ab ortu solis, habentem signum Dei vivi et cum eo reliquiae excussorum. Ascendet autem non gressu pedum aut immutatione locorum, sed quia dabitur ei plena libertas ad innovandam christianam religionem ad praedicandum verbum, incipiente iam regnare domino exercituum super omnem terram... Cfr. Dempf. *Sacrum imperium*, p. 273. We cannot accept Dempf's interpretation which sees this "angelus ascendens ab ortu solis" to be the reappearance of the *homo Christus* in the third age. Cfr. Tondelli, *Il libro delle figure* . . . p. 160A 1: Gioachino non ha mai posto all'inizio della terza età una riapparizione dell'homo Christus. The parallel to Christ involved the idea that that which had been present in Christ would be fulfilled on a higher level. This fulfillment, according to Joachim, was to be realized not in an individual, but in the new People of God, the *novus ordo*. This notion is compatible with the patristic view in which the *Christos pneumatikos* (i.e. the Church) is set above the historical *Christos sarkikos*. When he relates the Christ-likeness of this new people in a special way to the Prelates, Joachim gives this concept an emphatically ecclesial tone which is foreign to the Fathers. "Quia idem ordo non erit absque praelatis, qui gerant in eo vice Christi. Et si generalis intellectus totum ipsum ordinem tangit spiritualiter, tamen ipsos praelatos, in quibus regnavit Christus Jesus, quem opus dominari et regnari, donec ponat omnes inimicos suos sub pedibus suis (Ps. 109, 1) . . ." *Conc* V 18 f 69v; c 66 f 95v and 96r. Note also that the notion of the 42 generation, which was so important for Joachim, returns in Bonaventure. *Hex* XVI 31 p. 408b: Igitur cum sint septem tempora et in veteri testamento et in novo, et quodlibet triforme, vel in quolibet tria sint; septenarius multiplicatus per ternarium bis, quadraginta duo facit; et istae sunt quadraginta duo mansiones, quibus pervenitur ad terram promissionis.

41. This relationship goes so far that Bonaventure completely intertwines the event of Francis with the words of Scripture, as in *Hex* XXIII 14, p. 447a: Huic angelo apparuit signum expressivum . . . Scripture says nothing about a sign appearing to the angel, but apparently Bonaventure felt justified in expanding Scripture in the light of the events that had taken place.

42. Already in the *Sentence Commentary* the notion of "expressio" played an important role in Bonaventure. Cfr. Gilson, *Bonaventure*, p. 127ff. On p. 146 Gilson speaks of an "expressionism" in the case of Bonaventure. There are three steps involved here: expressivum—impressum—expressum.

43. Cfr. texts on p. 36 above; esp. XXII 23, p. 441 and parallels. In this instance, the Delorme text is very much shorter. But the decisive idea is preserved: V IV Coll III #3, 20-22, p. 256: Tertius ordo contemplantium est eorum, qui sursumaguntur in Deum: De quo videtur fuisse sanctus Franciscus, qui in fine

apparuit. To me it seems certain that the text of the *Opera omnia* (XXII 23) is authentic, and that the Delorme text represents a tendency to tone down the problems. This seems to be especially clear when we see the parallels to this text (XXII 23) in the Sermons: S. I de patre n. Francisco II. Vol. IX, p. 574b-575a: Item, expressum per exemplum perfectae virtutis . . . expressivum per zelum supernae salutis, secundum illud Apocalypsis: Vidi alterum angelum ascendentem ab ortu solis, habentem signum Dei vivi. Hoc quidem signum est zelus humanae salutis; unde in Ezechiele: Signa thau super frontes virorum gementium et dolentium super cunctis abominationibus etc. Hinc etiam est, quod in Aegypto percussit eos, qui hoc signo caruerunt.

44. Cfr. *Conc.* V 15 f 67v; 18 f 69v: Futurus est enim, ut ordo unus convalescat in terra similis Joseph et Salomonis . . ., ut compleatur in eo promissio illa psalmi dicentis: et dominabitur a mari usque ad mare et a flumine usque ad terminos orbis terrarum . . . Hic est populus ille sanctus, ordo sc. iustorum circa finem futurus, de quo in typo Salomonis dictum est . . . Ego ero illi in patrem et ipse erit mihi in filium (2´reg 7, 14). C 65 f 95r: Beatus est autem aut erit ordo ille, quem dominus diliget super omnes, utpote qui visione pacis fruiturus est et dominaturus a mari usque ad mare . . . c 66 f 96r sets up the following relations:

Saul	= populus primi status		Zacharias	= 1i
David	= 2i		Johannes	= 2i
Salomon	= 3i		Christus homo	= 3i

The other works of Joachim provide ample material on this point. Cfr. Grundmann, *Joachim* I, p. 112ff; Dempf, *Sacrum imperium*, p. 271, 278; Benz, *Ecclesia spiritualis*, p. 11ff. Of special interest is the draft of the constitution for the *novus ordo* which has come to light in the *Liber figurarum* edited by Tondelli and printed again in Grundmann, *Joachim* II, p. 116-121 with detailed commentary on p. 85-115. Above this draft, Joachim writes: "Dispositio novi ordinis pertinens ad tercium statum ad instar superne Jerusalem." The basic line of thought in this draft may be found already in *Conc.* V 22-23 f 71v-72r.

45. *Ecclesia spiritualis*, p. 67. As can be seen in the texts already given, Joachim frequently uses "ordo" as equivalent to "populus." Cfr. Bonaventure, *Hex.* XXII 17, p. 440a, where the Seraphic Doctor distinguishes between the ordo monasticus—laicus—clericalis. A more detailed study of the use of this word would certainly be valuable. Certainly the explanation given to the concept "ordo" in the Quaracchi-Scholion, p. 453b, is false.

46. The best source for the evaluation of the quality and sequence of the *Legenda* is still: W. Goetz, *Die Quellen zur Geschichte des Franz von Assisi*, p. 57.

47. In support of this view we have not only the writings of Francis himself, but also his use of the letter tau: cfr. n. 38 above. From among the *Legends*, the strongest evidence is found in the *Speculum perfectionis* [for the question of the source-value see: *op. cit.*, p. 216-221. The final redaction dates form the year 1318 (p. 148), but it involves material that goes back to Brother Leo]. C I (II) c 26, ed. Sabatier, p. 72ff: Quadam vice dixit Beatus Franciscus-: "Religio et vita fratrum Minorum est quidam pusillus grex, quem Filius Dei in hac novissima hora postulavit patri suo caelesti dicens: 'Pater, vellem quod faceres et dares mihi unum novum et humilem populum in hac novissima hora . . .' " Cfr. also: I Celano p. 2 c 1, 89 ed. Alencon, p. 92: Nam cum doctrina evangelica, esti non particulariter, sed generaliter ubique multum per opera defecisset, missus est hic a Deo, ut universaliter per totum mundum, apostolorum exemplo, per-hiberet testimonium veritati . . . Quoniam in novissimo tempore novus evangelista, quasi unus ex paradisi fluminibus, in toto terrarum orbe fluenta evangelii pia irrigatione diffudit . . .

48. Cfr. the Synoptic commentaries of J. Schmid in the Regens-burger New Testament. As a systematic study by a Catholic author, we cite: M. Schmaus, *Das Eschatologische im Christen-tum*, in: *Aus der Theol. der Zeit*, ed. G. Söhngen, Regensburg, 1948, p. 56-84; M. Schmaus, *Von den letzten Dingen*, Münster, 1948; J. Auer, *Das Eschatologische eine christliche Grund-befindlichkeit*, in: *Festschrift fur Kardinal Faulhaber*, Munich, 1949, p. 71-90; M. Schmaus, *Dogmatik*, IV, 2 for further literature.

49. For the understanding of the essence of Franciscanism, see: M. Bierbaum, *Bettelorden und Weltgeistlichkeit*, p. 398ff. Bierbaum gives the interpretations of L. Bracaloni (*Arch Franc Hist*, VIII, p. 467-481), A. de Sérent, *op. cit.*, p. 448-466, and E. d'Alencon, *L' âme franciscaine*, Paris, 1913. Bracaloni sees the essence of Franciscanism to lie simply in love in the broadest sense. De Sérent sees it to lie in poverty, sincerity, and kindness. Only d'Alencon singles out the historical element when he writes: C'est un esprit de retour à l'observance primitive du saint Evangile . . .; c'est un amour personnel et passioné de l'humanité de Jesus-Christ voila l'élément matériel,—le tout animé d'un ésprit de détachement absolu poussé jusqu'a la pauvreté la plus extrême—voilà l'élément formel. A. Gemelli emphasizes poverty and love (*The Franciscan Message to the World*, London, 1935, p. 23ff.). On p. 39ff. poverty — obedience — love are presented as the main pillars of Franciscanism. Valuable observations may be found also in: Nigg, *Das Geheimnis der Mónche*, p. 249-285, esp. p. 254ff. See also: W. Esser, *Mysterium paupertatis. Die Armutsauffassung des hlg. Franziskus von Assisi*, in: *Wissen-chaft und Weisheit* 14 (1951) p. 177-189. The eschatological meaning of poverty is treated on p. 187-189.

50. Esp. the Regula non bullata; *Analekten zur Geschichte des Franciscus von Assisi*, ed. Böhmer. p. 1: Hec est vita evangelii Jesu Christi . . .; esp. Nr. 14, p. 13f: Quando fratres vadunt per mundum, nihil portent in via "neque sacculum neque peram neque pecuniam neque virgam" (Lk. 9, 3). Et (Lk. 10, 4) "in quamcumque domum intraverint primum dicant: Pax huic domui . . . "Non resistant malo (Mt. 5, 39), sed si quis eos in maxillam percusserit, prebeant ei et alteram; qui aufert eis vestimentum, etiam tunicam non prohibeant. Omni petenti se tribuant; et qui aufert, que sua sunt, ne repetant (Lk. 6, 29-30). Cfr. nr. 22, p. 22 and especially the Testamentum, *op. cit.*, p. 36-40. The well-known citation in Nr. 12, p. 39: Et omnibus fratribus meis clericis et laycis precipio firmiter per obedientiam, ut non mittant glosas in regula neque in istis verbis dicendo: "Ita volunt intelligi." Sed sicut dedit michi Dominus simpliciter . . . scribere . . ., ita . . . sine glossa intelligatis. Cfr. I Celano (ed. Alencon) c 9, 22 p. 25; c 13, 32, p. 33; *Speculum perfectionis*, ed. Sabatier c 1, 8, p. 2; C I (II) c 3, 10, p. 11. Hardick-Esser gives reliable information concerning the various rules of Francis (*op. cit.*, p. 2-8) and emphasizes the unrealistic nature of these rules (p. 4 and 5). Here we read of the "Wirklichkeitsfremdheit dieses in der Liebe verlorenen Herzens" (p. 5). Actually, the rule of Francis raises the same problem as the Sermon on the Mount and cannot be realized in an institutional form.

51. *Speculum perfectionis*, ed. Sabatier c 26, 2 p. 72: . . . unum novum et humilem populum . . .; c 26, 13, p. 76: unum novum et parvum populum. The fact that the early Franciscan community was conscious of being the People of God is clear in I Celano c 11, 27, p. 29; II Celano c 117, 158, p. 288f.

52. *Vom Geheimnis der Mönche*, p. 273.

53. Benz, *Ecclesia spiritualis*, p. 11f.

54. *Testamentum*, nr. 12 ed. Böhmer, p. 39.

55. See note 50 above.

56. *Super Hieremiam*, Venice, 1516, esp. c 4 f 12v-f 13r; c 8 f 18v; c 12 f 23v. Cfr. Benz, *Ecclesia spiritualis*, p. 182f; Dempf, *Sacrum imperium*, p. 334.

57. *Conc.* V 38 f 76v, cited by Grundmann, *Joachim* II, p. 108. On page 95f, Grundmann indicates other significant texts. I have already called attention to the text of *Conc.* V 15 f 67v in another context.

58. Cited by Grundmann, *Joachim* II note 2, p. 109f and by Tondelli, *op. cit.*, I, p. 164. The following citations are related to this text.

59. Also in Ps.-Joachim, to be sure, there are indications of the opposite tendency, namely, to attribute a definitive character to only one Order. In *Super Hieremiam* c 13 f 25v we read: Tandem vero rediens Esau, ordo alter, dolebit de primogenitis clericorum sublatis, de benedictione praedicationis et eruditionis eorum et invidebit alteri, nesciens, quia (quod?) primi erunt novissimi et

novissimi primi. The real difference would seem to lie in the fact that Joachim proceeds from the triple-schema Zachary, John the Baptist, homo Christus Jesus (e.g. *Conc.* IV 35 f 57r; V 66 f 96r); from this basis he can ascribe a truly definitive character to only one Order. Ps.-Joachim, on the other hand, begins with a two-fold schema from which, eventually, one member is dropped. The relation between Joachim and Ps.-Joachim is in need of more precise study.

60. Cfr. Bonaventure, *Hex* XXII, 21.22, p. 440f. Here the relation between the *ordo cherubicus* and the eschatological *ordo seraphicus* is treated in a very similar way.

61. Esp. XXII 22, p. 440f (Delorme V IV C III #3, 20-23, p. 256), and all the other citations that treat of the *ordo futurus* (p. 37ff. above.)

62. XII 29, p. 408b; XX 29, p. 430b. Cfr. Ch. 2.

63. III 23, p. 347a; XIV 28, p. 397b; XV 26, p. 402b; XVIII 24, p. 418a; XXIII 30, p. 449b; in II 28, p. 341a this is joined with ideas from the mysticism of Pseudo-Dionysius. Cfr. the evaluation of St. Paul in III *Sent.* d 25 a 1 q 1 c 1 p. 534b.

64. III 23, p. 347a; XIII 14, p. 390a; see also XV 3, p. 399a in relation to III 23, p. 347a; also I *Sent.* d 27 p 2 a un c p. 490b.

65. III 23, p. 347a; XV 26, p. 402b; XXIII 29, p. 449a; cfr. *Apol. paup* 12, 2 Vol. VIII 316b.

66. Sermo de translatione S. Francisci Vol. IX, p. 534b; for the evaluation of the figure of Moses, *Hex* I 10, p. 331a; S. Christus unus omn mag 19, Vol. V, p. 572b.

67. III 23, p. 347a.

68. Rm. 11, 1 and Phil. 3, 5. Here Paul emphasizes his origin from the tribe of Benjamin. In I Cor. 15, 8 he calls himself the last of the Apostles. From among the Fathers, Augustine refers to this fact in Sermo 279 (s 14 de sanctis) 1, 1 PL 38, 1275.

69. There seems to be no doubt that the fact that there were twelve Apostles and seventy-two disciples (Lk. 10, 1; cfr. Ex. 1, 5) in the NT is related to the corresponding OT numbers. Cfr. F. M. Braun, *Neues Licht auf die Kirche*, p. 71f for further literature. The further development of these parallels was a self-evident step for later theology.

70. XV 26, p. 402b, XXIII 30, p. 449b (almost literal correspondence in the text of Delorme V IV C IV #2, 30, p. 273.)

71. I Cor. 2, 6-10. Bonaventure cites this freely in *Hex* II 28, p. 340f.

72. 2 Cor. 12, cfr. *Hex* II 30, p. 341; XXIII 12, p. 447a; Tract de plant par 3 Vol. V, p. 575b; cfr. II *Sent.* d 23 a 2 q 3 c, p. 544b; further material in: K. Rahner, *Der Begriff der ecstasis bei Bonaventura*, ZAM IX (1934) p. 1-19 and the literature indicated there, esp. the works of Longpré, Grünewald, Rosenmöller.

73. Cfr. the texts in note 62.

74. *Hex* XVI, 22, p. 406b; XVIII 7, p. 415b; III 31, p. 348b; esp. De perf ev q 2 a 2 ad 20, p. 148a. See also, Joachim, *Concordia*

IV 39 f 59 v: Necesse quippe est, ut succedat similitudo vera apostolicae vitae . . . Cfr. also IV 40 f 60r; and Grundmann, *Joachim* I, p. 104 f.

75. This is clear in the comparison of XIV 28, p. 397b with XX 29, p. 430b. In XIV 28, we read: . . . in Paulo, in quo consummantur actus apostolorum . . . nec mirum, quia ipse fuit Benjamin, et 'lupus rapax', (Gen. 49,27), ultimus apostolorum, per quem significatur ordo futurus. XX 29: Et iste ordo intelligitur per Joannem. See also XIII 14, p. 390b: . . . et dixit hic: iste (=Johannes) est istius ordinis specialiter. On the other hand we find in Ps.-Joachim, *Super Hieremiam* c 8 f 18v: . . . apparentibus duobus aliis (sc ordinibus) in fine secundi et initium tertii, quemadmodum Christus apparuit in fine primi et in initio secundi, designatur in bove et asino . . . in Moyse et Josue, in Paulo et Joanne evangelista. But also in Ps.—Joachim the relation of Peter—John, which is found in Joachim, is more common. Cfr. the praefatio (not numbered in the folio); c 4 f 12 v. In c 12 f 13 r John is presented as Benjamin; Joannes alter ordo minor, qui ab ipsis angelis minorabatur paulo, quia novissimus . . . Iste est frater Benjamin minimus. f 13 v switches to Paul: Paulus quoque minimus apostolorum se fatetur et tamen plus omnibus laboravit. It would seem that there is no fully consistent understanding.

76. XX 29, p. 430b: Et iste ordo intelligitur per Joannem, cui dictum est: "sic eum volo manere, donec veniam" (Jn. 21,22). Cfr. Joachim, *Liber figurarum*, ed. Tondelli (Il libro delle figure II) tav XIX; Grundmann, *Joachim* II, p. 103ff.

77. Hieronymus, *Adv. Jovinianum* I 26 PL 23, 248A.

78. XIV 28, p. 397b.

79. XX 29, p. 430b.

80. XXII 23, p. 441a.

81. XXII 22, p. 440b.

82. Vol. V, p. 453b (nr. 4). Similar in Gilson, *Bonaventure*, p. 18: ". . . And if he (=Bonaventure) grants that a new spiritual order must come into being, he has in mind not a religious order as an organized body, but an ideal order of perfect souls, to whatever religious order they may happen to belong." This mistake is similar to the error which I have pointed out elsewhere in the interpretation of the *Civitas-Dei*. It is correctly recognized that the "empirical" interpretation is not correct. If one overlooks the category of the pneumatic, which is actually the point here, then one reaches immediately to the category of the idealistic. Cfr. J. Ratzinger, *Herkunft und Sinn der Civitas-Lehre Augustins*, in: *Augustinus Magister*, II, Paris, 1954, p. 965-979.

83. XXII 23, p. 441a: Iste ordo non florebit, nisi Christus appareat et patiatur in corpore suo mystico. Here the text clearly speaks of a "florere" relative to this *ordo*, indicating an historical time which is yet to come. This would seem to be implied in the designation of this order as the *ordo ultimus* as well as in a whole series of

texts which will be treated. Furthermore, the context seems to indicate the probability that Bonaventure saw this appearance,
which is demanded for historico-theological reasons, to have taken
place already in the appearance of the Crucified Christ to Francis.
Furthermore, XX 15, p. 428a and XV 28, p. 402b indicate that
Bonaventure considered it possible that history had already moved
into the final tribulation, or was very near to it. XVI 29, p. 408b
is dubious.

84. Cfr. #1, n. 3 above concerning the attitude of Bonaventure relative
to John of Parma. Angelo of Clareno sees here the *quarta persecutio* of the Order. He writes about Bonaventure: "Tunc enim
sapiencia et sanctitas fratris Bonaventure eclipsata paluit et ob-
scurata est, et eius mansuetudo ab agitante spiritu in furorem et
iram conversa defecit in tantum, ut diceret: 'Si ordinis non respi-
cerem honorem, sicut hereticum eum facerem manifeste puniri.'"
(Ed. Ehrle, in: ALKG II, p. 285.)

85. Dempf points out in *Sacrum imperium*, p. 241, that an interpretation of the hierarchical schema very similar to that of Bonaventure is found already in Honorius of Autun, L XII quaestionum
c 8 PL 172, 1182.

86. We would be tempted to say the "hierarchical aspect" if it were
not for the fact that Bonaventure uses a wider meaning of "hierarchy" whereby he refers to the entirety as "hierarchical."

87. Cfr. the text in the central column of the schema, nr. 15, p. 440a.

88. For more material on this, see: Benz, *Ecclesia spiritualis*. Benz
structures his entire book from this perspective and consequently
over-emphasizes it.

89. XXII 16, p. 440a; Delorme V IV Coll III #3, 16-17, p. 255.

90. The statement concerning the *primi* and the *novissimi* (Mt. 19,30)
is not found here expressly, but it appears unmistakably from the
entire schema. The axiom of *Hex* III 13, p. 345b, is applied to
Christ: Hoc est maximum miraculum, ut quod Deus sit homo,
primus sit novissimus. Cfr. Ps.-Joachim, *Super Hieremiam* c 4
f13r:Joannes alter ordo minor . . . Sic revera erunt primi novissimi
et novissimi primi. c 13 f 25v: Tandem vero rediens Esau, ordo
alter . . . invidebit alteri nesciens, quia (quod) primi erunt
novissimi et novissimi primi.

91. XXII 22, p. 441a: quis autem ordo iste futurus sit vel iam sit, non
est facile scire. Concerning the *ordo cherubicus*, see nr. 21, p. 440b.

92. XXII 22 and 23, p. 440f.

93. Similarly, Gilson, *Bonaventure*, p. 75ff. On p. 75: "In a text of
capital importance . . . he places himself and the other members
of the Order on a plane other than that of St. Francis. p. 77ff:
"Thus St. Bonaventure's state of perfection is that of speculation,
St. Francis' that of ecstasy." Without doubt, these pages are
among the best in Gilson's book.

94. This development found its high point in the biography of Francis
written by Sabatier (*Vie de saint Francois*, Paris, 1893; 1902).

The exaggerated views of Sabatier were reduced to proper proportions already by W. Goetz, *Die Quellen zur Geschichte des heiligen Franz von Assisi*, Gotha, 1904. S. Clasen, *Franz von Assisi und Joachim von Fiore*, in: *Wissenschaft und Weisheit*, 1939, p. 68-83 writes against the unscientific rejuvenation of these views by D. Mereschkowski (*Franz von Assisi*. Tr. E. Kaerrick, Munich, 1938). Among current Catholic authors the actual difference between Francis and Franciscanism, which Bonaventure openly admitted, is often glossed over. Guardini makes some valuable remarks on the question in his epilogue to Rüttenauer's translation of the *Speculum perfectionis* (Munich, 1953, p. 245-259). An excellent treatment of the problem is found in O. Engelbert, *St. Francis of Assisi*, Chicago, 1965.

95. Cfr. n. 93. Gilson's treatment is not oriented to the strict historico-theological question.

96. We need only think of the detailed *Expositio super regulam ff. Minorum*, Vol. VIII, p. 391-437, a "gloss" of almost disturbing subtlety; or of the extensive *Determinationes quaestionum*, Vol. VIII, p. 337-374. Cfr. Gilson, *Bonaventure*, p. 43-57, where we find a number of details of this sort. Especially interesting is the case described on p. 55.

97. Cfr. what will be said under 3.

98. XXII 21, p. 440b.

99. Text in Böhmer, *Analekten*, p. 71: . . . Placet mihi, quod sacram theologiam fratribus legas; dummodo propter huius studium sanctae orationis et devotionis spiritum non extinguant, sicut in regula continetur. Vale. As regards the authenticity of this text. Böhmer remains undecided (p. XXX). Gilson decides against the authenticity of the letter (*Bonaventure*, p. 454). Goetz seems to favor it (*op. cit.*, p. 55.) Hardick-Esser, *Schriften des heiligen Franziskus*, p. 14 takes a positive position: "For a long time this little letter was a subject of controversy as regards its form. But recent research has shown it to be a genuine work of St. Francis as regards its content and its form." Hardick-Esser refers to K. Esser, *Der Brief des heiligen Franziskus an den heiligen Antonius von Padua*, in: *Franz. Studien* 31 (1949) p. 135-151. I believe we can follow this judgment. Cfr. also the detailed study of J. Cambell given in the list of literature. Recently O. Bonmann has taken a stand against its authenticity (cfr. literature.)

100. XXII 21, p. 440b. See the beautiful text in the *Verba admonitionis* of St. Francis: "Et illi religiosi sunt mortui a littera: qui spiritum divine littere nolunt sequi, sed sola verba magis cupiunt scire et aliis interpretari. Et illi sunt vivificati a spiritu divine littere, qui omnem litteram, quam sciunt . . . verbo et exemplo reddunt . . . altissimo Domino Deo . . . (Nr. 7, Böhmer, *Analekten* 44.) Cfr. *Regula non bullata*, Nr. 17, *op. cit.*, p. 16. *Speculum perfectionis* c III (IV) c 69, 1, ed. Sabatier, p. 199. II Celano p. 2, c 32 6, ed. Alencon, p. 217.

101. Cfr. p. 41.
102. XVIII 7, p. 415b; XVI 22, p. 406b; XV 28, p. 402b. Likewise already in Joachim, *Concordia* IV c 39 f 59v: Necesse quippe est, ut succedat similitudo vera apostolicae vitae, in qua non acquirebatur possessio terrenae hereditatis, sed vendebat potius, sicut scriptum est. In *Sacrum imperium*, p. 253, Dempf says that the prophecy of a poor church of monks is found already in Gerhoh von Reichersberg, and that here also it is connected with a distinction between Petrine and Johannine Christianity.
103. Cfr. especially the *Quaestiones de perfectione evangelica* (q. 2) and the *Apologia pauperum*. In both works, Bonaventure emphasizes that Franciscan poverty is a poverty "tam in communi quam in privato." Bonaventure never accepted the loose notion of poverty of the Conventuals. Cfr. the clear call to poverty in *Hex* XX 30, p. 430f; this will be treated later.
104. XV 28, p. 402b. Also, XVI 29, p. 408. See the schema given above, p. 21.
105. XXII 27, p. 441b.
106. XVI 29, p. 408b. See also, XX 29, p. 430b.
107. Above all the near-eschatology of XX 15, p. 428a and XV 28, p. 402b. This would seem to have been obsolete at the time of the *Hexaemeron*.
108. Esp. XX 30, p. 430f, and XXIII 26 and 29, p. 448f.
109. XX 30, p. 430f. Concerning the anti-Aristotelian polemic see Ch. 4.
110. See the following chapter.

Notes to Chapter 2, #6

1. *Hex* XV 24, p. 401b:...tunc impletum erit illud Isaiae: Non levabit gens contra gentem gladium, nec exercebuntur ultra ad proelium; quia hoc nondum adimpletum est, cum adhuc vigeat uterque gladius; adhuc sunt disceptationes et haereses . . . Also, XV 25, p. 402a; XVI 13, p. 405a: In novo testamento similiter sunt septem tempora:...pacis postremae (as seventh); XVI 30, p. 408b: In septimo tempore scimus quod haec facta sunt: reaedificatio templi, restauratio civitatis et pax data. Similiter in tempore septimo futuro erit reparatio divini cultus et reaedificatio civitatis . . . et tunc pax erit.
2. Englebert gives a lively picture of the turmoil and strife of the time in *St. Francis*, p. 41ff. The confusion of the period of Frederick II and the interregnum added to the problem. Bonaventure's *Hexaemeron* dates from the year in which the interregnum was ended by the election of Rudolph of Hapsburg.
3. XV 24,p.401b and 25,p.402a. Here reference is made to Is.2,4 (Non levabit gens contra gentem gladium, nec exercebuntur ultra ad proelium); XVI 30,p.408b is based on Ez.40ff.
4. See, *Conc* 1 V c 65 95r: Beatus est autem aut erit ordo ille, quem dominus diliget super omnes, utpote qui visione pacis

fruiturus est et dominaturus a mari usque ad mare . . . Similar in c 18 f 69v.

5. Cfr. the Franciscan greeting, about which Francis says in his Testament: Salutationem michi Dominus revelavit, ut diceremus: Dominus det tibi pacem. (nr.6,ed. Böhmer, p.38). Bonaventure emphasizes this basic character of the Franciscan message in: *It* prol 1 Vol.V,p.295a: . . . quam pacem evangelizavit et dedit dominus noster Jesus Christus; cuius praedicationis repetitor fuit pater noster Franciscus, in omni sua praedicatione pacem in principio et in fine annuntians, in omni salutatione pacem optans, in omni contemplatione ad ecstaticam pacem suspirans, tanquam civis illius Jerusalem, de qua dicit vir ille pacis, qui, "cum his qui oderunt pacem, erat pacificus: Rogate quae ad pacem sunt Jerusalem" (Ps 119,7 and Ps 121,6). Sciebat enim, quod thronus Salomonis non erat nisi in pace, cum scriptum sit: "In pace factus est locus eius, et habitatio eius in Sion" (Ps.75, 3). Cfr. Jörgensen, *St. Francis of Assisi*,p.61: "What he said was very simple and without art, — it only concerned one thing, namely, peace as the greatest good for man . . ."

6. *Hex* XXIII 4, p.445: Sex sunt tempora, quorum sextum tempus habet tria tempora cum quiete. Et sicut Christus in sexto tempore venit, ita oportet, quod in fine generetur Ecclesia contemplativa. Ecclesia enim contemplativa et anima non differunt, nisi quod anima totum habet in se, quod Ecclesia in multis. Quaelibet enim anima contemplativa habet quandam perfectionem ut videat visiones Dei. The Delorme text brings out more clearly Bonaventure's division of history on the basis of the double-seven-schema when it states in V IV C IV, II #1,4,p.265: In quibus etiam intellige signari sex tempora; et sextum tempus habet septem tempora cum quiete. Et sicut sex diebus factus est mundus et sexta aetate venit Christus, ita post sex tempora Ecclesiae in fine generabitur Ecclesia contemplativa . . . Cfr. *Hex* XX 27,p.430a: Unde non habetur illuminatio, nisi quando Ecclesia consideratur secundum sua tempora; Rachel adhuc concipiet et parturiet, et Beniamin nascetur.

Notes to Chapter 2, #7

1. This thesis cannot be based on positive citations; it can be justified only negatively, i.e. on the basis of the lack of statements that treat of "revelatio" as understood in our modern sense. The thesis is confirmed from another perspective by the important study of J. de Ghellinck, *Pour l' histoire du mot "revelare,"* in: *Rech.sc. rel.* 6 (1916) p.149-157; and indirectly by B. Decker, *Die Entwicklung der Lehre von der prophetischen Offenbarung von Wilhelm von Auxerre bis zu Thomas von Aquin,* Breslau, 1940. Decker treats of the area within which the most important authors of High Scholasticism apply the notion of "revelare"

without finding it necessary to treat of the problem of "one revelation." Beyond this, I know of no study that attempts to establish this theme.

2. Cfr. B. Decker, *op.cit.*, p.134-164, where manuscript material is given.

3. Esp. the impressive treatment in *Sermo Christus unus omnium magister*, 2 — 5, Vol.V, p.568a-b, nr.2:Christus namque secundum quod via est magister et principium cognitionis, quae est per fidem. Haec enim cognitio duplici via habetur, videlicet per revelationem et per auctoritatem . . . Cum igitur his duabus viis contingat devenire ad cognitionem fidelem, hoc non potest esse nisi per Christum datorem, qui est principium omnis revelationis secundum adventum sui in mentem, et firmamentum omnis auctoritatis secundum adventum sui in carnem. Nr. 3: Venit autem in mentem ut lux revelativa omnium prophetalium visionum . . . Nr.4: Venit etiam in carnem ut verbum approbativum omnium prophetalium locutionum . . . Nr.5: Et ideo tota Scriptura authentica et eius praedicatores aspectum habent ad Christum venientem in carnem tanquam ad fundamentum totius fidei christianae . . . . The most frequently used expression for the objectively enduring element is indeed 'faith.' Cfr. I *Sent*, d 2 a un q 4 c,p.57a (fides catholica docet); *ibid.* d 5 a l q l c, p.112b (fides vera dicit); *ibid.* d 19 p 2 a un q 2, p.358a (fides nostra ponit); *ibid.* d 11 a un q l c,p.211b (fidei veritas est) etc. Many such examples can be given. Of special significance for the relation between the objective 'fides quae creditur' and the subjective 'fides qua creditur' is III *Sent.* d 25 a l q l,p.535ff.

4. Concerning inspiration cfr. III *Sent.* d 25 a 1 q 2 ad 6, p.541b: At times when the 'revelatio aperta' of prophetism was lacking it did not follow that 'inspiratio' for the individual was lacking. A more general formulation is found in III d 19 a l q 3 c, p.406a: Apparuit autem lumen veritatis et interius per divinam inspirationem et exterius per humanam instructionem. In relation to this, the *Brev* p 4 c 1, Vol.V, p.242a and p 5 c 6,p.259b distinguishes between the 'verbum incarnatum' and the 'verbum inspiratum.' Regarding 'manifestatio' see I *Sent* d 15 p l a un q 3 c,p.263b and especially II *Sent* d 10 a 3 q l c,p.268f. In general, the meaning of 'manifestatio' seems to be broader than 'revelatio.' Concerning 'apertio' see *Hex* XX 29,p.430b; XVI 29,p.408b; XX 15,p.428a.

5. This meaning is practically always involved. Without refering to the special usages for the moment, this meaning appears in *Hex* III 2;22;32 p. 343a; 347a; 348b; XXI 20; 26; 33,p.434b;435b; 437b.

6. *Hex* XIII 17, p.390b; XIV 14, p.396a; XIV 25, p.397a; XIV 7 and 10,p.394f. The same meaning appears in the texts given by B. Decker (*op.cit.*) from the still unedited questions De prophetia, De raptu, De visione intellectuali et corporali, De divinatione.

7. Since *Hex* XVI 29, p.408b, connects the three words: intelligentia scripturae — revelatio — clavis David — with the word "vel," they seem to be practically synonymous for Bonaventure. 'Revelatio' is understood in the same sense in XXII 27,p.441b. For the interpretation of this text, see also XXII 21,p.440b and XV 28,p.402b; as well as II 12 and 19, p.338b; XIX 10,p.421b.
8. II 30,p.341a — b; XVIII 24,p.418a. Cfr. also #12.

Notes to Chapter 2, #8

1. *Hex* II 6, p.337a: Sine sanctitate non est homo sapiens . . . Sanctitas immediata dispositio est ad sapientiam.
2. II 8,p.337b.
3. II 9 and 10, p.337f. Bonaventure bases himself expressly on Aristotle. The Delorme text, Princ II Coll II #1,9 and 10, p.23f is more explicit than that of *Opera omnia*.
4. II 19, p.339b.
5. This is intended merely to establish that this wisdom belongs basically to *ratio* as such. The question raised by Gilson (*op. cit.*, p. 341ff.), Van Steenberghen (*Le mouvement* . . . 225ff.), Robert (*Le probleme de la philosophie bonaventurienne*, in: *Laval phil. et theol.*VII, 1951,9 — 58) as to how far this wisdom may be pursued by reason alone is not the object of this study.
6. II 11,p.338a.
7. II 19,p.339b.
8. II 12; 19,p.338b; 339b.
9. II 21,p.340a.
10. V 22,p.357b; II 20,p.339f.
11. II 30,p.341b; cfr. the entire section Nr.28 — 34,p.340ff.
12. II 28,p.340f; II 50,p.341 a — b.

Notes to Chapter 2, #9

1. This is not changed by the fact that, according to Bonaventure, the New Testament brings a new revelation of the meaning of the Old Testament. Cfr. III *Sent.* d 13 a 2 q 3 ad 6, p. 290b; d 25 a 2 q 2 c,p.548b; d 25 a 2 q 3 c,p.550b; IV *Sent* d 8 p 2 a l q 2 ad 9 and 10,p.194b. Not only is the word 'revelatio' lacking here, but furthermore the meaning is not that the text of the New Testament is a deciphering of the text of the Old Testament, but that the New Testament is a time of understanding, of 'revelata cognitio', after the time of darkness. Therefore, here also "revelation" is not a book, but the inner understanding.
2. *Hex* II 13 — 17,p.338f. A different and highly individual explanation of the four senses of Scripture is found in Eucherius, *Liber spiritualis intelligentiae*, Praef CSEL 31,p.3-6, esp.4f. This writer connects them with the so-called Platonic scientific schema, which actually appears for the first time in Xenocrates. The following schema emerges:

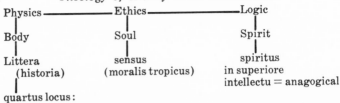

Physics ——————— Ethics ———————— Logic

Body   Soul   Spirit

Littera   sensus   spiritus
(historia)   (moralis tropicus)   in superiore
                                         intellectu = anagogical

quartus locus:

allegoria — the 'narratio gestorum' is understood as 'umbra futurorum.'

Cfr. Grundmann, *Joachim* I,28. Especially from p.23-40 we find important material on the general problem of Medieval exegesis. For the earlier history of the triple schema of the sciences see Grabmann, *Gesch. der schol. Methode* II, p.30 and especially Baur, *Dominicus Gundissalinus*, p.194.

3. *Hex* II 13,p.338b; XIII 11,p.389b: triplex intelligentia spiritualis: allegoria quid credendum; anagogia quid exspectandum; tropologia quid operandum . . . XX 15,p.428a; *De red* 5 Vol.V,p.321b: . . . allegoria . . . , secundum quod credendum est. See also the above references to Grundmann; also Lubac, *"Typologie" et "Allegorisme"*, in: *Rech th anc med* 14 (1947) p.180-226; M.D. Chenu,*Théologie symbolique et exégèse scolastique au XII et XIII siècle*, in:*Mélanges Joseph de Ghellinck*, Gembloux, 1951, Vol.II, p.509-526, esp. p.516 and 519. On p.519 we read: L' édifice de la pensée chrétienne se construit donc sur la base des textes scripturaires, mais s' élève et se fabrique par la méthode allégorique.

4. *Hex* XIX 8,p.421b.

5. Delorme, *Hex* ·V III Col VII #1,14,p.217.

6. *Hex* XIX 9,p.421b; *Brev* prol #4,p.206a. Cfr. Joachim, *Conc* V 9 f 65v: Haec de primo intellectu breviter dicta assignata sunt quoquo modo in cortice exteriore . . . It may be that the image was taken by Joachim from an already common usage.

7. See #16 B II 2b. Also, Sermo 2 in dom III adv. Vol.IX,63a.

8. *Hex* XIX 9,p.421b; XVI 23,p.407a; also XX 15,p.428a. For the notion of the 'Judaeus' see III 4,p.344a.

9. *Hex* II 19,p.339b and the other texts of the *Hex* that make use of 2 Cor.3,18.

10. P. Dempsey, *De principiis exegeticis S. Bonaventurae*, Rome, 1945,p.10-11. Dempsey bases himself on the unedited *quaestiones de prophetia* and *de visione intellectuali et corporali*. Unfortunately, despite much effort, I was unable to find a copy of Dempsey's work. The references given here are taken from the detailed review of Dempsey's book by Th. ab Orbizo, in *Coll Franc* XV (1945) p.240f.

11. Cassiodore, *Expos in Ps.*, Prol,PL 70,12 B. This is taken over by the *Glossa ordinaria* and by Peter Lombard (PL 191,58 B). On

this point, see the German 'Thomasausgabe', Vol.23: Special gifts of grace and the two ways of human life, with commentary by H. U. von Balthasar (1954), p. 6 (II-II q 171 a 1 opp 4 and ad 4) and p.296f.

12. According to Decker, *op. cit.*, Bonaventure is dependent on Alexander of Hales, William of Auxerre, and Philip the Chancellor; and very probably on Albert the Great or on a third source from which they both work. (Cfr. p.135; 143f; 164.) He in turn had influence on Thomas Aquinas (p. 161). Also the studies on the ancient, patristic, Judaic, and Arabian sources for the Scholastic doctrine of revelation indicated on p.5 — 38 are important. In his important development in Vol. 23 of the *Deutsche Thomasausgabe*, p.293f., Balthasar points out a very important scholastic source which was not available to Decker, namely, the *Quaestiones* of the Manuscript of Douai 434 (Cfr. Glorieux, *Les 572 questions de manuscrit de Douai* 434, in: *Rech th anc med* 10 (1938) p.123-152;225-267). Here we find several groups of questions on prophecy.

13. Rupert of Deutz, *Comm in Apoc* 1 c 1 PL 169,851f; Kamlah, *Apokalypse und Geschichtstheologie*, p.105 — 114. Besides providing a brief statement of the most significant Scholastic material on this point, the text has the further advantage of standing in the precise direction of historical thought which was to be characteristic of the later Bonaventure. See Ch.3,#13.

14. *De gen ad litt* XII 6 — 34,PL34,458-480. Also S. Zarb, *Le fonte agostiniane del trattato sulla profezia di S. Tomaso d' Aquino*, in: *Angelicum* 15 (1938) p.169 — 200; Decker, *op. cit.*, p.6 — 9; *H.* Sasse, *Sacra Scriptura. Bemerkungen zur Inspirationslehre Augustins*, in: Festschrift F. Dornseiff zum 65. Geburtstag, Leipzig, 1953, p. 262—273. Sasse insists strongly, indeed too strongly, on the pagan-apologetic origin of Augustine's mystical doctrine of inspiration.

15. Rupert, *op. cit.*, 851; Augustine, *op. cit,* c 28, 56,478.

16. Rupert, *op. cit.*, 851 D — 852A. This idea seems not to have an exact parallel in Augustine.

17. Cfr. Decker, *op. cit.*, p.134-164, and Dempsey, *op. cit.*, for the texts. The three 'visiones' are named expressly in *Hex* III 23, p.347a; *Brev* p 5 c 6, Vol.V,p.260a.

18. *Hex* III 22 and 23, p.347a: (22) Tertia clavis est intellectus verbi inspirati, per quod omnia revelantur; non enim fit revelatio nisi per verbum inspiratum: Daniel intellexit sermonem. Intelligentia enim opus est in visione. Nisi enim verbum sonet in aure cordis, splendor luceat in oculo, vapor et emanatio omnipotentis sit in olfacto, suavitas in gustu, sempiternitas impleat animam; non est homo aptus ad intelligendas visiones. Sed "Danieli dedit Deus intelligentiam omnium visionum et somniorum" (Dan 1,17). Per quid? Per verbum inspiratum. (23) Visio autem est triplex, ut communiter diciter: corporalis, imaginaria, intellectualis. Duae

primae nihil valent sine tertia. Unde parum valuit Balthasari visio corporalis in visione manus . . . et Pharaoni visio in spicis et bobus, sed Danieli et Joseph. Joseph respondet Joanni, Daniel Paulo. Cfr. the entire Collatio III; II 34, p.342b (revelation to Moses) ; Sermo IV Christus unus omnium magister 2 — 3, Vol.V, p.568f.

19. I *Sent* d 15 a un q 1 ad 2, p.271a (Saul; *Comm in Eccli* Prooem q 4 Vol.VI p.8b (Bileam, Solomon) ; See also C. van den Borne, *Doctrina Sancti Bonaventurae de inspiratione et inerrantia sacrae scripturae,* in: *Antonianum* 1 (1926) p.312f. It is clear that Bonaventure held this as an exceptional case; cfr. I *Sent* d 15 a un q 1 ad 2, and especially ad 3, p.271a.

20. II *Sent* d 4 a 2 q 2 c, p.138a: . . . praedicere . . . quod non voco revelare, sed certam interius illuminationem dare . . . , hoc voco revelationem. In ad 1 it is said that as far as the recipient of revelation is concerned, revelation involves a "simpliciter intelligere." Van den Borne, *op. cit.,* p.312, speaks expressly of the identity of inspiration and revelation in Bonaventure. The visionary character of Bonaventure's notion of 'revelatio' arises from the essentially Platonic basis of his doctrine of being and knowledge, for here the inner truth is grasped not in discursive thought but in an illuminative vision. Cfr. B. A. Luyckx, *Die Erkenntnislehre Bonaventuras* . . . p.124.

21. See the treatment below on page 69, especially n.32; and also what was said above, page 62.

22. . . . ut sicut Christus fuit panniculis involutus, ita sapientia Dei in scripturis figuris quibusdam humilibus involveretur. *Brev* prol #4, Vol.V,p.206a; van den Borne, *op. cit.,* p.311. We find the same idea in Luther, *Vorrede auf das Alte Testament,* 3 (cited by W. Vischer, *Das Christuszeugnis des Alten Testaments,* Vol.I, Zurich 1946,p.17) :". . . this is the Scripture which confounds the wise and clever, and which stands open to the small and the simple. Here you find the swaddling clothes and the crib wherein Christ lies, and to which the angel directs the shepherds. The swaddling clothes are poor and base, the treasure that lies within is precious; it is Christ."

23. See # 10 II 1, p.72ff. Cfr. J. Ratzinger, *Offenbarung-Schrift-Überlieferung, ein Text des hl. Bonaventura und seine Bedeutung für die gegenwärtige Theologie,* in: *Trierer Theologische Zeitschrift* 67 (1958) p.13-27.

24. *De don Sp* coll IV 13ff., Vol.V, p.476: in nr. 13 he says that the 'scientia theologica', which thereafter is referred to as 'sacra scriptura', is 'super fidem fundata.' Here, as elsewhere, he understands the 'fides' to be that which is contained in the Symbolum: sicut scientiae philosophicae super prima principia sua fundantur, ita scientia scripturae fundatur super articulos fidei, qui sunt duodecim fundamenta civitatis. See III Sent d 25 a 1 q 1, p.534ff. It is from this viewpoint that we must understand the pair 'fides

— scriptura' that occurs so frequently in Bonaventure, e.g. I *Sent* d 13 dub 6 r,p.241a; I d 27 p l a un q 4 c,p.478a; II d 30 a l q l c,p.715b; III d 3 p l a l p l q l Epil,p.64a; IV d 44 p 2 a l q l c,p.921b.

24a This we find consistently and expressly in the Prologue to the *Brev.* For the previous history see below #12, n.18, p. 90 and 206.

24b Prooem Vol. I, 4 b and 5 b.

25. As the lowest level parallel to "revelation" to sinners we have the 'fides informis.' I *Sent* d 15 a un q l opp 4;p.270.

26. These stages of faith, which are also stages of mystical vision and thus stages of revelation, form the structure of the *Hexaemeron* which recognizes a "visio intelligentiae per contemplationem suspensae, per prophetiam illustratae, per raptum in Deum absorptae" beyond the "visio intelligentiae per naturam inditae, per fidem sublevatae, per scripturam eruditae." III 24, p.347a. See also the treatment in the following paragraphs.

27. Denifle, *Das Evangelium aeternum und die Commission zu Anagi,* ALKG I 60: "Gerard considers the three principle works of Joachim to be the canonical works of the third age. He considers them all together under the word "opus", and calls Joachim the 'scriptor huius operis' . . . Thus, Joachim would be the evangelist of the third age." Concerning the viewpoint of Joachim himself, we read on p.56f.: "It is clear that Joachim did not consider the *Evangelium aeternum* to be a written gospel . . . The teacher would be not a book nor a writing, but the Holy Spirit Himself. In relation to this point, Joachim applied the Victorine doctrine of contemplation to his own theory of the third age, which was unknown to the Victorines." Denifle, *ibid.,* points out that Joachim designates the *novus ordo* as ecclesia contemplativa, ecclesia contemplantium, ordo contemplantium, viri spirituales. All these notions are found in Bonaventure, at times literally and at times by way of allusion.

28. XVI 2 p.403b. It is expressed in briefer form in Delorme V III C IV 2 p.180: . . . post Novum autem Testamentum non succedet aliud, quia aeternum est.

29. *Hex* X 3 and 4 p.377, and the entire Coll X in general.

30. *Hex* XXII 21 and 22 p.440f; Nr.27 p.441b; XXI 20 and 26 p.434b and 435b; Nr. 23 and 33 p.435 a and 436b.

31. H. U. von Bauthasar gives numerous references in the *Deutsche Thomasausgabe,* Vol.23 p.280. Here we single out only Abaelard, *Exp. in Pauli ad Rom lib IV* PL 178, 939, where the *gratia interpretandi* is used as a definition of prophecy.

32. Cfr. the texts indicated in foot-note 30 above which clearly express this conviction. See also, XV 28 p.402b.

33. The reader is referred to the competent presentations of the history of philosophy. The rapid upsurge of theology is presented well by O. Englebert, *St. Francis of Assisi,* p.271ff. On p.276 we read: "And Dominic succeeded so well in his purpose that half

a century after his death his Order possessed around seven hundred doctors of theology; whereas in 1220 one could not have found more than a hundred in all Christendom."

34. XX 15 p.428a: Et ideo figurae nondum explanatae sunt; sed quando luna erit plena, tunc erit apertio Scripturarum, et liber aperietur, et septem sigilla solventur, quae adhuc non sunt aperta. —Credite mihi, tunc videbimus quasi per plenilunium, quando leo noster de tribu Juda surget et aperiet librum, quando consummabuntur passiones Christi . . . The time of the full moon is not the time after the Parousia, for that will be the time of the sun and not of the moon. Rather, the period indicated here is the inner--historical time of the *ecclesia contemplativa*, as is clear from the text of Coll XX. See also XX 27-29 p.430a-b; XXII 22 and 23 p.440ff; XXIII 2 — 4 p.445 a — b; in a certain sense the text of XV 28 p.402b belongs here also. (Cfr. #5, the end.)

35. Of all the texts indicated already, *Hex* XXII 22 and 23 p.440ff gives the clearest expression of the orientation of the final revelation which lies in the direction of the Dionysian. *sapientia nulliformis*. This must be compared with XXI 33 p.436b, and above all with II 30 — 31 p.341a-b, which is the primary text on the *sapientia nulliformis*. Also, XXIII 30 p.449b. Already in the *De red* 5 Vol.V 321b, Dionysius is presented as the Father of the final age. Here Bonaventure attempts to give a theological meaning to the history of theology: Circa primum (=sensum allegoricum scripturae) insudare debet studium doctorum, circa secundum, (=sensum moralem) studium praelatorum, circa tertium (=sensum anagogicum) studium contemplativorum. Primum maxime docet Augustinus, secundum maxime docet Gregorius, tertium vero docet Dionysius. The situation indicated at the conclusion of #8 works itself out naturally here. According to *Hex* II 30, Bonaventure held a double "revelation" at the beginning of Christian history: a general one, and one granted only to the *perfecti*. The tension between these will be resolved at the end of time in that then there will be only the *perfecti*. We find the same approach to the concept of revelation already in Pseudo-Dionysius: *Epist IX ad Tit* #1 PG 3,1105 D; in the translation of Eriugena (PL 122 1189 C-D) we read: Sed itaque et hoc intelligere oportet, duplicem esse theologorum traditionem: unam quidem arcanam et mysticam, alteram vero manifestam et notiorem: et eam quidem symbolicam et perfectivam, hanc vero philosophicam et approbativam, et complectitur effabili ineffabile. In the extract of Thomas Gallus (*Dionysiaca* I p.715a) the text reads as follows: . . . ad excusationem sensibilium signorum attendendum est quod duplex traditio est theologorum de divinis in sacra scriptura . . . una . . . secreta et clausa. Alia autem evidens et notior est . . . The translation of John Sarracenus: *Dionysiaca* p.637 b,c. If we wish to understand both of these texts properly, we must keep in mind that Dionysius does not

use the word "theologi" in the modern sense. Rather, for him it signifies the sacred writers themselves; and in accordance with this, he understands traditio differently. Cfr. J. de Ghellinck, *Le mouvement théologique du XII Siècle*, 1948², p.91-93; R. Roques, *L' univers dionysien*, Paris, 1954, p.209-234; R. Roques, *Note sur la notion de "Theologia" selon le Pseudo-Denys*, in: *Melanges Marcel Viller* (RAM 25, 1949) p.200-212.

36. Francis as the type of the final state of revelation. *Hex* XXII 22-23 p.440f. (It is briefer but no less clear in Delorme V IV C III #3,20-23 p.256) ;cfr. also XIX 14 p.422b in comparison with XVII 28 p.414b; XXIII 14 p.447b in comparison with XXII 23 p.441a and *Leg mai* Prol, Vol. VIII 504b (see the explanation of this text given above p. 32f.). Mt.11,25 is used expressly in relation to the concept of revelation in II 12 p.338b. For Bonaventure's attempt to apply the text to Francis, see the following foot-note.

37. *Leg mai* c 11,14 Vol.VIII 538b; *Leg Miracula* #X 8 p.564; *S. I de s.p.n. Francisco* I. Vol. IX 573b; S. V, I Vol. IX 593a. The same text is applied not directly to Francis, but clearly to Franciscanism in *Apol paup* c 9, 26 Vol. VIII 302f. Note also the peculiar double-concept of *humilitas* which Bonaventure develops in *De perf evang* q 1 c Vol.V 122a. In this context, there is a *duplex esse* — *esse naturae* and *esse moris et gratiae*; corresponding to this, there is a *duplex nihilitas* — *nihilitas veritatis* and *nihilitas severitatis*, and thus a *duplex actus humilitatis* — *humilitas interior* and *humiliatio exterior*. A higher form of humility is here added to that ontologically grounded *humilitas veritatis* which is proper to human existence as an existence mixed with nothingness. This new form is determined by saving history and is made possible only through Christ; it is the *humilitas severitatis*. The historical determination of this type of humility is clearly stated in ad 1 p.123a: Hic autem actus humilitatis fundatur in fide Jeus Christi, qui est actus super rationem et excedit terminos naturae. Similarly in ad 3 p.123a, ad 5 p.123b, ad 8 p. 124a. The peculiar relationship of the Franciscan Order to *humilitas* becomes clear when we see how Bonaventure understands the factual realization of this *humilitas severitatis* to take place in the act of *humiliatio exterior*; this in turn is seen as the proper possession of the Mendicant Orders and is to be defended as such; and particularly is this true of the Franciscan Order which is called to follow Francis.

38. *Hex* II 12 p.338b; also in the texts indicated in note 37. Similarly already in the *Comm in sap* c 6 to 5,24 Contra Vol.VI 150b: Item, abscondenda superbis sapientibus, sed revelanda parvulis humilibus . . .

39. See particularly the texts in note 37 that relate to St. Francis.
40. Cfr. note 35.

41. Besides the texts indicated in note 35, we must also keep in mind the texts which are yet to be analyzed in #16 in which Bonaventure predicts the end of Scholasticism: XIX 14 p.422b; XVII 28 p.414b.

42. C. van den Borne, *Doctrina S. Bonaventurae de inspiratione*, p.315,326. H.U. von Balthasar, *Deutsche Thomasausgabe* Vol.23, p.276ff.

43. Balthasar, *op. cit.*, p.310-320 together with the literature indicated there.

44. Balthasar, *op. cit.*, p.317 provides important material for the proper understanding of the multiple aspects of the concept involved here which is inadequately covered with the notion of "angel."

45. E. Gilson, *La philosophie au moyen âge des origines patristiques à la fin du XIV siècle*, Paris, 1947, p.382:Nous retrouverons plusieurs fois ad XIII siecle, cette subordination de la noétique d'Avicenna à celle de saint Augustin, que l'on a désigné par la formule, plus respectueuse de la complexité du fait, "d'augustinisme avicennisant." One might get the impression that Gilson found the expression ready-made. But Van Steenberghen (*Le mouvement . . .* 295 Note 1 to p.294) points out: Or M. Gilson a créé lui-meme la formule "augustinisme avicennisant." Also, *ibid.*, 202. Van Steenberghen would like to see this concept applied to the theory of William of Auvergne, who had held God Himself to be the *intellectus agens* for man. But in a wider sense, we would without doubt have to consider all those theories which arise from the same problem and which attempt to form a synthesis between the epistemology of Augustine and that of Avicenna.

46. O. Keicher, *Zur Lehre der älteren Franziskanertheologen vom "intellectus agens,"* in: *Abhandlg. aus dem Gebiet der Phil. und ihrer Geshichte*. Festgabe zum 70. Geburtstag G. v. Hertling, p.178. Concerning Rupella, cfr. D.H. Salman, *Jean de la Rochelle et les débuts de l'averroisme latin*, in: *Arch Hist Doctr Litt MA* 16 (1947/48) p.133-144. Salman's treatment confirms the thesis that there was already an incipient Averroism in Rupella's treatment of the soul. Concerning the so-called *Summa Halensis*, cfr.: M.M. Curtin, *The "Intellectus Agens" in the Summa of Alexander of Hales*, in: *Franciscan Studies* 5 (1945) p.418-433. Alfredus Anglicus can be seen as a predecessor of Rupella in the theory of mediate illumination; cfr. *De motu cordis*, ed. Cl. Baeumker, Münster, 1923 (=Baeumker-Beiträge XXIII, 1—2). Prol. 1,p.2f.: in se enim considerata (anima) substantia est incorporea, intellectiva, illuminationum quae a primo sunt, ultima relatione perceptiva. This definition, which Baeumker sees as undoubtedly Arabian, is found also in Rupella, *Summa de anima*, ed. Domenichelli (Prato, 1882) p.106. There are also indications of it in the *Summa Halensis* I/II inq 4 tr 1 sect 2 q 3 tit 1 membr 2 c 2

a 2 sol and ad 1.2. Vol. II,p.452b. In the case of Bonaventure, it appears in the *oppositiones*: II *Sent* d 10 a 2 q 2 opp 2 p.265a. Furthermore, Alfredus bases himself justifiably on Pseudo-Dionysius, whose influence on this question will be treated immediately.

47. For the entire question of the inferior knowledge, Bonaventure simply took over the Aristotelian theory of abstraction. Cfr. B. A. Luyckx, *Erkenntnislehre Bonaventuras*, esp. p.124 and 197. For a good summary with indications of the most important citations, cfr. Geyer, *op. cit.*, p.390-393.

48. *Q. disp. de sci Christi* q 4 Vol.V p.23a: Et ideo dicere, quod mens nostra in cognoscendo non extendat se ultra influentiam lucis increatae, est dicere, Augustinum deceptum fuisse, cum auctoritas ipsius exponendo non sit facile ad istum sensum trahere; et hoc valde absurdum est dicere de tanto patre et doctore maxime authentico inter omnes expositores sacrae scripturae.

49. II *Sent* d 24 p 1 a 2 q 4 c p.568/70, where Bonaventure clearly rejects the notion of God as the *intellectus agens* which could still be found in the *Summa Halensis*, and develops a theory of the *intellectus agens* which is quite thoroughly Aristotelian; from this point on, Aristotle remains for him the genuine authority in this area. "Et iste modus dicendi verus est et super verba philosophi fundatus"(p.569a). Cfr. also: III *Sent* d 39 a 1 q 2 p.904b; IV *Sent* d 5 a 3 q 1 ad 3 p.128b — 129a. The fact that there is no strict Aristotelianism present here does not do away with the fact of the clear intention to follow Aristotle on this point which is obvious in these citations.

50. *Q. 4 de sci Chri* f 16 Vol. V p.18b — 19a where Aristotle is presented as a witness for theory of Illumination. The *oppositiones* are not emphatically based on Aristotle; rather, in accordance with the Scholastic method, they take their proofs from the same authors as do the *fundamenta*: Augustine (4 times), Gregory (1 time), Dionysius (1 time), Aristotle (2 times). In the Corpus, Bonaventure gives a rather sharp critique of the Thomistic theory of knowledge, which would have already been worked out by this time (cfr. note 48); he views it as a variant of the Illumination-theory and rejects both the Thomistic theory and radical Augustinianism(cfr. note 48 above).

51. Therefore, Gilson's observation must be somewhat limited when he says: "In 1250 there was nothing to foreshadow all the troubles of the Averroist movement" (p.4). Actually the Averroism of Siger was still a thing of the future. But, as we have seen, there were already some related phenomena operative here.

52. Bonav. II *Sent* d 9 praenot p.240a; II *Sent* d 10 a 1 q 2 p.261ff *Hex* XXI 16.20.21.30 p.434 — 436; Ps. Dionysius, *De coel hier* c 6 #2 PG 3,200-201; c 13 #2 col. 300. The theological problem involved here is indicated, for example, by O. Semmelroth, *Die Lehre des Ps. Dionysius Areopagita vom Aufstieg der Kreatur zum göttlichen Licht*, in: *Scholastik* 29 (1954) p.24-52. On p.26

we read: "Does not Dionysius attempt to reconcile two contradictory things when he determines the task of all creatures in
such a way that they are called into being for the purpose of
participating in the divine goodness, and yet each of the existing
beings is limited ċorresponding to its proper analogy? How can
a creature rise to communion with God when it is determined in
such a way as to remain always on its proper analogical level?"
Cfr. *ibid.*, p.27 for the solution.

53. *Hex* XXI 16 p.434a; Ps. Dionysius, *De coel hier* c 4 #2 PG, 180
A — B.

54. *Hex* XXI 21 p.435a and the texts of Dionysius indicated.

55. I do not desire to enter into the controversy concerning Dionysius
himself but merely to point out to what dangers his influence gave
rise independently of the problem of his own theology. As is
well known, there is no unanimity concerning Dionysius himself.
Strongly on the positive side is E. von Ivanka, *La signification
historique du "Corpus areopagiticum"*, in: *R sc rel* 36 (1949)
p.5-24. Ivanka attempts to show that Pseudo-Dionysius did not
intend to neo-Platonize Christianity, but, on the contrary, was
engaged in polemics against neo-Platonism which was still felt
to be a danger. Indeed, it was an inner polemic in which the external form was taken over so that the danger could be overcome
precisely from within. He himself states that this is his intention
in the sixth letter when he says: qu'une représentation convai-
cante de la vérité, sans polémique explicite, est une meilleure
réfutation de l'erreur qu'une attaque directe (p.19). The immediacy of man to God is fully preserved, for the diminishing
degrees of the neo-Platonic participation become, for Dionysius,
"une multiplicité des formes de la participation immédiate au
divin" (p.18). Nevertheless, Ivanka allows for the possibility
that the influence of Dionysius took quite a different course.
'Toute tentative d'introduire de pareils êtres intermédiaires con-
tredit . . . à l'intention de Denys, et si une semblable tentative
se férèr à Denys, elle le fait absolument a tort.' " Semmelroth's
evaluation is not so positive, *op. cit.*, p.36. To me, the judgment
of R. Roques seems to be the most sober; it seems to come to
terms with the complexity of the situation more adequately
(*L'univers dionysien*, Paris, 1954, p.339). Le syncrétisme et le
concordisme dionysien décevront toujours parce qu'ils ont retenu
trop d'éléments radicalement inassimilables au platonisme, et trop
d'autres éléments profondément étrangers au christianisme. Mais
la confrontation généreuse pour laquelle Denys s'est passionné, la
fermeté de ses positions essentielles, dans la pleine et loyale con-
science des vrais désaccords, doivent imposer à notre intention
et à notre respect: "Qu'on dise: il osa trop, mais l'audace était
belle."

56. In this sense Bonaventure gives numerous citations, e.g.: II *Sent*
d 1 p 2 opp 1 p.45b; II *Sent* d 10 a 2 q 2 f 1 p.265a; II *Sent* d

23 a 2 q 3 ad 7 p.546b ("cum ipse sit immediatus rationali creaturae"); III *Sent* d 1 a 1 q 1 ad 4 p.11 . . . pro eo,quod natura
rationalis, eo ipso quod est imago Dei, nata ordinari ad ipsum
immediate . . .). The citations from Augustine that lie at the
basis of this are noted in Vol. II,p.45 A 5; of particular significance are: *De vera relig* c 55, 113 PL 34/172; *En in ps* 118 s
18,4 PL 37,1553; Ps-Augustine (Alcher of Clairvaux), *De spir et
an* c 10 f PL 40,785ff.

57. Cfr. the remarks of H.U. von Balthasar, *Deutsche Thomasausgabe*, vol.23,p.318f. Balthasar indicates that this notion can be
found already in Augustine (p.318), but he does not fail to point
out the danger of this idea (p.318).

58. *Hex* III 32 p.348b; *De don Sp.S.* VIII 15 Vol.V 497a. For parallels
from other Scholastics, cfr. Balthasar, *op. cit.*, p.318.

Notes to Chapter 2, #10

1. *L de div qu* 83, q.48 PL 40,31.

2. In my study *Volk und Haus Gottes* . . . I have attempted to
clarify in detail how the early approach of Augustine, which was
almost purely ontological, gave way more and more to historical
thinking. In this context, *De civ Dei* XVII 3 CSEL 40,2,p.207ff.
is worthy of note. Here three levels of prophetic sayings of the
OT are set up: they are to be understood partly in a purely spiritual sense; partly in a purely earthly sense; but also partly
"ad utramque pertinere intelliguntur." Is there not already in
this third group of sayings a remarkable penetration of history
and intelligibility? Regarding the problem of categorizing the
historical, Alexander is important, *S Theol*, tr intr c 1 q 1 ad 1
and 2,2f. These statements are taken up by Bonaventure in *QD
de theologia* q 1 ad 4,ed. Tavard, *R theol anc med* XVII (1950)
213. Concerning Augustine's position on the problem of historical understanding, see; H.J. Marrou, *The Meaning of History*
(Baltimore, 1966). For further treatment of the entire problem-
atic, see: J. de Ghellinck, *Patristique et argument de tradition
au bas moyen âge*, in: *Grabmannfestschrift*,p.403-426; Ghellinck,
Pour l'histoire de mot 'revelare', in: *Rech sc rel* VI (1916) p.149-
157; P. de Vooght, *Les sources de la doctrine chrétienne d'après
les théologiens du XIV siécle* . . . Paris, 1954.

3. *Hex* X 4 p.377f; a somewhat different accentuation is found in
XII 17 p.387b.

4. See the powerful Praefatio to the *Concordia*. The same thing is
expressed clearly and often in the text as well.

5. *Hex* XIX 10 p.421b.

6. *Methode* II, p.210 with a reference to *De sacr* prol c 7 PL 176,186;
in the same place, Grabmann points out the opposite position
of Abaelard.

7. Grabmann, *Methode* II, p.346-349; also, the texts here which are taken from the Prologue of the Book of Sentences. Concerning Robert, see: Landgraf, *Einführung*, p.69ff; Geyer, p.276-278. Geyer emphasizes more the relation between Robert and Hugo, while Landgraf emphasizes the fact that they belong to the school of Abaelard. For the text itself, cfr: R.M. Martin, *Oeuvres de Robert de Melun* III,p.19,19-21,20. The text is worked into the treatment of the value of the *Glossa*, which begins on p.9.

8. The text is given by Ghellinck, *Le mouvement theologique* . . . 515f and by Ch. Turot, *Comptes rendus des séances de l'académie des Inscriptions et Belles-Lettres, nouvelle série* t VI,1870 p.249-250. Concerning Almeric, see: Ghellinck, *Patristique et argument* . . . p.420. It is well known that, besides these fundamental problems concerning the Canon, the concrete determination of the canonical books remained unresolved during the whole of the MA. The canon of Hugo of St. Victor, for example, (*De sacr* prol c 7 PL 176,186) is more limited than that of Trent, while Bonaventure's is more extensive (*Brev* prol #1 Vol V 202b and note 10 with the reference to the pseudo-Bonaventurian *Centiloquium*). In both cases, a number-speculation plays a great role. For the history of the Canon, cfr.: B. Walde, *LThK* V 775ff; Bertholet *RGG* I 975ff.

9. Cfr. the text of the *Brev* given above and P. Dempsey, *op. cit.*, though he does not seem to be free of apologetic tendencies (cfr. the review of Fr. C. Frins in *Franz Studien* 32 [1950] p.427f).

10. *Hex* XIX 10 p.421b. Furthermore, it amounts to essentially the same thing when Trent (D.785 and 786) and a series of later ecclesiastical statements (esp. the Syllabus of Pius X, D.2001ff) declare the exegesis of the Fathers to be a normal principle of Scriptural exegesis as such. Such statements can hardly be related meaningfully to the literal explanation, i.e. to the purely historical exegesis; they are concerned rather with that 'allegoria' which has as its object the 'quid credendum' (Bonav *De red* 5). In other words, it has to do with the dogmatic-ecclesial exegesis. Only when they are thus understood do these statements have a consistent meaning.

11. Cfr. the beginning of the Regula non bullata: Hec est vita evangelii Jesu Christi (Böhmer, *Analekten*, p.1). Nr.22: Theneamus vitam et doctrinam et sanctum eius Evangelium (*op. cit.*,p.22). Testamentum Nr.4: . . . nemo ostendebat michi, quid deberem facere, sed ipse Altissimus revelavit michi, quod deberem vivere secundum formam sancti Evangelii (*op. cit.*, p.37). Also, I Thomas of Celano c 9,22,ed. Alencon,p.25: Non enim fuerat evangelii surdus auditor, sed laudabili memoriae, quae audierat cuncta commendans, ad litteram diligenter implere curabat. In a Sequence written by Thomas of Celano it is stated: Novus ordo, nova vita/mundo surgit inaudita;/restauravit lex sancita/statum evangelicum (Alencon, *op. cit.*, p.446). Also, Bonaventure, *Apol*

paup c 3, 8 — 10 Vol. VIII 246f; c 8, 19.20,p.293a; c 10,4,p.305a. Here Bonaventure acquiesces to the "ad litteram" of the Spirituals . . . nudis pedibus incedunt . . ., ut illud evangelii verbum ad litteram impleant . . . Cfr. Hardick-Esser, *Die Schriften des heiligen Franziskus von Assisi*,p.4; Jörgensen, *op. cit.*, p.78; W. Nigg, *Vom Geheimnis der Mönche*, p.254, as well as the literature on Francis in general. See also #5, note 51 above.

12. Especially the text of the Testamentum just cited (4,Böhmer, p.37).

13. *De perf ev* q 2 a 1 c Vol. V 130b.

14. This view should be held in preference to the widely circulated but false notion that already the pre-Scholastic period and the period of early Scholasticism were determined by the controversy about universals. Cfr. Grabmann, *Methode* I, p.216; J. de Ghellinck, *Le mouvement theologique* . . . p.68-71; Geyer, *op. cit.*, p.181ff.

15. *De perf ev* q 2 a 2, adv obi postea factas IV,p.153a: *Apol paup* c 10,4 Vol. VIII, p.305a: Quod si verum est, per omnem modum apostolica erravit ecclesia . . .; esp. c 11,15 —-17, p.315f. Nr. 16:Te igitur, sacrosancta Romana Ecclesia, tamquam alteram Esther elevatam in populis ut Ecclesiarum omnium matrem, reginam atque magistram . . . fiducialiter interpellat tuorum pauperum coetus, ut quos genuisti ut mater, educasti ut nutrix, nunc etiam ut regina potenter ac juste defendas . . . Nr. 17: Sed et tu, Regina mundi dignissima, defensatrix pauperum et humilium, advocata, longe sublimius quam Esther exaltata in populis et praeparata in tempore, Mardochaei tui, Francisci videlicet, excitare clamoribus . . .

16. *De perf ev* q 2 a 2 adv obi postea factas IV Vol.V, p.153a.

17. *De perf ev* q 2 a 2 f 22 and 23 Vol.V,p.138b. The sanctity of the founders of the Orders was admitted even by those who opposed the Mendicants. As Bierbaum points out, Nicholas of Lisieux refers to Dominic and Francis as "gloriosi sancti" (*op. cit.*, p.366). The position of William of St. Amour is not as clear; cfr. his Annotationes to Bonaventure, *Quaestio reportata de mendicitate*, (to ad 17 end),ed. Delorme, *op. cit.*, p.339. In contrast, Gerard of Abbeville has a thoroughly positive image of Francis; cfr. his Tract "Contra adv perf Christ",ed. Clasen *AFH* 32 (1939) p.89-200; l II p 1, p.91,14ff; l II p 4,p.132,34ff.

18. *De perf ev* q 2 a 2 ad 20,p.147f; *ibid.*, adv obi postea factas I, p.150a; *ibid.*, V p.155b. Cfr. #14 below.

19. Cfr. # #5 and 14.

20. *Hex* II 17,p.339a. Also, XV 11,p.400a and XV 20,p.401a.

21. See the schemata from *Hex* XV and XVI given in #5.

22. *Hex* XIII 6 and 7,p.388b and 389a. Significantly in the parallel text of the Delorme recension (V III Coll I #1,6 and 7,p.148) the eschatological outlook is entirely absent; the New Testament as such is seen as the fulfillment of this prophecy. The fact that

we have genuine Bonaventurian thought in this case can be seen by the parallels in the text of the *Opera omnia* (XVI 29,p.408b; XX 29,p.430b) as well as by a text which has remained in the Delorme recension: V III Coll IV 29,p.192: . . . in quo tempore dabitur uni personae vel multitudini . . . scientia et revelatio sive clavis David et intelligentia scripturae. — The text of *Hex* XIII 6 and 7 provides a vivid example of Bonaventure's often sharp eschatological critique of time; cfr. XII 11, p.439a; . . . in ecclesia primitiva, quando ecclesia optime erat disposita; sed modo porcus et canis intrant. V 9,p.355b; V 19,p.357a; XXII 18,p.440b; *De don Sp S.* III 9 Vol.V,p.470b: Ubi est pietas hodie? Non est medium, quia Deus abstulit extrema; tanta est hodie crudelitas, quod homo non potest satiari de vindicta, regnat hodie impatienta et iracundia: male iudicat homo: etiam si non offendit me homo, male tamen iudicabo de ipso. *De don Sp S.* VII 17, p.492a-b; *Serm. V in dom II post Pascha II* Vol IX,p.304b; S feria II post Pascha Vol.IX,p.281b: Et ideo ego valde invitus praedico, quia "non est bonum sumere panem filiorum et mittere canibus" (Mt.15,16) ad manducandum, quia ea, quae recte dicuntur, quidam prave et perverse interpretantur; p.287b: . . . in dombus scholarium varia fercula et vina sunt, ita ut non clerici, sed emptores vinorum iudicentur (cfr. J. d'Albi, *op. cit.*, 23 Note 146), etc.

Notes to Chapter 2, #11

1. Cfr. II Celano c 124, 165 (ed. Alencon 293): Per impressa rebus vestigia insequitur ubique dilectum, facit sibi de omnibus scalam, qua perveniatur ad solium. Gilson, *Bonaventure*,p.64; esp. 185-214 where the formation of the Bonaventurian image of the world is sketched from the general symbolism indicated here. Regarding Francis' relation to the world of nature, cfr. W. Nigg, *Grosse Heilige*, p.91f.

2. *Hex* II 20,p.339f and V 22,p.357b.

3. II 20,p.340a.

4. The parallel between the 'Judaeus' and the 'Philosophus' is clearly emphasized in those places that work with the imagery of the "lignum scientiae boni et mali." See #16 B II 2 b below; Gilson, *Bonaventure*, p.205.

5. *Comm in Joa* 1,43 (to verse 18). Vol. VI 255b-256a: . . . est cognoscere Deum in se et in suo effectu. Et cognoscere Deum in effectu, hoc est videre per speculum, et hoc dupliciter: aut per speculum obscuratum et sic videbat primus homo ante lapsum; aut per speculum obscuratum et sic videmus nos modo, quia propter peccatum et oculi nostri caligaverunt et omnes creaturae obtenebratae sunt; unde videmus nunc per speculum in aenigmate, primae ad Corinthios decimo tertio. Cfr. the schema of the *Hex* coll III 24 — 31,p.347f; also, *Hex* XIII 12,p.389f; *S Chr unus omn mag* 2 — 6 Vol.v,p.568.

6. *Hex* V 24,p.358a; *Brev* p 2 c 12,p.230b.
7. *Itin* c 2,15 Vol. V,p.299b. Also, E. Sauer, *Die religiöse Wertung in Bonaventuras Itinerarium mentis in Deum*, Werl i.W. 1937. Creation as a "ladder" to God,e.g. also in: I *Sent* d 3 a un q 3 arg neg 2,p.74b; *Itin* c 4,2,p.306a; c 7,1p.312b. Cfr. also #1, note 18 above for the citation from Thomas of Celano.
8. A few examples of this: R. Bultmann, *Die Frage der natürlichen Offenbarung*, in: *Glauben und Verstehen* II Tübingen, 1952, p.79-104; O. Cullman, *Christ and Time*, p.177ff; A. Nygren, *Der Römerbrief*, Gottingen, 1951, p.75-83. Cfr. especially G. Söhngen's discussion with K. Barth and E. Brunner (G. Sohngen, *Die Einheit in der Théologie*,p.212-264); also, H.U. von Balthasar, *Karl Barth*,p.148-168, and esp. p.314 — 355. The danger which Protestants fear is well expressed by Oepke in his somewhat overstated formulation: "According to the Greek concept, man reveals God; but according to the biblical concept, God reveals Himself to man. On the one side stand the proofs of God's existence and the glory of man; on the other side stands the glory of God!" (*Th W* III 576,28ff; 576,19ff).

Notes to Chapter 2, #12

1. *Hex* II, 28-34,p.340-342.
2. Esp. II 30,p.341b: . . . non est cuiuslibet, nisi cui Deus revelat.
3. Cfr. texts indicated in #9, note 32.
4. The gradual development of Aristotle's influence is depicted well in Geyer, *op. cit.*, p.342 — 351. Cfr. also the various writings of F. Van Steenberghen, especially *Aristote en Occident*, Louvain, 1946.
5. Concerning the scattered effects of the systematic works of Eriugena, see: Grabmann, *Methode* I,p.206ff; Geyer, *op. cit.*, p.176. See the following notes concerning his translation of Dionysius.
6. *Prol of Hier cael*, ed. Grabmann, in: *Mittelalterliches Geistesleben*,I,p.459.
7. *Ibid.*
8. John Sarracenus writes thus in the letter with which he sent his translation of the *De divinis nominibus* to Abbot Odo of St. Denis. Cfr. Grabmann, *op. cit.*, p.456.
9. In: *Dionysiaca* I,p.CIX; printed again in H.F. Dondaine, *Le corpus Dionysien de l'université de Paris au XIII siècle* (Rome, 1953) p.31, note 27.
10. Dondaine, *op. cit.*, p.29 (the text of Gregory involved here is *Hom 34 in evang* PL 76,1254 B). We cannot agree with Grabmann when he says that the translation of John Scotus Eriugena had a great influence on early Scholasticism as well as on the High Scholasticism of the thirteenth century (*Die mittelalterlichen Übersetzungen der Schriften des Pseudo-Dionysius Areopagita, Mittelalterl. Geistesleben*,I,p.454). Regarding High Scholasticism,

see note 11 and 12; to what has already been said concerning early Scholasticism we must add that Grabmann himself indicates (*op. cit.*, p.460) that the commentary on Dionysius by Hugo of St. Victor is the only one of the entire twelfth century. Furthermore, Hugo did not use the translation of Eriugena, but a new recension which possibly was his own work; cfr. Dondaine, *op. cit.*, p.79f.

11. P. Minges, *Über Väterzitate bei den Scholastikern*, Munich, 1923, p. 17, and Dondaine, *op. cit.*, p. 108, note 99.

12. Minges, *op. cit.*, p.17; Dondaine, 114 note 121. Even before reading Minges and Dondaine, I myself undertook a comparison of texts which indicated that Bonaventure frequently cites the text of Sarracenus literally or almost literally; e.g. *De sci Chr* q 7 c Vol. V 40 a = *Dionysiaca* I 385f; *ibid.* q 3 opp 3,p.11a = *Dionysiaca* I 360 a-c; *Hex* III 32,p.342b = *Dion.* I 313; at times with suggestions of Hilduin, e.g. *De sci Chr* q 4 opp 6,p.21b= *Dion* 606d — 607b (cfr. Dondaine 114 note 121).

Naturally there are also texts that use the version of Eriugena. Regarding these, one must be careful as the following remarks will indicate: *Itin* c 7,5 Vol V 313a uses texts from the translation of Eriugena, but the Quaracchi editors themselves point out that they have improved the text of Bonaventure according to the text of Eriugena; *Hex* III 32,p.342 a-b makes use of the same texts, and this time clearly according to the recension of Sarracenus. This should not be taken as a denial of the fact that Bonaventure used Eriugena also; cfr. the schematic presentation of the Corpus Dionysiacum of the University of Paris in: Dondaine, *op. cit.*, p.72.

13. III *Sent* d 1 a 2 q 2,p.24,note 8; *Hex* XXII 24, p.441a.

14. Text in: *Dionysiaca* I,p.673-717.

15. II *Sent* d 9,p.237-257. There would seem to be also some awareness of the basic lines of the mysticism of Dionysius; but this likewise does not exceed the limits of the School Theology and reveals no more intimate knowledge of the works of the Areopagite. Cfr. note 18.

16. See the schematic presentation of the structure of the *Summa* in A. Walz, *Thomas von Aquin, Lebensgang und Lebenswerk des Fürsten der Scholastik*, Basel, 1953, p.86.

17. *De perf ev.*q 4 a 3, Vol.V,p.189-198.

18. For the Dionysian concept of theology see: J. de Ghellinck, *Le mouvement* . . . p.91; R. Roques, *Note sur la notion de "Theologia" selon le Pseudo-Denys*, in: *RAM* 25 (1949) p.200-212. In general, Pseudo-Dionysius understands the term "theologia" to refer to the Sacred Scriptures. The equation of theologia=sacra scriptura is missing in the *Sentence Commentary* of Bonaventure. However, it does appear in the *Quaestiones disputatae de theologia* from the year 1256, which have been edited by Tavard; and especially in the *Breviloquium* which comes from the same period.

The *Breviloquium* uses the equation throughout the entire Prologue (cfr. the very beginning, Vol. V,p.201a: . . . sacrae scripturae, quae theologia dicitur . . .), whereas the *Quaestiones* attempt to strike a balance with the usual concept of theology as
found in the *Sentence Commentary*: Ad ultimam quaestionem,
utrum scilicet sit idem subjectum vel materia hujus libri et Sacrae Scripturae, potest dici, quod sic, secundum Magistrum, qui
dicens in principio libri (d 1 n 1) quod "tota continentia Novae
et Veteris Legis est de rebus et signis," in fine eiusdem capitis
dicit quod de eisdem vult dicere, ita tamen quod illa, prout habet
rationem credibilis, sunt subiectum Sacrae Scripturae, sed, prout
ulterius habent, vel transeunt in rationem intelligibilis, sunt subiectum huius libri. This concept of theology is still influential in
Hex I 1,p.329a: . . . quibus debet loqui: quia ecclesiae; non
enim dandum est sanctum canibus, nec margaritae spargendae
sunt ante porcos. We find a clear parallel to this theological *disci-
plina arcani* in a text of an anonymous Dionysian theologian
from the circle of Alan of Lille, which has been edited by Parent.
Cfr. Parent, *Un nouveau témoin de la théologie dionysienne au
XII siecle, Grabmannfestschrift*, p.293. A reading of Bonaventure's sermons indicates that his own position arises from a very
concrete background; e.g. in feria II post Pascha, Vol.IX,p.281b;
see also J. d'Albi, *op. cit.*, p.122, note 145 and 225-227.

19. Ps.-Bernard, *Tract. de contemplando Deo* c 8 n 17, cited in II
Sent d 23 a 2 q 3 ad 4, p.545b; also note 5 (the real author is
William of St. Thierry, see the text in PL 184,376).

20. III *Sent* d 27 a 1 q 3 c, p.597a: . . . cum ipsa voluntas sit su-
premum in anima. III *Sent* d 17 a 1 q 1 opp 4 indicates the same
thing when compared with ad 4, p.364. Regarding the problem of
the Bonaventurian voluntarism, see: Gilson, *Bonaventure*, p.164.

21. II *Sent* d 23 a 2 q 3 c, p.544b.

22. *Ibid.*, ad 6,p.546a.

23. *Comm in Joa* c 1,43 r Vol.VI,p.256a. Cfr. K. Rahner. *Der Begriff
der ecstasis bei Bonaventura*, in: *Zeitschrift f. Aszese und Mystik*
9 (1934) p.1-19; against Rahner, Grünewald, *Zur Mystik des
hlg. Bonaventura, op. cit.*, p.124-142; 219-232. Also the works of
Gilson, Longpré, Rosenmöller indicated in the literature in this
study.

24. *Hex* II 30, p.341b; cfr. Nr.33 and 34, p.342b; other material in
Rahner and Grünewald, *ibid.*

25. *Itin* 7,4. Vol. V, 312b; *Hex* II 30, p.341b; cfr. Delorme, Princ Coll
II 30,p.30.

26. M. Scheler, *Moralia*, Leipzig, 1923, p.140, cited by Schmaus, *Die
psychologische Trinitätslehre des hlg. Augustinus*, p.376.

27. Against Scheler, see Schmaus, *op. cit.*, Harnack, DG III 121
note 1; favorable towards the voluntaristic interpretation of
Augustine, see: Seeberg, *DG* II 433ff. It is generally recognized
that the theses of Scheler lack textual foundation.

28. Paraphrase of the *theologia mystica,* c 1, *Dionysiaca* I,710a.

29. Benz has shown well the connection between mysticism and salvation history in the case of Olivi (*Ecclesia spiritualis,*p.268). The same thing can be said in the case of Bonaventure. When nothing to the contrary is said, the textual basis for what is developed here is to be found in the schema of *Hex* XXII given above, p. 47.

30. The pre-eminence of the Apostles is preserved by means of the connection between the processus-schema and exercitia-schema; the church of the final age is of identical rank with the primitive church, and is seen as the definitive, pneumatic recurrence of the latter.

31. This idea is jeopardized by the notion of the intellectual *nulliformitas* of that highest form of mysticism which will dominate in the church to come. Without a doubt Bonaventure did not see this contact with God to be an enduring state for the church while still in history (XVI 30,p.408b) ; rather we must keep in mind what has just been said (note 28 and text) about that love which "effectiva est verae cognitionis." *Hex* XXII 22 and 23, p.440f provides the justification for conceiving the form of live in the seventh age in terms that would be parallel to the life of Francis. Cfr. *Leg mai* c 11, 2 Vol.VIII,p.536a concerning the character of the theological thinking of Francis; also, *De sci Chr* q 7 ad 19.20.21 Vol.V,p.43a: . . . qui quidem excessus est ultimus modus cognoscendi et nobilissimus, quem in omnibus libris suis laudat Dionysius . . . De quo etiam mystice est tota scriptura divina et de quo Apocalypsis secundo: Dabo ei calculum et in calculo nomen novum scriptum, quod nemo scit, nisi qui accipit (Apoc. 2,17) . . . It is clear that all one has to do is add the precise historical determination in order to arrive at the finished doctrine of the *Hexaemeron.*

32. *Hex* XV 24,p.401b. Here the distinction between Bonaventure and Joachim becomes clear. Joachim described this time as "Finis novi testamenti": *Liber figurarum,* ed. Tondelli, t IV,col 3. For Bonaventure, the New Testament is in the process of coming to its true fullness; for Joachim it is in the process of passing away in order to make place for a greater one.

33. *Itin,* Prol 2 Vol.V,p.295a-b. From here onwards, the vision is frequently mentioned; aside from the well known sections of the *Legenda* and the *Hexaemeron,* cfr. also: *De sex alis Ser* c 1,4 Vol.VIII,133; *Apol paup* c 3,10 Vol.VIII 247a; *S. IV de s.p.n. Franc* II Vol. IX,p.589b; *S. V de s.p.n. Franc* I Vol.IX,p.593b.

34. It is not yet fully clear how Bonaventure arrived at such a synthesis. Certainly both Joachim and Pseudo-Joachim contributed significantly (cfr. Ps.-Joach., *Super Hieremiam* c 20 f 44v: "*Masculus*" est ordo seraphicus in ecclesia oriundus; see also what is said below in #13 concerning Honorius of Autun, following Dempf, *Sacrum imperium,*p.241.) It is interesting to note that

every indication of the extension of this idea to the historical is absent in the primary texts concerning the concept of the hierarchy in the *Sentence Commentary*: II *Sent* d 9; IV *Sent* d 18 p 1 a 3 q 2,p.480ff; IV *Sent* d 24 p 2 a 2 q 4,p.634ff.

35. II *Sent* d 9 a un q 6 c,p.250b; q 7 c,p.253f. In q 6 f 4,p.250a we find the first indication of the later Franciscan concept of the Seraph. As far as I can see, this is the only instance in the *Sentence Commentary*: . . . in via videmus, quod aliqui assimilantur Seraphim in usu gratiae, aliqui Cherubim et sic de aliis. In the *Hexaemeron*, this notion of a functional ordering "in via" is expanded while the idea that these men will be distributed among the corresponding choirs of angels in heaven is no longer mentioned. But there is no reason to assume that this idea has been abandoned in the meantime; rather, it is presupposed as self-evident since it corresponds to a generally recognized tradition: cfr. the following note.

36. Lombardus, II *Sent* d 9 c 6 and 7,p.236f.

37. *Ecclesia spiritualis*, p.83.

38. *Speculum perfectionis* C III (IV) c 60, ed. Sabatier, p.165-167; De visione fratris Pazifici quam vidit et audivit sedem Luciferi reservari humili Francisco. Nr. 3, p.166 the basic text states: "Haec sedes fuit Luciferi; et loco illius sedebit in ea Franciscus humilis." Certainly Bonaventure is aware of the tradition, but he tones it down to such an extent that the real point is lost and he is able to take a position against rather than in favor of this idea: *Leg mai* c 6,6 Vol. VIII p.521a-b. Here we find a parallel to the text just cited: "Sedes ista unius de ruentibus fuit, nunc humili servatur Francisco."

39. *Hex* XVI 30,p.408b; XV 24,p.401b; cfr. #6 above.

Notes to Chapter 3, Introduction

1. P.229-398.

2. W. Kamlah, *Apokalypse und Geschichtstheologie. Die mittelalterliche Auslegung der Apokalypse vor Joachim von Fiore*. Berlin, 1935.

3. Cologne, 1884, esp. p.32-56. Also, H. Meyer, *Gesch. der abendl. Weltanschauung* Vol.III p. 140-153. Valuable material is found also in: Erich Seeberg, *Gottfried Arnold, Die Wissenschaft und die Mystik seiner Zeit*, Meerane, 1923, esp. p.257-280 for a study of the notion of decadence. Also, J. Spörl, *Grundformen hochmittelalterlicher Geschichtsanschauung*, Munich, 1935.

Notes to Chapter 3, #13

1. Cfr. references in my article, *Herkunft und Sinn der Civitas-Lehre Augustins*, in: *Augustinus Magister* II, p.965 note 3, especially the work of E. Peterson, *Der Monotheismus als politisches Problem*, in: *Theol. Traktate*, Munich, 1951, p.45-117; also, K.A. Schöndorf, *Die Geschichtstheologie des Orosius*, Munich, 1951

(Diss.). Concerning the notions of a 'Theologie der Weltgestaltung', and 'Weltüberwindung' together with a basic evaluation, see: G. Söhngen, *Zur Frage eines "christlichen Sozialismus"*, in: *Politische Studien* 5 (1954) p. 6-20, esp. 16ff.

2. Cfr. my above-mentioned article. Important material is to be found also in: W. Kamlah, *Christentum und Geschichtlichkeit*, Stuttgart, 1951; I have discussed his view at length in the article indicated.

3. M. Werner, *Die Entstehung des christlichen Dogmas*, Bern-Tübingen, 1941, p.82ff. Werner points out how this idea was reinterpreted and practically done away with already in the work of Eusebius; but it was not until the Latin Middle Ages that these early beginnings became fully effective.

4. *De cat rud* c 22, 39 PL 40,338f; *De gen contr Man* I 23, 35-24,42 PL 34,190ff; and the well-known texts of *De civ. Dei.*

5. For general orientation on Rupert, see: *LThK* IX,15-16 (A. Manser); Grabmann, *Methode* II 100-104; J. Beumer, *Rupert von Deutz und seine "Vermittlungstheologie"*, *MThZ* IV (1953) p.255-270. For material more pertinent to the present question, see: Grundmann, *Joachim* I, 91; Dempf, *Sacrum Imperium*, p.233-238; P. Séjourné, *Rupert de Deutz*, in: *DThC* XIV (1939) p.169-205, though Séjourné does not treat the theology of history as such.

6. I cannot agree fully with Grundmann (*Joachim* I 91) when he follows Hauck (*Kirchengeschichte Deutschlands* IV 436ff) in saying: Rupert did not possess any great ideas, but he sought them. Without a doubt Rupert's importance lies more in the seeking than in the finding; it was a seeking of unique power and genuine greatness.

7. For example, in Geyer's outstanding presentation of the history of Medieval philosophy, Rupert of Deutz and Anselm of Havelberg are not treated while a figure of less significance such as Otto of Freising receives a relatively detailed treatment on p.241f. Here again we can see how a primarily philosophical orientation can threaten to distort the perspective. Also in Landgraf's *Einführung* Rupert of Deutz is not treated.

8. *De sancta trin*, prol PL 167, 197 — 200.

9. PL 167,199.

10. Col. 200; p 3 1 1 c 1 Col. 1571f. Augustine, *De civ Dei* XX 6 and 7 CC 48,p.706-712. Further material in: Ratzinger, *Volk und Haus Gottes*, p.232, note 44. From Augustine onward, this doctrine became traditional. We find it, for example, in Bonaventure, IV *Sent* d 43 a 1 q 4 ad 1,p.887b.

11. *De sancta trin*, prol col.197; p 1 1 3 c 36 col.324ff.

12. Prol col. 199-200.

13. Col.200.

14. P. 3 1 1 c 31 col.1603. The text of 1 2 c 24 and 25 col 1630ff. c 24 contains the following caption: Quomodo eadem sapientia lusit hic et illic, et quod lusit illic bene coram domino, sed hic melius, ubi sic illusit coram Deo, ut illuderet diabolo. This is reminiscent of a text of St. Bernard of Clairvaux (*Epist* 87, 12 PL 182,217 C) to which Bonaventure refers in the *Q. de perf ev* q 1 sol end Vol V, p. 122: "Ludam et vilior fiam" (2 Kg.6,22), ludam scilicet et illudar. Bonus ludus, quo Michol irascitur et Deus delectatur: bonus ludus, qui hominibus ridiculum, sed angelis spectaculum praebet; bonus inquam ludus, in quo efficimur "opprobrium abundantibus et despectio superbis" (Ps.122,4). Hoc casto et religioso ludo ludebat, qui dicebat: "Spectaculum facti sumus huic mundo et angelis et hominibus" (1 Cor.4,9). Hoc ludo etiam nos interim ludamus, ut illudamur et confundamur et humiliemur, donec veniat qui "potentes deponit et exaltat humiles" (Lk.1,52), qui nos laetificet, exaltet et glorificet in aeternum. Cfr. also H. Rahner, *Man at Play* (Westminster, 1967).
15. Col.1604. There and all that follows.
16. Especially the two chapters on Jerome and Augustine: P 3 1 7 c 18 and 19 col.1781ff.
17. Dempf, *Sacrum imperium,* p.236 says that the sixth age comprehends the decline from the cultural heights of the Church Fathers to the simplicity of the migration of nations. But in the text of Rupert I cannot find any foundation for this statement. Cfr. the following note.
18. This conception of the church is not identical with what Dempf calls the descending Augustinian line of Rupert's understanding of the world (*Sacrum imp,* p.236). According to Dempf, Augustine would have replaced the original faith in progress by the pessimistic picture of a declining world; and only in Anselm of Havelberg would the original optimism have re-asserted itself (*op. cit.,* p.241). We cannot treat the details of the problem here; but it is clear that this view involves a simplificaion of a complex situation. We would simply point out that the Augustinian consciousness of the end age is in no way necessarily connected with a pessimistic notion of decadence. Precisely the opposite is the case in Rupert of Deutz. Presumably Dempf develops his position from the text of *De sancta trin* p 3 1 1 c 31 col.1604 where we read: Nam in illis (= in the seven ages before Christ) a timore ad sapientiam ascendebamus, hic (= in the seven ages after Christ) autem a sapientia ad timorem descendimus . . . The declining line of the gifts of the Spirit is in no way simply identical with a declining line of history. Indeed, history is moving toward an end; but the final age is precisely the fullness of time, the time of maturity and wisdom; it alone is the true time of the Spirit; it is in this age alone that all which was indicated figuratively will be given truly: " . . . illic tanquam in imagine, hic autem in re ipsam nobis adesse intuemur personam Dei sancti spiritus."

19. I do not wish to decide on an answer to the question as to how far Rupert could base his view of this type of theology of history on predecessors. It would be necessary to study the early Scholastic literature on the Hexaemeron in order to decide this.

20. *De victoria verbi Dei* XII 5 and 6 PL 169,1490f for Rupert's concept of history and its understanding of the final age. Also, Dempf, *Sacr Imp*, p.238. For a full evaluation of Rupert's theology of history, it would be necessary to give a detailed treatment to: *De glorificatione trinitatis et processu spiritus sancti* (PL 169,13-202; Dempf,p.237) and his commentary on the Apocalypse (PL 169, 827—1214). This would take us too far afield for our present purpose.

21. Dempf, *op. cit.*, p.240 speaks of "Rupert, whom Honorius still revered as one per visionem illuminatus . . ." For the life of Honorius, see: Geyer, *op. cit.*, p.203 (concerning his doctrine, p.203-205); Also the detailed monograph of J.A. Endres, *Honorius Augustodunensis*, Kempten-Munich, 1906.

22. *Expos in cant cant* c 7, 5 PL 172,460f; Dempf, *op. cit.*, p.240; Grundmann, *Joachim* I,p.90.

23. For the history of this idea from the beginning to the present, cfr: Y. Congar, *Ecclesia ab Abel*, in: *Abhandlungen über Theologie und Kirche, Festschrift f. K. Adam*, ed. by Elfers-Hofmann, Düsseldorf, 1952, p.79-108.

24. In the case of Augustine, for example. Cfr. J. Ratzinger, *Volk und Haus Gottes*, p.296ff.

25. *Expos in cant cant*, col. 460: Per denarium quippe notantur decem status ecclesiae, quorum quinque erant ante adventum Christi, quinque post eius adventum. Thus, in fact, Christ appears as the turn of the ages. But it remains merely a fact. The detailed enumeration that follows simply runs from beginning to end; it seems to be mere chance that the sixth period was "sub evangelio," "sub quo ab ipso sponso Christo . . . ad nuptias agni invitabatur . . .": This is one event among many; apparently history continues after this event without entering a new level.

26. This arises from an interpretation of the members of the bride; cfr. the interpretation which precedes this one: c 7, 1-4, col.455-459. Col. 456: Antichristus . . . cum decem regibus ecclesiam impugnabit, contra quem haec Sunamitis bellum suscipiens, decem ordines iustorum . . . ordinabit . . ., quos ordines rex enumerat, dum decem membra Sunamitis laudat . . . Other treatments of Honorius are given in Dempf, *op. cit.*, p.240.

27. Concerning the following presentation, cfr. Dempf, *Sacr Imp.*, p.241-243. The important data of Anselm's life are given on p.241. Cfr. also: Grundmann, *Joachim*, I,p.92-95. On p. 92, Grundmann points out that Anselm was in contact with the Greek Church just as was Joachim. Cfr.: M. van Lee, *Les idées d'Anselme de Havelberg sur le développement des dogmes*, in: *Analecta Praemonstratensia*, 1938, p.5-35; G. Schreiber, *Studien über Anselm*

von *Havelberg zur Geistesgeschichte des Hochmittelalters*, in: *Analecta Praem.*, 1942,p.1-90; G. Schreiber, *Anselm von Havelberg und die Ostkirche*, in: *ZKG* 60 (1942) p. 354-411; *Spörl, Grundformen hochmittelalterlicher Geschichtsanschauung*,p.18-31.

28. *Dialogi* 1 1 (De unitate fidei et multiformitate vivendi ab Abel iusto usque ad novissimum electum) c 1 PL 188,1141-1143.

29. *Ibid.*, c 2 col.1143f; cfr. c 5 col.1147: ... In istis duabus transpositionibus sive mutationibus divina sapientia tanta varietate paulatim usa est . . . c 6 col.1149: . . . per diversos status sibi invicem paulatim succedentes usque in hodiernum diem sicut iuventus aquilae renovatur et semper renovabitur. Also, c 10 col.1157.

30. *Ibid.*, c 6 col.1147f. Cfr. 1 2 (De processione Spiritus sancti) c 23, col.1200-1202.

31. L 1 c 7—13, col.1149-1160. On the basis of the texts, it cannot be clearly determined whether Anselm identifies the present with the fourth or fifth period. They cannot be clearly distinguished from one another in a temporal sense; rather, they involve different orderings of reality. Dempf, *Sacr. Imp.*, p.242 takes a position which identifies the present with the fifth age. We find almost the same historical schema in a work written by William of St. Amour after 1257, *De antichristo et eius ministris* P 2 c 1 Nr. 5-12. Nr. 5 (ed. Martène-Durand, col.1336 E): Equus albus ecclesia in baptismo, secundum Glossam, dealbata . . . Nr. 6 (col.1337 B): . . . per rufum enim equum aperti ecclesiae persecutores et sanguinolenti figurantur . . . Nr.7 (col.1337 E): Per equum nigrum illi haeretici designantur, qui numquam fidei sacramentum susceperunt (Porphyrius and the Platonists of his time are given as examples). Nr.8 (col.1338 C): Per pallidum ergo equum signati sunt hypocritae . . . (e.g.: Arius, Macedonius, the Manichaeans). Nr. 14 (col.1340 A): In hac ergo sigilli quinti apertione persecutores praemittit in fine scilicet huius pacis ecclesiae (which, according to Nr. 10-12 col.1339 should come first), qui exercitum eius congregent . . . In P 1 c 1 col.1277ff, William presents quite a different typology of history on the basis of his typological interpretation of the temptations of the Lord. When we see how William, who was an avowed opponent of Joachim's theology of history, uses divisions of history in his own polemic which are not unlike Joachim's, then it is not surprising that a Franciscan like Bonaventure could have felt justified in making even more extensive use of Joachim's ideas. We do not yet have an exact dating of the work of William. But on the basis of a number of texts, I hope to show that it must be placed in 1263/64.

32. This sacrifice of eschatological thought is to be identified with what Dempf (*op. cit.*, p.242) has called the "progressive philosophy of culture" no more than the eschatological attitude is to be equated with pessimism(cfr. note 18). We do not mean to

deny that, in some sense, the idea of progress is present in Anselm (l 1 c 6 col. 1149; c 10 col. 1157).

33. *Op. cit.*, l 1 c 6 col. 1148: . . . ab adventu Christi usque ad diem iudicii, quae sexta aetas distinguitur . . .

34. We cannot take up the important statements of the brothers Gerhoh and Arno von Reichersberg. Cfr. Hippler, *op. cit.*, p.40f; Dempf, *Sacrum Imp.*, p.252-254; also the related articles in *LThK* (I 688f: M. Schmaus; IV 421f: V.O. Ludwig). Literature in Landgraf, *Einführung*, p.109f.

35. Dempf's statement that Joachim was a guest of the Prior Ebbo of the Cistercian house at Eberbach near Bingen (*Sacr. Imp.*, p.268) and made trips through France and Germany (p.269) is untenable. Cfr. Grundmann, *Joachim* II, p.78, note 1.

36. Grundmann demonstrates this in opposition to the Italian research on Joachim which had denied it.

37. Cfr. Grundmann, *Joachim* II for a compilation of the most important materials. Also, Francesco Russo, *Saggio de bibliografia gioachimita*, in: *Archivio storico per la Calabria e la Lucania* VI (1936) p.102-141.

38. It is certain that there were such intermediary figures. We need only think of the unfortunate attempt of Gerard of Borgo San Donnino; of John of Parma and his circle of followers; and of the pseudo-Joachimite literature. Cfr. especially J. Chr. Huck, *Joachim von Floris und die joachitische Literatur* (Freiburg, 1938) p.190-226, where the author treats a number of lesser known and partly unpublished pseudo-Joachimite texts. Another line of tradition has become accessible in the new publication in the Monumenta Germaniae Historica: Alexander Minorita, *Expositio in Apocalypsim*. Ed. by A. Wachtel (*MGH Quellen zur Geistesgeschichte des Mittelalters*, Vol. 1) Weimar, 1955; see the review of the same by J. Koch, in: *Theol. Revue* 53 (1957) p.119-126; also, A. Wachtel, *Die weltgeschichtliche Apokalypse-Auslegung des Minoriten Alexander von Bremen* (*Franz Stud* 24, 1937). From 1249, the Franciscan author of this commentary on the Apocalypse worked pseudo-Joachimite material into his work (MGH, *op. cit.*, XXXff). The fact that Bonaventure indicates historical details in his great historical schema that find no parallel in Joachim himself also serves as a sure indication that he was aware of such sources. Cfr. also note 107 #5.

39. *Apokalypse und Geschichtstheologie*, p.117. Kamlah takes a different position in "Christentum und Geschichtlichkeit", p.111 note 196, where, in opposition to Cullmann, he clearly rejects the idea of Christ as the center of the ages. Cfr. the following note.

40. We refer here to the fact, which Cullmann points out on p.17 of *Christ and Time*, namely, that the reckoning of time as "before the birth of Christ" became common only in the 18th century. Hipler, *op. cit.*, p.87f. names some precursors of this practice. According to Hipler, John Nauklerus (d.1510) would seem to

have been the first to have divided his world chronicle into time before and after the birth of Christ. On the other hand, the reckoning of time from the birth of Christ onward — that is, the determination of years "after the birth of Christ" — is much older; and, according to Hipler, p.35, is found for the first time in the case of Bede: " . . . for the first time, Bede took the decisive step of dating the events of the sixth age not only according to the years since the creation of the world, but according to the years since the birth of Christ as well . . ." In view of these circumstances, it is surprising that Cullmann should see this to be a fitting reflection of the New Testament consciousness of time and history (*op. cit.*, p.19; cfr also p.81ff; also, Kamlah's critique of Cullmann indicated in note 39 above). For related theses, see: H. Conzelmann, *The Theology of St. Luke*, N.Y., 1960 and the critique by P. Winter, in: *Theol. Lit. Ztg.* 81 (1956) p.36-39.

41. On this point, cfr. Benz, *Ecclesia spiritualis*. This viewpoint is preferable by far to that of Grundmann (*Joachim*, I,p.185ff.) according to which the real influence of Joachim is not to be found in the circles of the Franciscan Spirituals related to him from a literary viewpoint, but in the various free-thinking sects which involve a break with Christian religiosity as such. This is related to the core elements of Grundmann's interpretation of Joachim. According to Grundmann, the central idea of Joachim would be the notion of a 'liberation' of religion 'from all rules to a life of the spirit,' (p.187). Later, following Tondelli, Grundmann practically admits that this interpretation is no longer tenable (*Joachim*, II,p.103ff). Those texts which seem to prophecy the dissolution of the hierarchical church (*Conc* II 1 c 28f 18r; p.103 note 1), can well be explained in another way; indeed, they must be given a different interpretation since Joachim expressly says the opposite on a number of occasions and with full clarity. (Cfr. esp. *Conc* V c 18 f 69v: . . . quia idem ordo non erit absque praelatis, qui gerant in eo vice Christi. Other texts can be found in Tondelli and in Grundmann himself). Another fact is of significance here. In *Joachim* I, Grundmann sees the difference between Joachim and the Franciscans (whom he treats with some disdain because of their strict Christian-ecclesial religious spirit) above all in the fact that Joachim sought the *intellectus spiritualis* while the Franciscans made the "ad litteram" their motto. But this contradiction is only apparent. The same Francis who was so insistent on the "ad litteram" writes in the *Verba admonitionis* Nr.7 (Böhmer, *Analekten*, p.44): Dicit apostolus (2 Cor.3,6): "Littera occidit, spiritus autem vivificat." Illi sunt mortui a littera, qui tantum sola verba cupiunt scire . . . Et illi religiosi sunt mortui a littera: qui spiritum divine littere nolunt sequi . . . Et illi sunt vivificati a spiritu divine littere, qui omnem litteram, quam sciunt et cupiunt scire, non attribuunt

corpori, sed verbo et exemplo reddunt ea altissimo Domino Deo, cuius est omne bonum. On the other hand, Joachim, the defender of the *intellectus spiritualis* maintains that in the church of the Spirit, the Sermon on the Mount will be fulfilled "sine glossa" (Benz, *Eccl. spir.*, p.11f). Certainly there are differences and problems. But at least it is clear that we may not understand the *intellectus spiritualis* in an idealistic sense. Here again we come up against a mistake which we have already pointed out: the lost category of the "pneumatic" is confused with the category of the Idealistic so that they become identified. In my opinion, it. is only with great reserve that we can accept Kamlah's thesis (*Apokalypse und Geschichtstheologie*, p.117) that Joachim introduced the secularization of eschatological hope which led to the epochal consciousness of the Renaissance and the modern age. It is correct to say that in the case of Joachim a change in the eschatological hope did take place; but we would have to be very cautious in any attempt to see as the initiator of the Renaissance such a man of contemplation who prophecied a contemplative and monastic age of pure interiority.

42. In a certain sense, this happened quite naturally already in the Patristic writers. But, while in the earlier period, it was purely a factual thing, in the later development it becomes a basic theory.

43. Cfr. the distinction between *initiatio* and *fructificatio* (e.g. *Conc IV c 33 and 34 f 56v and 57r*; c 36 f 57v). According to this, the third age is under way since the time of Benedict. Cfr. Dempf, *Sacrum Impr.*, p.274f. and the literature on Joachim.

44. One limitation remains also in the interpretation of Joachim: the persecution of the Anti-Christ must precede the *tertius status*: Tondelli, *Il libro delle figure* II Tav IV col 3: Sub eiusdem apertione sigilli continetur validissima Anti Xristi tempestas. Finis novi testamenti. Helias cum venerit ipse restituet omnia. Tav VII presents the following schema, which we give here in very simplified form:

Adam	Ozias
Noe	Zorobabel
Jacob	Xristus
David	Silvester Papa
Ezechias	Zacharias Papa

P	P
Johannes Baptista	Helias propheta
(In the Dresden ms.,	
P=persecutio Babilonis	Persecutio Babilonis nove).

Regarding this text, B. Hirsch-Reich points out (*Rech th anc med* 21 [1954] p.147) that in both cases the better Oxford manuscript has *Percussio* instead of *Persecutio*.

Notes to Chapter 3, #14

1. At the time of his *Sentence Commentary*, Bonaventure seems not to have known Joachim, but to have satisfied himself with the general judgment of the Scholastics that Joachim had spoken "ignoranter" (I *Sent* d 5 dub 4 r,p.121a).

2. III *Sent* d 1 a 2 q 4 c, p.32a; IV Sent d 2 a 1 q 2 c.p.51a-b.

3. Also, dub 1 (III *Sent* d 1,p.33a-b). We will come back to this again.

4. Prol #2, Vol. V,p.203b; p 2 c 5,p.223b; p 4 c 4,p.245a.

5. Hipler, *op. cit.*, esp. p.34.

6. *Brev* p 4 c 4,p.245a; cfr. p 6 c 4,p.269a: Medio autem tempore et fuit regeneratio et ecclesiae ordinatio et spiritualis cibatio . . .; *Hex* I 20,p.333a. Tondelli, *Il libro delle figure* I,p.217 tries to show that the *Breviloquium* already is related to Joachim; it seems questionable whether the material at hand is adequate to support such a thesis. In *S Th* III q 1 a 6, Aquinas does not use the expression "Christ the center of the ages," but actually he seems to sacrifice the interpretation of Christ as coming at the end of time even more decisively than does Bonaventure. An indication of this may be seen in the question: Utrum incarnationis opus differri debuerit usque in finem mundi. *Brev* p 4 c 4,p.245a is of significance. Here the time of Christ alone is designated as the *tempus remedii* while in IV *Sent* d 2 a 1 q 1 c,p.49b we read: . . . tempus remedii incepit a lapsu et profecit in lege et consummatum est in evangelio . . . As long as the Christ-event is seen as the end of the ages, the whole of time can be seen as "tempus remedii", even though with a difference of intensity. But as soon as Christ is seen as the center of time, then we find the well-known division of the ages which affirms a time of sin and darkness next to a time of redemption and light — a schema which can find no adequate support in the facts of history.

7. III *Sent* d 1 dub 1 r,p.32f.

8. R. Silic, *Christus und die Kirche. Ihr Verhältnis nach der Lehre des hlg. Bonaventura*, Breslau, 1938, p.75-89, and Guardini, *Die Lehre des hlg. Bonaventura von der Erlösung*, passim. A. Stohr, *Die Trinitätslehre des hlg. Bonaventura*, p.190, sees the real significance of Bonaventure to lie in the way he worked out and developed the *opinio media et sobria*. As a matter of fact, it is one of Bonaventure's heuristic principles that the truth lies *in medio*, and that when other criteria fail, the *via media* is to be chosen. III *Sent* d 5 a 2 q 2 c, p.133a; *De perf ev* q 2 a 3 c Vol. V,p.160a; I *Sent* d 32 a 1 q 1 c,p.558a, *ibid.*, q 2 c,p.560b and frequently. *Hex* I 10-39,p.330 — 335b brings the development of the Medium-idea to a high point.

9. *Brev* p 4 c 2 Vol.V,p.242a: . . . Mediatoris namque est esse medium inter hominem et Deum ad reducendum hominem . . . Nullum autem magis decet esse medium quam personam, . . . quae

est media trium personarum . . . Here the mediating position
of the Lord in the history of salvation is related to the trinitarian middle-position of the Logos; in *Hex* I 12-17, p.331f the mediation relative to creation developed from the doctrine of ideas
is brought into the same context. Nr. 14,p.331f: Istud est medium
personarum necessario: quia, si persona est, quae producit et
non producitur, et persona, quae producitur et non producit,
necessario est media, quae producitur et producit. In I *Sent* d
27 p 2 a un q 2 ad 5,p.486b the following is said about the Son
and the Spirit, namely, that they "secundum rationem intelligendi
et appropriandi quasi medium sunt inter nos et Deum." The concept of the *verbum medium* which is developed in the above-mentioned Quaestio is of great importance for the entire line of
thought, and it betrays a strongly economical tone in Bonaventure's trinitarian theology. Concerning the historical context and
the peculiar characteristics of Bonaventure's trinitarian theology, cfr. the work of A. Stohr indicated above in note 8.

10. Cfr. the doctrine of the seven-fold mediation of Christ in *Hex* I,
    10-39, p.330b — 335b.

11. IV *Sent* d 48 a 1 q 4, p.988f (the place where Thomas speaks of
    the problem of Joachim while Bonaventure says nothing). The
    Quaestiones de novissimis edited by Glorieux are from the year
    1255-56 (Glorieux, p.XXVII), and as regards their content they
    are close to the *Sentence Commentary* just as we would expect
    (see the comparison of texts on p.XII — XVIII). On this point,
    the *Quaestiones* offer nothing new.

12. Denifle, *Das Evangelium aeternum und die Commission zu Anag-
    ni*, p.84ff. Also, E. Faral, *Les "Responsiones" de Guillaume de
    Saint Amour, Arch. hist. doctr.* 25/26 (1950/51) p.346f (= III
    15); E. Aergerter, *L'affaire du De perculis novissimorum tempor-
    um*, in: *Rev. del'hist de rel* 56 (1935) p.242-272; all the works
    of William, especially the late *De antichristo*, are characterized
    by a sharp polemic against Joachim.

13. *Tractatus brevis de periculis novissimorum temporum*, ed. Bier-
    baum, c 8 p.19; also p.20 and 21. Cfr. Bierbaum's commentary.
    p.262-267.

14. *Ibid.*, prol p.2; *ibid.*, c 1 p.5 ("appropinquante finali ecclesia").

15. This is the general tendency of the entire tract *De periculis novis-
    simorum temporum*: cfr. esp. c 8 p.21f. Also, in the editions of
    Faral cited above: Responsiones V,p.356-359.

16. *Sacrum Imperium*, p.336.

17. *Op. cit.*, p.267. Faral's judgment (p.384-387) is somewhat cau-
    tious. Aegerter shows great sympathy for William (p.272), and
    summarizes his view as follows: Voici donc quelle fut son oeuvre
    veritable: la défense, le renforcement d'un esprit universitaire.
    Certes, l'Université de Paris fut longtemps impregnee d'une ten-
    dance au conservatisme, mais ille montra aussi un sens très vif
    de son autonomie spirituelle. Et dans son devéloppement ultérieur

. . . il y eut toujours un peu de la liberté véhémente, de l'indépendance sérieuse que défendit par la parole, par l'écrit, et au détriment de sa réussite temporelle, l'auteur du De periculis. In reality, it would be difficult to come to an unbiased conclusion. It can hardly be denied that William was lead by a genuine conviction for which he paid with the loss of his position (cfr. in the "Responsiones" III 35, *op. cit.*, p.352: . . . scit se passurum multa et gravia . . . pro hiis quae praedicat; sed non curat, . . . quia paratus est mori pro ista veritate). On the other hand, if the tendency to play with the eschatological terminology often reveals a considerable lack of seriousness, we cannot in justice forget that to a degree even a man such as Thomas Aquinas allowed himself this type of play in his answer (cfr. note 22 and 23).

18. Concerning the literary form and origin of the text, cfr. the commentary of Faral, *op. cit.*, p.361-368.
19. V,p.357. For the entire section of the text, p.356-359; also IV 39,p.354; III 34,p.352; III 21,p.348.
20. *De per nov temp* c 8, Bierbaum, p.19: Nos sumus, in quos fines saeculorum devenerunt (1 Cor 10,11); glossa: "quia in ultima aetate saeculi sumus"; post istam vero sextam aetatem, "quae est pugnantium," cum qua currit septima aetas, "quae est quiescentium," non est ventura aetas alia nisi octava, "quae est resurgentium." Ergo nos sumus in ultima aetate huius mundi . . . The idea expressed here is really the same as what is found in the texts edited by Faral; it is presented more clearly in Faral's texts. It can hardly be denied that this represents a faithful expression of the *sententia communis ecclesiae* of that time.
21. In *De antichristo* the temporal proximity of the end is even supported by elaborate historical schemata; cfr. note 31 #13 for the texts.
22. Esp in the Prooemium (. . . qui prius occulte contra te loquebantur, nunc in publico loqui non formidant. Ut enim dicit glossa, novissima tempora Antichristi designat, quando hi, qui modo premuntur metu, in liberam vocem erumpent; and similar statements.).
23. Bierbaum, *op. cit.*, p.270. The most reserved on this question is Thomas of York (Ps.-Bertrand of Bayonne; concerning the authorship of this work, cfr. M. Bihl, in: *LThK* II 233 and M. Grabmann, *LThK* X 136) (*op. cit.*, p.269. Text, p.37-168); certainly his reasons for reserve are not always the best. The Joachimite influence indicated by Bierbaum (p.285) I see as unproven. In the text of the Master of Gerhard of Abbeville (p.169-207) eschatological statements are more frequent, but the question is not touched in the text of Nicholas of Lisieux (p.220-234).
24. This is not intended as an answer to the question as to when a direct literary awareness of the works of Joachim is present.
25. *De perf ev* q 2 a 2 opp 20,p.136a.

26. *Ibid.*, ad 20, p.148a Cfr. Delorme, *op. cit.*, for the *Quaestio reportata de mendicitate cum annotationibus Guilelmi de S. Amore* (for literary-critical remarks, see Delorme XXIV-XXVI). Ad 11,p.352f: Similiter dico quod primitiva ecclesia fuit in maxima paupertate per voluntatem Dei, deinde medio tempore ditata Sancto Spiritu operante, sed in fine revolabit omega ad alpha, scilicet ecclesia in quibusdam erit in maxima paupertate et hoc similiter operatione spiritus sancti. On this point, further, the marginal gloss of William: Vide periculosum verbum et suspicione non carens, quod dicit, ecclesiam redituram in quibusdam ordinibus ad pristinam paupertatem. Hoc enim sapit sententiam Joachim, qui ponit imperium Petri et ecclesiae Romanae imperium babylonicum eo quod ditata est ecclesia et imperium Romanum habere meruit. In contrast with the *De perf ev*, the eschatological theme recedes into the background in the *Apologia pauperum*. It is hardly possible to decide whether the frequently occuring "diebus istis novissimis" (prol 2 Vol VIII, p.233b; c 12,1,p.316a) is intended to be eschatological or whether it merely means "in days recently past." Relevant passages in *De perf ev* are q 2 a 2 adv obi postea factas I,p.150a; q 2 a 3 ad 12,p.164. The eschatological statements in *De don Sp S.* III 7 Vol.V,p.469b; coll VII 17, 18, p.492f are also a development from the thematic of the poverty controversy.

27. *De perf ev* q 2 a 2 adv obi postea factas V,p.155b.

28. *Ibid.* q 2 a 3 ad 12,p.164b.

29. In *De perf ev* the eschatological thought is still quite limited by the idea that the Church presently lives "in pace": q 2 a 1 ad 2, p.131b; q 2 a 2 f 3,p.136b. The eschatological feeling acquires its full concrete quality only after the rise and development of a very sharp criticism of time which we can see reflected in the *Coll de decem praec* and in the *Coll de don Sp S.*

30. Certainly one should not overlook the fact that *de facto* the eschatological consciousness fades into the background in the work of Thomas; cfr. note 6.

31. *ZKG* 53 (1934) p.52-116: Joachimstudien III. Thomas von Aquin und Joachim von Fiore. In *ZKG* 50,p.24ff., we find the first article in this series: Die Kategorien der religiösen Geschichtsdeutung Joachims; *ZKG* 51,p.415ff: Joachimstudien II: Die Exzerptsätze aus dem Evangelium aeternum; Cfr. also *ZKG* 52,p.90-121: Die Geschichtstheologie der Franziskanerspiritualen des 13. und 14. Jahrhunderts nach neuen Quellen. The essential ideas can be found in Benz, *Ecclesia spiritualis.*

32. *ZKG* 53, esp. p.116. The book, *Ecclesia spiritualis*, above all is formed on the basis of this notion. For a critique, cfr. A Dempf, *Ecclesia spiritualis oder Schwarmgeisterei?*, in: *Hochland* 32,2 (1936) p.170-173; A. Mirgeler, Ernst Benz, *Ecclesia spiritualis*, in: *ZKG* 55 (1936) p. 286-294. Here Benz's thesis is rejected on good grounds from the viewpoint of systematic theology.

33. The theses which Benz offers about Bonaventure in *Ecclesia spiritualis* are based exclusively on the *Legenda* and overlook the *Hexaemeron* completely.

34. IV *Sent* d 43 a 3 q 2 and sol 2. As Hipler shows (*op. cit.*, p.52), Aquinas had already come to know the works of Joachim in Italy in the year 1250. Cfr. Dempf, *Sacrum imperium*, p.281. On p.51-53 Hipler gives a brief but pointed statement concerning Thomas' position toward Joachim.

35. *Op. cit.*, q 2 opp 1.

36. *Ibid.* opp. 3.

37. *De civ Dei* XVIII 52 CC 48,p.650-652.

38. Sol 2 ad 3. It is significant that even Thomas had to admit that part of what Joachim had predicted had already happened.

39. It is recognized, for example, that in trinitarian theology Thomas represents a purer "Augustinianism" than Bonaventure; cfr. Stohr, *op. cit.*, p.188.

40. Cfr. the summary presentation which I have attempted to give on p. 104f above. According to the source material, it seems in no way possible to deny all relationship between Bonaventure and Joachim as S. Clasen has attempted to do (*Die Sendung des hlg. Franziskus. Ihre heilsgeschichtliche Deutung durch Bonaventura*, in: *Wissenschaft und Weisheit* 14 (1951),p.212-225). For all the patristic texts which Clasen points out cannot clarify the decisive and the peculiar character of the *Hexaemeron*; this becomes understandable only in relation to Joachim. Therefore, the summary statement of Clasen's position (p.222) overlooks the real character of these texts: "Therefore, though both Joachim of Fiore and Bonaventure work from the same tradition of the Fathers, each of them has developed an independent theology of history from this tradition . . ." Such a position becomes impossible as soon as we call to mind the basic difference between the simple seven-schema of the Patristic period and the double-seven schema of Joachim.

41. Cfr. #4. See the text of *Hex* XVI 2,p.403b.

42. Collatio I, 11-end, p.331-335.

43. Kamlah, *Apokalypse und Geschichtstheologie.* p.117. See also what was said above on page 106.

44. Cfr. the schema in Dempf, *Sacr. Imp.*, p.274. The distinction between initiatio and fructificatio is entirely lacking in Bonaventure.

45. The parallel treatment of the two periods of the OT and the NT is more consistently developed by Bonaventure on the basis of the notion of the middle than it is in Joachim.

Notes on Chapter 4, #15

1. J. d'Albi, *Saint Bonaventure et les luttes doctrinales de 1267-1277*. Cfr. *Revue d'histoire franciscaine* 1926, p.506-510; Gilson, *Bonaventure*, p.427; F. Tinivella, *De impossibili sapientiae adeptione . . .*, in: *Antonianum* 11 (1936), esp. 154-163. One could

be tempted to say that the credit goes not to d'Albi but to Ehrle. To this we would have to say that Ehrle did indeed point out Bonaventure's "Augustinianism," but not his anti-Aristotelianism. In line with Ehrle's understanding of Augustinianism, these would be two quite different things. Ehrle never speaks of an express anti-Aristotelianism in Bonaventure, cfr. note 9 and 12. A good treatment of the development of the understanding of this question together with further literature may be found in: F. van Steenberghen, *The philosophical movement in the thirteenth century*, 1935, p.3-18.

2. Gilson, *The Philosophy of St. Bonaventure*, New York, 1938. This book was originally written in French and published in Paris in 1924. The second French printing which appeared in Paris in 1943 left the text essentially unaltered and added an appendix with a discussion of the new literature. The work appeared in German in a translation by Philotheus Böhner in 1929. A second German translation by Paul Alfred Schlüter appeared in 1960. This version is based on the third French printing of 1953, which is an unaltered reprinting of the second French printing. The first English translation appeared in 1938, and was the work of F. Sheed and Illtyd Trethowan; it is based on the first French edition. In 1965, this English translation was reprinted by St. Anthony Guild Press as a volume in their Bonaventure series. It is unaltered; and the reader is referred to the *Introduction to the Works of Bonaventure* by J. Guy Bougerol in the same series for the latest bibliographical research.

3. Angelo da Vinca, *L'Aspetto filosofico dell'aristotelismo di S. Bonaventura*, in: *Coll Franc* XIX (1949) p.41.

3a.Van Steenberghen, *The philosophical movement . . .* p.60: "In short, the attitude of St. Bonaventure towards Aristotle in the Sentences was not essentially different from that of all the great theologians of the thirteenth century, and, in particular, from that of Albert the Great or Thomas Aquinas . . . Now, the examination of his Commentary leads to this conclusion. St. Bonaventure retained a very large part of the Aristotelian heritage." Cfr. also p.59 and 68.

4. *Op. cit.*, p.169.

5. *Ibid.*, p.170.

6. P.178.

7. Especially the final chapter, "The Spirit of St. Bonaventure."

8. Esp. F. Ehrle, *Beiträge zur Geschichte der mittelalterlichen Scholastik* II: *Der Augustinismus und der Aristotelismus in der Scholastik gegen Ende des* 13. *Jahrhunderts*, in: *ALKG* V (1889) p.603-635; Ehrle, *Zur Geschichte der Scholastik im* 13. *Jahrhundert*, in: *ZkTh* 13 (1889) p.172-193. Ehrle, *L'Agostinismo e l'Aristotelismo nella scolastica del secolo XIII*. Ulteriori discussione e materiali, Xenia Thomastica III (1925) p.517-588; Ehrle, *Der hl. Bonaventura, seine Eigenart und seine drei Lebensauf-*

gaben, Franz Stud 8 (1921) p.109-124. A brief treatment may be found in the article on Augustinianism by J. Koch in *LThK* I 826f.

9. Ehrle clearly states that this is the way he wants to be understood; cfr. the first article cited above in *ALKG* V p.603-635. On p.605f, Ehrle describes the Augustinianism of Alexander of Hales and the influence which he had on the Franciscan school. Thus, when Bonaventure comes on the scene, he and his disciples develop this already present Augustinianism to a climactic point. Ehrle concludes that the rise of the Franciscan school in Paris did not create a new direction of doctrinal development (.. . . *keine neue Lehrrichtung* [emphasis by Ehrle himself]), but merely gave a new representative to the already dominant Augustinianism. The same idea can be found on p.606, 607, 609, as well as in the other articles indicated above.

10. Gilson presents his new conception of Bonaventure at the very beginning of his book. p.3: "St. Bonaventure, say they, differs from St. Thomas only because he built up his doctrine on narrower foundations and could never command the time necessary to work it out in complete detail. This is why the state of his thought has been up to the present comparatively neglected. If he is only a potential and incomplete St. Thomas, to study him would be a futile occupation . . . Now it will be one of my duties to examine whether the fact that he had to govern his Order really prevented St. Bonaventure from reaching his full intellectual development and bringing his doctrine to completion. But right at the beginning it is important to realize that St. Bonaventure did not set out upon a way that would have led to Christian Aristotelianism if he had not stopped too soon. The truth is that from the first he had attached himself to a doctrine which was its radical negation. It was neither through ignorance nor by reason of a mere chronological chance that he did not become Aristotelian . . ." p.4. "St. Bonaventure was never to forget his lesson. He knew Aristotle well, quoted him constantly, adopted a large part of his technical vocabulary, he admired him sincerely and regarded him as the man of knowledge *par excellence* . . . but did not place him on a pedestal, nor suppose for a single instant that true philosophy must coincide with his teaching, nor that theology, the guardian of faith, must modify itself by a hair's breadth to come into harmony with him. From his first contact with the pagan thought of Aristotle, St. Bonaventure is as one who has understood it, seen through it, and passed beyond it . . ." p.33. "From the moment of this change (= his appointment as General), St. Bonaventure's thought appears as if bent with all its powers towards the creation of a new synthesis, a synthesis wherein he should find a place for all the philosophical and religious values of which he had had living experience . . ." Similar texts can be found in great numbers through-

out Gilson's book which is based on this fundamental concept. Cfr. especially the final chapter, "The Spirit . . ." p.440ff: "In order to make clearer the line of our argument, we may contrast two different interpretations of the evolution of philosophy in the thirteenth century. One, which we may consider classic, sees all that took place in the perspective of Thomism: the thirteenth century began with the Augustinian tradition, but threatened by the invasion of Averroism and reacting with Albertus Magnus against this invasion, absorbed from it all that was true in the system of Aristotle. The thesis of the anarchy of Augustinianism is necessarily involved in this, since obviously, if Augustinianism had been adequate, Thomism would have had no reason to exist. The second interpretation sees the scholasticism of the thirteenth century as reaching its height in two summits: the powerful movement at work within Christian thought threw up two high peaks, to say nothing of the secondary heights which formed a double chain about them: of these two peaks one is the doctrine of St. Bonaventure; the other, that of St. Thomas Aquinas. We have said elsewhere what the signification of the second has appeared to us to be; here we should like, in the light of the study made in this book, to insist upon the historic significance of the first . . . p.445: And in this sense it may be said that if the success of Thomism seems at a distance to have brought the development of mediaeval Augustinianism to an end, it may be simply because with St. Bonaventure the mystical synthesis of medieval Augustinianism was fully formed, just as that of Christian Aristotelianism was fully formed with St. Thomas."

11. Gilson, *op. cit.*, p. 449:". . . that both men were involved in the construction of the scholastic synthesis of the Middle Ages and that today both men must be seen as representing it: 'duae olivae et duo candelabra in domo Dei lucentia.' "

12. Gilson, *op. cit.*, p.440 as cited above. Here again we can see clearly the distinction between Gilson and Ehrle. Ehrle had helped in the creation of the very concept that Gilson so emphatically rejects: the notion of an Augustinianism which ultimately rests on an ignorance of Aristotle (and hence cannot be an anti-Aristotelianism). Thus, for example, Ehrle writes that, unfortunately, Bonaventure was elected to the office of General already in 1257 and thus was drawn out of his scientific work. He was, then, only about 36 years old when he began the almost uninterrupted travelling which was demanded of him by his new position. The difference in the life of the two men (Thomas and Bonaventure) becomes clear, and the facts of Bonaventure's life must be taken into account in an evaluation of his writings. (Cfr. Ehrle, *Der heilige Bonaventura, seine Eigenart und seine drei Lebensaufgaben*, in: *Franz Stud* 8 (1921) p.109-124.)

13. P. Robert, *Le problème de la philosophie bonaventurienne*, in: *Laval phil et theol.* 6 (1950) p.147.

14. This expression in F. van Steenberghen, *Siger de Brabant* II, p.459; also P. Robert, *op. cit.,* p.147f.
15. Esp. the valuable article on Bonaventure in: *Dict. d'histoire et de géographie ecclesiastiques* T IX Paris, 1937,p.741-788. P.751f: Au confluent de tous ces courants d'idées, tres informé aussi de la pensée d'Aristote et des philosophes, qu'il utilise largement . . . saint Bonaventure a elaboré la synthèse definitive de l'augustinisme médiéval sous le signe d'Assise. p.786f: Métaphysicien à l'égal des princes de la scolastique, il a constitué la synthèse définitive de l'augustinisme médiéval ou triomphent la métaphysique de l'exemplarisme et de l'analogie universel et l'idee du Christ centre de tout et maître unique du savoir . . . See also, Longpré, *Saint Augustin et la pensée franciscaine*, Paris, 1932, and the other works of Longpré.
16. J. Squandrani, *S. Bonaventura christianus philosophus*, in: *Antonianum*, 1941, p.103-130 and 253-304.
17. F. J. Thonnard, *Augustinisme et aristotélisme au XIII siècle*, in: *L' annee theol.* 4 (1944) p.442-466.
18. G. H. Tavard, *Transiency and permanence.* 1954, esp. p.163-165.
19. B. Rosenmöller, *Religiöse Erkenntnis nach Bonaventura*, Munich, 1925.
20. J. Auer, *Die Entwicklung der Gnadenlehre in der Hochscholastik* I, Freiburg in Breisgau, 1942; II,1951. Esp. I,p.25 note 9. Also worth reading is L. Meier, *Bonaventuras Selbstzeugnis über seinen Augustinismus*, in: *Franz. Stud.* XII (1930) p.342-355, where the critical reservations of Bonaventure relative to Augustine are well treated.
21. A. Dempf, *Metaphysik des Mittelalters*, Munich-Berlin, 1930, p.110-119; also, Dempf, *Etienne Gilson*, in: *Phil Jahrbuch der Görresgesellschaft* 62 (1953) p.253-266.
22. P. Robert, *Le problème de la philosophie bonaventurienne*, in: *Laval theol et phil* 6 (1950) p.145-163; 7 (1951) p.9-58. Also, P. Robert, *St. Bonaventure, Defender of Christian Wisdom*, in: *Franc. Stud* III (1943) p.159-179. Confer the end of this section for a more precise determination of Robert's position.
23. L. Veuthey, *Sancti Bonaventurae philosophia christiana.* Rome, 1943. Cfr. note 76 to #16.
24. B. Geyer, *Die patristische und die scholastische Philosophie*, p. 386-396.
25. *Gesch. der abendl. Weltanschauung* III, p.256-272.
26. *Geschichte der Philosophie* I, p.380-383. Only Gilson is named in the literature on Bonaventure. According to Van Steenberghen, *The philosophical movement . . .* p.62, the thesis of Gilson was quite generally accepted by the Franciscans.
27. Compare the expression of the Louvain school, above all: M. de Wulf, *History of Medieval Philosophy*, Vol. II, 1937 (Bonaventure on p. 79-93). Concerning De Wulf, see: Van Steenberghen, *The Philosophical Movement . . .* p.7.

228   *Theology of History in St. Bonaventure*

28. Vol. II, 979. Following De Wulf, he says that Bonaventure "malgré des sympathies augustiniennes non dissimulees . . . lui aussi est peripatéticien dans le sens scolastique du mot."
29. F. van Steenberghen, *Siger de Brabant d'après ses oeuvres inédites* I 1931; II 1942. Concerning Bonaventure, Vol. II, p.446-464. In the second edition of his book on Bonaventure, Gilson takes a position relative to Van Steenberghen's view, but does not give up his original thesis.
30. *Aristoté en Occident. Les origines de l'aristotelisme parisien* (Essais philosophiques 1), Louvain, 1946. Unfortunately, I was unable to find this book at any library that I consulted.
31. A. Forest-F. van Steenberghen-M. de Gandillac, *Le mouvement doctrinal du IX au XIV siècle.* Paris, 1951. Cfr. p.179-305. Following the view of Van Steenberghen is A. Hayen, *Thomas von Aquin gestern und heute* (German by R. Scherer), Frankfurt, 1953. Similarly, D. A. Callus, *La condenacion de Sto. Thomas en Oxford*, in: *Revista di Filosofia* VI (1947) p.347-416. Regarding the general understanding of the line of development, Callus agrees with Van Steenberghen. On the other hand, there is the out-dated thesis of R. Lazzarini, *S. Bonaventura filosofo e mistico del Christanesimo*, Milan, 1946. This thesis is rejected by Z. Alszeghy, *Studia Bonaventuriana*, in: Gregorianum 29 (1948), p. 142-151. Alszeghy, however, takes exception to Van Steenberghen's view as well.
32. The only exception so far, to my knowledge, is the book on Thomas Aquinas by A. Hayen translated from the French (cfr. note 31). The fact that a critical discrepancy has arisen is not even mentioned by A. Dempf in his article: *Etienne Gilson*, in: *Phil. Jahrbuch der Görresgesellschaft* 62 (1953) p.253-266. He speaks of Gilson's Bonaventure-study on page 257f.
33. E. Gilson, *Die historisch-kritische Forschung und die Zukunft der Scholastik*, reproduced by A. Hayen, *op. cit.*, p.103-119 (first printed in: *Antonianum* XXVI (1951), p.40-48), esp. p.118f.
34. Van Steenberghen, *Le mouvement* . . . p.189-191, 219-221.
35. *Op. cit.*, p.190f.
36. *Op. cit.*, p.191.
37. P.201. Also in Grabmann, *Methode* II, p. 551. It is not quite enough when Gilson describes the situation in the year 1250 as follows: "The Masters in the Faculty of Arts had not yet taken the step of declaring that Aristotle's philosophy was equivalent to Philosophy itself . . ." (p.3)
38. Van Steenberghen, *op. cit.*, p.201. He writes that in the case of William of Auxerre Aristotle is cited around 100 times; in the case of Philip the Chancellor, already about 300 times; in the case of William of Auvergne, the citations are 'innombrables.'
39. *Op. cit.*, p.203.
40. P.204.

41. *Ibid.*, also, *Siger de Brabant* II, p.730; and, *The Philosophical Movement*, p.51.
42. P.205.
43. P.205f. Also, *Aristotle in the West* . . . p.130—The philosophical movement . . . 54: . . . which Maurice de Wulf called "pro-Thomistic' or 'ancient scholasticism,' was not an Augustinian current, as Mandonnet believed, nor even a traditional current, going back through the twelfth century to St. Augustine and Plato. It was a new and Aristotelian current . . .
44. P.233. Prof. Söhngen has pointed out to me that Richard Harder, a man so thoroughly conversant with Plotinus, has rejected the term "neo-Platonism;" for he sees in this term a distortion of the historical and philosophical situation relative to Platonism. It is possible to conceive of something rather definite under the term "aristotélisme augustinisant" but not under the term "aristotel-isme néoplatonisant", for this was already an essential aspect of ancient neo-Platonism. Actually, it is difficult to see the rather monstrous formula as especially fortunate. Nevertheless, despite the evident terminological weakness of the formula, it seems to me that the meaning he is trying to express does come through, and that this meaning actually corresponds to the historical facts. Perhaps there is an improvement in: *The philosophical movement* . . . p.61 where we read: . . . the philosophy of St. Bon-aventure is an eclectic and neoplatonic Aristotelianism, subor-dinated to an Augustinian theology. In philosophy Augustinian-ism is one of the sources of his thought, but is a secondary source, compared with Aristotelianism.
45. P.296.
46. P. 296. Esp. see what is said about Thomas on this page in the section on neo-Augustinianism: . . . par ses remarquables com-mentaires sur Aristote et par une série d'options philosophiques, il apparaît aux yeux des théologiens (et aussi des artiens) comme un partisan du péripatétisme, comme l'allié des philosophes et comme l'adversaire de la théologie traditionelle.
47. P.297.
48. P.297. We could be tempted to raise the same objection to the concept of a neo-Augustinianism as is raised against the notion of a neo-Platonism. But here there is a different situation. Neo-Augustinianism is really not an "Augustinianism"; it is not a new, creative development of Augustinian thought, but merely a restoration, and in this sense a "Neo-Augustinianism!"
49. P.299 and 298.
50. P.232f.
51. P.300. The *Correctorium fratris Thomae* of William of Mare is called a codification of neo-Augustinianism.
52. P.301.
53. Van Steenberghen, *The philosophical movement* . . . p.66. Cfr. the work of Veuthey cited in foot-note 23.

54. In: *Gregorianum* 29 (1948) p.142-151.

55. Alszeghy distinguishes between the *Sentence Commentary* and the "free writings" of Bonaventure as Guardini already had done (Guardini, *Erlösungslehre*). But A. Stohr had shown that this distinction was untenable (*Die Trinitätslehre . . .* p.2-5). In the light of a further group of "free writings" which have been published, it has become clear that this distinction simply cannot be maintained. The *Qu. disp. De prophetia, De raptu, De visione intellectuali et corporali, De divinatione* edited by B. Decker, as well as the *Qu De theologia* edited by G. H. Tavard, and the *Qu De caritate* and *De novissimis* edited by Glorieux show a stronger Aristotelianism than does the *Sentence Commentary*. They clearly show that Bonaventure does not break the line of development leading to Thomas, but rather, that he develops it consistently further and shows a very close approximation to the position of Thomas. It is surprising that these *Quaestiones* have not been brought into the discussion thus far. In my opinion, they are sufficient to decide definitely in favor of Van Steenberghen's view concerning Bonaventure's position prior to 1257.

56. *L'Aspetto filosofico . . . Coll Franc* XIX (1949) p.40, see summary on p.42.

57. Cfr. the studies of Baeumker (cfr. Literature) and R. Klibansky on Medieval Platonism; for example, Klibansky, *The Continuity of the Platonic Tradition during the Middle Ages*. Outline of a "Corpus Platonicum Medi Aevi" 1939. Also in agreement with this is a statement made in a quite different context by Th. Crowley (in: *Rev. Neosc. de Phil.* 1939, p.648-50; cfr. Van Steenberghen, *Aristotle in the West*, p.113): The term Augustinianism cannot be used to describe the philosophical teaching of the period prior to St. Thomas. The influence of St. Augustine on Bacon is practically absent . . .

58. *Augustinisme et aristotélisme au XIII siècle*, in: *L'année théol.* 4 (1944) p.442-466.

59. *The philosophical movement . . .* p.71. Van Steenberghen's answer to his critics, *ibid.*, p.68-73.

60. *Ibid.*, p.73.

61. Gilson, *Bulletin thomiste*, Vol. 6 (series nr. 17-19, 1940-1942), p.5-22; S. Brounts, *Siger von Brabant en de wijsgeerige stroomingen aan de Parijssche Universiteit in de XIII eeuw*, in: *Tydschrift voor Philosophie* 8 (1946) 317/48, esp. 323f.; Van Steenberghen, *The philosophical movement . . .* p.63f.

62. *The philosophical movement . . .* p.73.

63. *Ibid.*

64. *The philosophical movement . . .* p.112f; *Le mouvement . . .* p.221 note 1; p.224f.; p.226 note 1. Indeed, Van Steenberghen also recognizes that the unity of Christian wisdom is a central theme of Bonaventure's thought. E.g. *Le mouvement . . .* p.220f.; 227.

65. *Le mouvement* . . . p.303; *The philosophical movement* . . . p.100f.

66. Aside from the general presentation of *Le mouvement*, it seems to me that this line is drawn out clearly in *The philosophical movement*, p.19-37 ("The organization of studies and its repercussions on the philosophical movement"). On p.62 Van Steenberghen remarks that M. Grabmann and O. Lottin also had seen the development in this way.

67. In this context, see the position of such an outstanding scholar as P. Robert. He began his series of articles "Le problème de la philosophie bonaventurienne" (*Laval phil. et theol.* 6 [1950], p.145-163; 7 [1951] p.9-58) with the intention of defending Gilson against Van Steenberghen in the essential lines of his thought even if not without reservations (esp. 1950,p.152 to end; 161: Dans l'esprit de saint Bonaventure, il existe manifestement une philosophie augustinienne . . .) The situation changes, however, in the course of the presentation; the second series is a sharp critique of Gilson. The concept of "Augustinianism" is only very cautiously defended: "Jusqu à plus ample informé, on nous permettra donc de considérer la philosophie de saint Bonaventure essentiellement et fondamentalement comme un augustisme médiéval, sans aucun doute fortement influencé par l'aristotélisme néoplatonisant de son milieu doctrinal, mais non spécifiquement caractérise par lui." (1951, p.57). An essential step further is taken in the "Note additionelle" appended to the article (p.58): "Cet article était déjà sous presse lorsque, grâce a l'aimable coursoisie de M. Van Steenberghen, nous avons pris connaissance des pages suggestives consacrées a la doctrine de Docteur Séraphique dans l'important ouvrage qu'il vient de publier avec MM. A. Forest et M. de Gandillac ... Nous constatons avec plaisir que cette étude confirme pleinement la critique que nous venons de faire de l'ouvrage de M. Etienne Gilson . . . Nous ne croyons pas qu'il existe entre nous aucun désaccord irréductible sur les autres points de son interprétation."

68. Cfr. the texts cited in foot-note 55. The *Qu D de theologia* seem to me to go the furthest in this direction. For example, in *Qu* 1 I it is said that there are sciences which proceed ex principiis notis solo lumine naturali intellectus sicut arithmetica, geometria, et huiusmodi; quaedam vero procedunt ex principiis notis et notificatis lumine superioris scientiae sicut perspectiva . . . Et hoc modo Sacra Scriptura est scientia, quia procedit ex principiis notis lumine superioris scientiae, scilicet Dei et beatorum . . . (ed. Tavard, p.212). Similar notions can be seen in the other texts cited in note 55. B. Decker, *Die Entwicklung der Lehre von der prophetischen Offenbarung* . . . p.161 says that, in his analysis of prophetic knowledge in the *Qu de prophetia* and *De visione intellectuali et corporali*, Bonaventure is closer to Thomas' analysis of revelation than all the pre-thomistic theologians.

Notes to Chapter 4, #16

1. *De decem praec* II 25 and 28, Vol. V,p.514f. Nr.28,p.515: Audivi, cum fui scholaris, de Aristotele, quod posuit mundum aeternum; et cum audivi rationes et argumenta, quae fiebant ad hoc, incepit concuti cor meum et incepit cogitare, quomodo potest hoc esse? Sed haec modo sunt ita manifesta. ut nullus de hoc possit dubitare. Cfr. also Gilson, *Bonaventure*, p.486ff; J. d'Albi, *op. cit.*, p.145ff.

2. Comprehensive presentation of material in d'Albi, *op. cit.*, p.190-227.

3. Coll VIII 16, Vol.V,p.497.

4. A comparison of this citation with *De red* 4 Vol.V,p.320b indicates an exact agreement with the scientific-theoretical structure of Bonaventure.

5. *Op. cit.*, Isti errores significantur in Apocalypsi in numero bestiae. Cfr. below, II.

6. *Sermo I de sancto Marco II* Vol. IX, p.524a. D'Albi takes a convincing position contrary to that of the Quaracchi edition concerning the dating of this sermon in 1255 (*op. cit.*, p.225-227). J. d'Albi dates it in the year 1273; in any event it comes from the period after 1257.

7. *Hex* VII 1, p.365a.

8. *Hex* VI 3, p.361a.

9. *Hex* VI 2, p.360f and Nr.5,p.361b. The same Apocalyptic expressions which are here referred to Aristotelianism are applied to the opponents of the Mendicants in *Apol paup*, prol 2, Vol.VIII, p.234a, so that we must say that, at least in part, they belong to the cliche-material of the literature concerning controversial questions. In the instance just cited, it says: . . . dogma quoddam pullulasse iamque in scriptis redactum comperimus, quod tamquam fumus teter et horridus a pueto abyssali prorumpens ipsiusque solis iustitiae splendentibus radiis se directe obiiciens, christianarum mentium hemisphaerium obscurare contendit . . . We have already shown that in the case of Bonaventure it is not merely a question of cliche, but a case of genuine eschatological conviction.

10. Van Steenberghen, *Le mouvement* . . . ,p.229: L'attitude de notre docteur se modifie vers la fin de sa carrière . . . Mais même à cette époque l'hostilité de saint Bonaventure va bien plus aux disciples chrétiens d'Aristote qu' à Aristote lui-même.

11. Van Steenberghen, *ibid.*, On this, P. Robert is in agreement with Van Steenberghen against Gilson: *Laval theol et phil* 1950, p.160: . . . la connaissance que Bonaventure avait d'Aristote . . . était assez étendue, mais peu approfondie. Bonaventure himself never hid this, but expressed it openly; cfr. II *Sent* d 1 p 1 a 1 q 2 c,p.22f: concerning the various interpretations of Aristotle, he says expressly on p.23a: Quod horum magis verum sit, ego

nescio, etc.; the same thing is practically repeated in *Hex* VII 3,p.365b: Sed quidquid senserit . . .

11a Following a suggestion of Prof. Söhngen, the author uses the German terminology 'thomanisch' and 'antithomanisch' to refer to Thomas himself and not to Thomism. For the substantive form, the word "Antithomismus" is used since it would be difficult to find another form and the context makes it clear where it is a case of Thomas or of Thomism in individual instances. In the translation we have used the terms "Thomist" and "anti-Thomist" to correspond to the German usage of "Thomanisch" etc., as referring to Thomas; and the terminology of "Thomistic"etc., to refer to Thomism.

12. *Hex* VII 2, p.365b.

13. Esp. *De sci Chr* q 4 c, Vol.V,p.23a.

14. *Hex* II 22-29, p.340f. Also, J. d'Albi, *op. cit.*, p.231-238.

15. *Hex* II 26, p.340b. Also, *Hex* IV 10, p.351f.

16. *Super Hieremiam* c 13 f 25v. In general, regarding the question of Bonaventure's anti-Thomist view, F. Tinivella is correct when he says: "a) Factum datur, Collationes in Hexaemeron positiones aliquas doctrinales adversantes thomismum defendere. b) Probabilius Seraphicus solummodo data occasione hoc fecit, non ex professo et multo minus ex intentione thomismum aggrediendi . . ." (*Antonianum* 1936,p.163.)

17. II *Sent* d 1 p 1 a 1 q 2, p.23a. We would have to agree with Gilson when he says that Bonaventure's position on this point was objectively anti-Aristotelian from the start.

18. II *Sent* d 1 p 1 a 1 q 2 f 2,p.21a. Gilson, *Bonaventure*, p.171ff.

19. *S Theol* I q 46 a 2 ad 7.

20. II *Sent, ibid.*, p.21a. Also, Gilson, *Bonaventure*, p.171ff.

21. I *Sent* d 37 p 1 a 3 q 2 c, p.648b; IV *Sent* d 43 a 2 q 2 c,p.898a; q 3 c,p.898f.

22. Thomas, II *Sent* d 1 q 1 a 5 arg 7: . . . quia tempus accidens motus. Also, arg 5 and 6.

23. II *Sent* d 2 p 1 a 2 q 3 c, p.68a. As far as I have been able to determine, the question as to what was created first is not even asked by Thomas. We merely indicate in passing such important texts as II *Sent* d 2 p 1 a 1 q 2 c,p.59f (unity of time, distinction between physical and cosmic time), a 2 q 1,p.64f (four-fold concept of time), q 2 c,p.66b (the "saeculum" as properly human time), d 2 p 2 a 2 q 1 c p.76f (the time of the angels as bound up with person, the time of man as cosmic time). Cfr. P. Robert, *Hylémorphisme et Devenir chez St. Bonaventure*, Montreal, 1936.

24. Gilson, *Bonaventure*, p.174.

25. Thomas, in IV *Sent* d 43 q 1 a 3 sol 2. Thomas takes a position against the authority of Augustine who explains the indeterminability of the duration of the world by means of the indeterminability of the years of old age. Thus Augustine employs a concept of time which involves limits as an essential element.

26. Prof. Söhngen has pointed out to me that this eternal circle of time is most clearly expressed in 1. Logos, 1. half of the Platonic "Phaidon," following the lead of Heraclitus. All the essential texts that express this circular understanding of time are to be found in K. Löwith, *Weltgeschichte und Heilsgeschehen*, Stuttgart, 1953, p.223 note 15. See also, Cullmann, *Christ and Time*, p.51 and 61. The notion of the *circulus intelligibilis* in Bonaventure is pointed out by R. Guardini, *Eine Denkergestalt des hohen Mittelalters*: *Bonaventura*, in: *Unterscheidung des Christlichen*, Mainz, 1935 (p.389-403), p.402. B. Rosemmöller, *Religiöse Erkenntnis* . . . p.36 speaks of express references on this point in Guardini's unpublished *Habilitationsarbeit*, but they seem to stand in a different context.

27. Newly edited in: Cl. Baeumker, *Studien und Charakteristiken zur Gesch. der Phil., insbes. des Mittelalters*. Edited by M. Grabmann, *Baumker-Beiträge* XXV, 1-2 (1927) p.207-214, Commentary, p.194-207. Bonaventure mentions this work expressly in I *Sent* d 37 p 1 a 1 q 1 ad 3. p.369b to the surprise of the Quaracchi editors who did not know of it. There seem to be some indications of it also in II *Sent* d 2 p 2 a 2 q 1 c,p.76b below and 77a above (Cfr. *Ps.-Hermes* III, ed Baeumker 208) ; otherwise, as far as I can see, it is only the *propositio* II that is cited; but it is cited very frequently.

28. *Reg* 7 PL 210, 627 A. Cfr. Geyer, p.247.

29. *Ps-Hermes*, prop. II *op. cit.*, p.208. Cfr. Bonaventure, I *Sent* d 37 p 1 a 1 q 1 ad 3, p.639b; *De myst trin* q 5 a 1 ad 7,8 Vol.V 91b; *Itin* c 5,8, Vol.V 310a; *Sermo IV* in vig nat Dni, Vol IX, p.94a.

30. I *Sent* d 45 a 2 q 1 c, p.804f. Ps. Dionysius, *De div nom* c 4 #14 PL 3, 713.

31. *De myst trin* q 8 ad 7 Vol. V,115b.

32. This is developed extensively in *Hex* XXII and XXIII, p.437-449; esp. XXIII 4,p.445b. Concerning the patristic teaching see: J. Ratzinger, *Volk und Haus Gottes* . . . p.197-218.

33. *Brev* p 5 c 1 end, Vol. V, p.253a; p. 6 c 3,p.267a.

34. *De red* 7, Vol.V,p.322a; *Brev* p 2 c 4,p.221b.

35. Actually the meaning of *De red* and *Hex* I is understandable only if it is seen as an allegory which clarifies the deeper meaning of things which is seen first in faith.

36. *Hex* I 24, p.333b. Cfr. Delorme, Princ Coll.I # 3,24,p.11. In line with the character of the Delorme text, the mathematical problem is treated more extensively here than in the *Opera omnia*; the theological meaning remains the same.

37. *De perf ev* q 2 a 2 ad 20, p.148a; *Hex* XVI 22, p.406b.

38. *De don Sp S*, VIII 16, Vol V., 497b. For a clarification of the notion of the "numerus cyclicus", see the text of Boethius, *II Arithmet.* c 30 PL 63,1137, which is given in note 5.

39. For Bonaventure's interpretation of the number six, cfr. I *Sent* d 2 a un q 4 c, p.57b: Senarius autem dicitur primus perfectorum,

quia constat ex omnibus partibus suis aliquotis, scilicet tribus, duobus et uno; included in the interpretation of the number ten, IV *Sent* d 1 p 2 a 1 q 3 c, p.35b; *Brev* p 6 c 12, Vol.V, p.278b: quia senarius est primus numerus perfectus; *De sex alis Ser c* 1,4 Vol. VIII, p.132b; also important is *Apol paup* c 3,8, Vol.VIII, p.246b and *Apol paup* c 7, 40, p.285b. The texts of Richard of St. Victor and Rupert of Deutz given by the Quaracchi edition do not make an interpretation possible (Vol. V,p.497b). The text can be understood only in relation to the parallels in Bonaventure's own work. Without a doubt, the meaning of Bonaventure is: the number six is, in itself, a perfect number — it is a cyclic number; placing this cyclic number three times in succession produces a number of more intense cyclic character; furthermore, it points very concretely to the threefold heretical teaching of the philosophers who have created a triple heretical circle with the affirmation of the aeternitas mundi, the necessitas fatalis, and the unitas intellectus.

40. *Hex* VI 4, p.361a. Also, II *Sent* d 1 p 1 a 1 q 2 c,p.23a.
41. Peter Lombard, I *Sent* d 3 p 1 c 1,p.63b; Bonaventure's commentary on this in d 3 a un q 4 opp 2,p.75b and ad 2,p.76b; also, William of St. Amour, *De periculis nov temp* c 11, ed. Bierbaum, p.25.
42. *Hex* XII 16 and 17, p.386f. For the notion of the "liber scriptus intus et foris" see *Brev* p 2 c 11, Vol.V,p.229a; also the indication given there concerning the origin of the idea in Hugo of St. Victor, *De sacr.* I p 6 c 5 PL 176,266f.
43. *Hex* VII 5,p.366a.
44. *Hex* VII 8ff, p.366f.
45. *Hex* VII 13,p.367b; also Joachim, *Conc* V 11 f 66r: Secundo tempore factum est firmamentum in medio aquarum. Firmamentum est ecclesia Petri, qui specialiter assumpta cruce secutus est Christum . . . Aquas enim ab aquis firmamentum divisit, quia fideles ab infidelibus mater ecclesia segregavit . . . G. Söhngen refers to the citation from Bonaventure in: *Die biblische Lehre von der Gottebenbildlichkeit des Menschen*, in: *Die Einheit in der Theol*, p.210.
46. *Hex* IV 1,p.349a; V 22,p.357b. Actually the Bonaventurian schema of sciences embraces 3 x 3 sciences, which are not reduced immediately to "beatitudo", but find their reduction by way of Scripture. If we may be allowed to take this into consideration in this context, then the two interpretations of the magicians of the Pharao are identical at least in their basic structure. Cfr. the schema of the sciences in *De reductione*, Vol. V, p.319ff.
47. *Hex* II 30, p.341b; cfr. Nr. 32-34,p.342. See what was said above in #12.
48. The minor side-remark against Thomas does not change this. Bonaventure rejects Thomas' concept of beatitude, which is primarily intellectual (II 29,p.341a: Unde patet, quod non est tota

beatitudo in intellectiva). But the total direction is not anti-Thomist, but anti-intellectual in a very general sense.

49. *Hex* XVII, 27, p.413b. Significantly the decisive second sentence of this section is missing in Delorme (V III Coll V #2, 27,p.201). But the idea can be seen to be genuinely Bonaventurian because the motif appears frequently in the work of the Seraphic Doctor; other indications in the Delorme text point in this direction as well. See the following. Furthermore, the first inspiration for this interpretation goes back to Francis himself. He says in the *Verba admonitionis* 2 (Böhmer, *Analekten*, p.42): Ille enim comedit de ligno boni et mali, qui sibi suam voluntatem appropiat et se exaltat de bonis, que Dominus dicit et operatur in ipso; et sic per suggestionem diaboli et transgressionem mandati factum est ei pomum scientie mali; unde oportet, quod sustineat penam. Cfr. Nr. 7 (Böhmer, p.44): Illi sunt mortui a littera, qui tantum sola verba cupiunt scire, ut sapientiores inter alios teneantur . . . Related to this also is Bonaventure's *Sermo V in dom II post Pascha* II, Vol. IX, p.304b: Quid igitur valent omnes aliae scientiae, nisi ad istam (sc. sapientiam salutarem) ordinentur? — Vae illis! qui toto tempore vitae suae student in logica, physica vel in decretis et nihil saporis in ista scientia inveniunt; si in ligno crucis studerent, scientiam salutarem ibi invenirent; est enim lignum vitae . . . Also, J. d'Albi, *Les luttes doctrinales* . . . 207. In *Hex* XIV 17, p.396a the image is used in a wider sense to symbolize the church of the anti-Christ as such.

50. *Tract de plant* par 8 Vol.V, p.577a.

51. *Hex* XVI 22 and 23, p.406f.

52. Unfortunately I was not able to determine the source for this interpretation. Most likely we would not be entirely wrong if we were to think of Joachim. But perhaps the history of the idea goes back further. The statement of St. Francis given above would seem to indicate this, for it was certainly formulated under the influence of some traditional view.

53. *Hex* XVI 23, p.407a.

54. *Sermo II in dom III adv*, Vol. IX 63a. Cfr. J. d'Albi, *op. cit.*, p.193-196.

55. See #15, 3 above

56. *De don Sp S* VIII 16, Vol. V, p.497b.

57. *Hex* VI 5, p.361b. The formulation of this text in Delorme is significant, V I Coll III #1,5,p.92: Hi ergo taliter ponentes inciderunt in hos errores, quorum intelligentia clauditur clave putei abyssalis, unde nimia caligo ascendit. Cautius ergo est dicere quod Aristoteles non senserit mundum aeternum, sive senserit sive non, quia tantus fuit quod omnes ipsum sequerentur et assererentur idem dicere; sic omnis lux determinata in praecedentibus extingueretur. Sequamur autem nos eum in quibus bene dixit, non in eis in quibus fuit tenebrosus, quae nescivit vel quae celavit. Unde in hac vita sunt homines in praecipitio infinito.

58. *Hex* II 7,p.337b. Again, the formulation in the Delorme text is weaker; Princ Coll II,II 7,p.22f.

59. *Hex* XIX 18,p.423a. Prof. Söhngen has made the following remarks on this point: By way of comparison, it is enlightening that Luther's "alte Vettel und Hure Vernunft" is directed not against reason itself, but against a reason that desires to have and actually does have the decisive word in theology. But in the case of Bonaventure, we see how difficult it is to succeed in placing the proper limits on such images. Apocalyptic images are like a torrent of water that overflows the banks and is difficult to keep in bounds. And regardless of all efforts to mollify the imagery, the apocalyptic tone predominates. Even a Mozart cannot make a trumpet forget to sound like a trumpet!

60. G. Söhngen, *Die Theologie im "Streit der Fakultäten,"* in: *Die Einheit in der Theologie,* p.13f. Therefore, when Dempf (*Metaphysik des Mittelalters,* p.112) says that Luther's statement concerning the "prostitution with the Aristotelian reason" is found already in the case of Bonaventure, we must add that the previous history of this statement is actually much older.

61. *Hex* II 7 end, p.337b and *Hex* I 9,p.330b.

62. *Hex* IV 1,p.349a: . . . superbientes de sua scientia luciferiani facti. *Hex* XXII 42, p.444a-b applies the designation of "luciferianus" to the proud contemplative.

63. *Hex* XVII 28, p.414b. It is significant that this is missing in Delorme. This seems to be another text which is based on a statement of St. Francis, or on a statement attributed to him. *Speculum perfectionis* C III (IV) c 69,4 (ed. Sabatier, p.200): Nam et ventura est tribulatio, qua libri, ad nihilum utiles, in fenestris et latebris proiicientur.

64. This distinction between the present and a coming, but not yet present, eschatological situation corresponds to the position which Bonaventure assumed relative to the problem of the Order as such in as far as he distinguishes between the present Franciscan Order and the eschatological Order of Francis (cfr #5). This remains the real distinguishing characteristic of Bonaventure's view, setting him off from the Spirituals who desired to have in the present what Bonaventure reserved for the future. For this reason, such anti-Aristotelian statements as were commonplace for Olivi would have been impossible for Bonaventure. Olivi, for example, says: ". . . licet eius auctoritas mihi valde displiceat" (ed. Jansen, I, 548); ". . . licet mihi non sit cura quid hic vel alibi senserit" (*ibid.* 337); cfr. Vol. III, Index C (Allegationes philosophorum), Aristoteles F (De auctoritate Aristotelis Aristotelicorumque et generatim philosophorum) p.578 ff. For Bonaventure, Aristotle is really an authority *now*, and his opinion is in no way a matter of indifference. In as far as Olivi draws the eschatological "then" of Bonaventure into his own "now", he destroys the real eschatological anti-philosophi-

cal attitude of Bonaventure and reduces it to an inner-philosophical dispute. Unfortunately, a number of scholars have not escaped the danger of placing Bonaventure in the same tracks as Olivi and of attributing to him a form of anti-Aristotelianism which he actually never held. See what follows.

65. *Hex* XXII 21 f,p.440f; see the previous note. This final position of Bonaventure is clearly different from the position which he held at the end of his *Magisterium* and at the time when he began to be more intensively interested in the historical problem in *Epist de 3 quaest* 13 Vol. VIII, p.336: "Fateor coram deo, quod hoc est, quod me fecit vitam beati Francisci maxime diligere, quia similis est initio et perfectioni ecclesiae, quae primo incepit a piscatoribus simplicibus et postmodum profecit ad doctores clarissimos et peritissimos; sic videbis in religione beati Francisci, ut ostendat Deus, quod non fuit per hominum prudentiam inventa, sed per Christum; et quia opera Christi non deficiunt, sed proficiunt, ostenditur hoc opus fuisse divinum, dum ad consortium virorum simplicium etiam sapientes non sunt dedignati descendere . . ." This development was overlooked by P. Robert, who has produced an otherwise outstanding analysis of the essential contents of this *epistola* (*Laval theol. et phil.* 1950, p.157ff).

66. See the *Testamentum* of St. Francis Nr. 4 (Böhmer, *Analekten*, p.37) : Et eramus ydiotae et subditi omnibus. Similarly in the *epist ad cap gen* c 5 (Böhmer, 61) : quia ignorans sum et idiota. Also, the introduction by Böhmer, p.XI. Likewise, II *Celano* p 2 c 145, 193, ed. Alencon, p.314: Volebat denique religionem pauperibus et illiteratis, non solum divitibus et sapientibus esse communem. Similarly, *Speculum perf* C IV (V) c 81,4, ed. Sabatier, p.239: Et statim dixit illi Dominus: "Dic mihi, o simplex et idiota homuncio, quare tantum contristaris . . ." c 81,7: Sed elegi te simplicem et idiotam, ut scire valeas, tam tu, quam alii, quoniam vigilabo super gregem meum. Also, c 45,3, p.118 and 68,5,p.196. See also the fragment of the Tres socii given by Sabatier, *op. cit.*, p.290 note 3: Sic et multa alia verba simplicia in fervore spiritus loquebatur, quia idiota et simplex electus a Deo non doctis humanae sapientiae verbis, sed simpliciter in omnibus se habebat. Bonaventure, *Hex* XVIII 26, p.418b: Sic ecce, quod una vetula quae habet modicum hortum, quia solam caritatem habet, meliorem fructum habet quam unus magister, qui habet maximum hortum et scit mysteria et naturas rerum. Here the Delorme text is clearly weaker (V III C VI #3, 26,p.211). See also, J. Jörgensen, *St. Francis of Assisi*, p.236; here the text is clarified by means of a conversation between Brother Giles and St. Bonaventure taken from the Chronica XXIV Gen.Min. (*Analecta Franciscana* III, p.101).

Cfr. the sigh of Br. Giles recounted on p. 238: "Our ship leaks and must sink; let him flee who can! Paris, Paris, thou ruinest

St. Francis' Order!"; also the statement of Jacopone da Todi which is quoted at the same place: "Paris, thou hast ruined Assisi." Similarly, Gilson, *Bonaventure*, p.40ff and p.454ff. Thus William of St. Amour adroitly makes use of genuine Franciscan material when he says: "Similiter non licet eis procurare ut fiant magistri, quia magisterium honor est." (*Responsiones* I, 2 ed. Faral, *op. cit.*, p.340.)

67. Cfr. the previous foot-note, especially the reference to Gilson where we find a discussion together with the pertinent literature.

68. Benz, *Ecclesia spiritualis*, p.36ff., esp. p:39; also the texts given in Grundmann, *Joachim*, II, p.109f. See also the treatment by Salimbenes which is based on Ps.-Joachim, and which is given by Gilson, *Bonaventure*, p.455.

69. *De red* 5 Vol.V, p.321b. The relation of Gregory to Bernard which is expressed in this text is found also in John of Salisbury, *Historia pontificalis*, M.G.SS. 55 XV, 526; See: Grabmann, *Methode*, II, p.411f. Without a doubt, Bonaventure could have made use of many predecessors in drawing up his schema.

70. II *Sent.* d 12, a 1, q 2 c, p.296b: Quidnam enim sancti in hac quaestione magis secuti sunt viam theologicam, trahentes rationem ad ea quae sunt fidei. Quidam vero, inter quos praecipuus fuit Augustinus, magis secuti sunt viam philosophicam, quae illa ponit, quae magis videntur rationi consona . . . Et haec positio multum fuit rationabilis et valde subtilis. Verumtamen, quia ad hanc positionem videtur intellectus scripturae distrahi, et securius est et magis meritorium, intellectum nostrum et rationem omnino scripturae supponere, quam ipsam aliquo modo distrahere: ideo communiter alii doctores et qui praecesserunt Augustinum, et qui secuti, sic intellexerunt . . . Should we try to clarify this text on the basis of the fact that the *Commentary* was not intended to be an "independent writing?"

71. II *Sent.* d 13, a 1, q 1 c, p.312f; II d 33 a 3 q 1 c, p.793f, (also, *Brev* p 3 c 5,Vol.V,p.235a); IV *Sent* d 44 p 2 a 1 c,p.924a; II *Sent* d 8 p 1 a 1 q 1 c, p.211a. Cfr. also L. Meier, *Bonaventuras Selbstzeugnis über seinen Augustinismus*, in: *Franz Studien* 17 (1930) p.342-355, where the limits of this Augustinianism are clearly indicated.

72. *Hex* XIX 10,p.422a; Delorme, V III C VII #1 10-11, p.216.

73. *Hex* XIX 14, p.422b. The encounter with the Sultan is treated at greater length in Sermo II de s. P. n. Franc II, Vol.IX, p.579b-580a. We find an interesting addition in Delorme, *op. cit.*, 14, p.217: . . . ecclesiae primitivae, quando clerici de novo conversi ut Dionysius libros philosophorum dimisit et libros sacrae scripturae assumpsit. On the other hand, the statement about burning philosophical books is missing.

74. II *Sent* d 1 p 1 a 1 q 2 c, p.22b: . . . etiam ille excellentior inter philosophos, Aristoteles . . .; also, *Hex* VII 2, p.363b. This is expressly admitted by P. Robert (*op. cit.*) and strengthened

with new arguments; cfr. esp. p.162: Al' encontre de ce que soutient M. E. Gilson, l' aristotélisme n' est donc pas uniquement pour le Docteur Séraphique 'une doctrine condamné' ou 'une erreur qu'il juge." L' aristotélisme est en effet beaucoup plus que cela pour lui. Il est la plus haute expression de la pensée antique et la plus parfaite explication de l' univers jamais concue par la raison humaine laissée a ses seules lumières. It seems to me that there is no longer any possibility for doubt in this matter.

75. Gilson, *Bonaventure*, p.26: "It was not St. Bonaventure who changed, but the world that changed about him." Similarly, p.178 and elsewhere. F. van Steenberghen, *Le mouvement* . . . p.223f and 228ff. P. Robert, in: *Laval phil et theol.* 7 (1951) p.36-56.

76. L. Veuthey, *Sancti Bonaventurae philosophia christiana*, Rome, 1943.

77. Compare with the conclusion of G.H. Tavard, *Transiency and Permanence*, p.164: This·can be dismissed as extravagant.

78. This is the indisputably correct point to which the works of Gilson, Van Steenberghen, and Robert (note 75 above) point, each from a different perspective. In this respect, the judgment of the scholion-writers of Quaracchi is also correct when they say: "Sanctus Bonaventura semper sibi constans ubique fere utitur eadem doctrina vel saltem iisdem principiis" (Vol.I, p.XXXVI. This is cited with emphasis by B.A. Luyckx, *op. cit*: p.234 and 288). Concerning less significant developments on individual points in the thought of Bonaventure even within the inner-Scholastic framework, see the list of literature for the works of R. Silic and F. Henquinet.

79. Cfr. the indications in #5 above.

Conclusion

1. Delorme, p.275; *Op. omnia*, Vol.V,p.449f, additamentum (p.450a, bottom).

2. These ideas are indicated by the Delorme text: V III Coll III #2 24-25,p.177: . . . ita esse deberet secundum Evangelii doctrinam.

LITERATURE

Articles from the *LThK* as well as other literature that is not related to the work as a whole will be indicated at the proper places and will not be repeated here.

1. General Works

Bach, J. *Dogmengeschichte des Mittelalters vom christologischen Standpunkt*, 2 vol. 1873-1875.

Cayre, F. *Patrologie et histoire de la théologie*, vol. 2, 3. ed., Paris, 1947.

Copleston, F., *A History of Philosophy*. Vol. II. Medieval Philosophy. Augustine to Scotus. London, 1950.

Curtis, S.J., *A Short History of Western Philosophy in the Middle Ages*, London, 1950.

Dekkers, E., *Clavis Patrum Latinorum*. Bruges, 1951 (Sacris Erudiri, Vol. III).

Forest, A. -Van Steenberghen, F. -Gandillac, M. de, *Le mouvement doctrinal du IXe au XIVe siècle*, Paris, 1951 (= A. Fliche-V. Martin, *Histoire de l' église* . . . Vol. 13), cited: Van Steenberghen, *Le mouvement*.

Geyer, B., *Die patristische und scholastische Philosophie*, Basel 1951 (unaltered reprint of the 1927 edition) = Vol. 2 of Überweg's *Grundriss der Gesch. der Phil.*, cited: Geyer.

Ghellinck, J. de, *Litterature latine au moyen âge* (Bibliothèque catholique des sciences religieuses), 2 vol., Paris, 1939.

Gilson-Böhner, *Christliche Philosophie von ihren Anfängen bis Nikolaus von Cues*. Paderborn, 1954³.

Grabmann, M., *Die Geschichte der scholastischen Methode*. 2 vol. Freiburg, 1909-1911, cited: *Methode* (unaltered reprint Darmstadt, 1956).

Harnack, A. von, *Lehrbuch der Dogmengeschichte*, 3 vol. Tübingen, 1931-32⁵ (unaltered reprint of the 1909-1911 edition), cited: DG.

Hirschberger, J., *Geschichte der Philosophie*, Vol. I, Altertum und Mittelalter, Freiburg, 1949.

Landgraf, A.M., *Einführung in die Geschichte der theol. Literatur der Frühscholastik*, Regensburg, 1948, cited: *Einführung*.
Dogmengeschichte der Fruhscholastik, Vol. I-IV, Regensburg, 1952-1956, cited: DG.

Meyer, H., *Geschichte der abendländischen Weltanschauung*, Vol. III: Die Weltanscrauung des Mittelalters. Würzburg, 1948.

Wulf, M. de, *Histoire de la philosophie medievale*, Vol. II, Louvain-Paris, 1936⁶. Also, the English: *History of Mediéval Philosophy*, Vol. II, 1937.

2. Monographs and articles

Abate, Gius., *Per la storia e la cronologia di San Bonaventura, O. Min.* (c. 1217-1274), Rome, 1950.

Aegerter, E., *L' affaire du De periculis novissimorum temporum,* R Hist Rel 112 (1935) p.242 — 272.

Albi, J. d' *Saint Bonaventure et les luttes doctrinales de 1267 —1277,* Paris, 1923.

Alencon, E. d', art. *Frères mineurs. DThC* VI 1 col. 809/15.

Alszeghy, Z., *Studia Bonaventuriana,* in: *Gregorianum* 29 (1948) p.142-151.

Andrew, J. Mc., *The Theory of Divine Illumination in St. Bonaventure,* in: *New Scholasticism* 1932, p.32-50.

Auer, J., *Die Entwicklung der Gnadenlehre in der Hochscholastik,* 2 vol., Freiburg, 1942 and 1951 (Freiburger theol. Studien, Vol. 62 and 64).

Augustinus Magister, Congrès international augustinien. 3 vol. Paris, 1954.

Balthasar, H. U. von, *Die deutsche Thomasausgabe,* publ. by the Albertus-Magnusakademie Walberberg bei Köln, vol. 23, 1954 (The special gifts of grace and the two ways of human life, *S Theol* II-II, p.171 — 182).

Baeumker, Cl., *Studien und Charakteristiken zur Geschichte der Philosophie, insb. des Mittelalters,* publ. by M. Grabmann. Münster, 1927 (Baeumker-Beiträge XXV 1 — 2), esp.:
Geist und Form d. mittelalterl. Philos. p.58 — 100;
From the annual reports on Western philosophy in the Middle Ages, p.101 — 139;
Der Platonism im Mittelalter, p. 139-179.
Witelo, Ein Philosoph und Naturforscher des 13. *Jahrh.,* Münster, 1908 (Baeumker-Beiträge III 2).
Studien zur Geschichte der Philosophie, Festgabe zum 60. Geburtstag Cl. Baeumker, Münster, 1913 (Baeumker-Beiträge, suppl., vol. 1) cited: Baeumkerfestschrift.

Baur, L., *Das Licht in der Naturphilosophie des Robert Grosseteste,* in: *Hertlingfestschrift,* p.41-55, Freiburg, 1913.
Dominicus Gundissalinus, *De divisione philosophiae,* analyzed from the perspective of the history of philosophy and publ. by L. Baur, Münster, 1903 (Baeumker-Beiträge IV 2 — 3).

Benz, E., *Ecclesia spiritualis*: Kirchenidee und Geschichtstheologie der franziskanischen Reformation. Stuttgart, 1934.
Die Geschichtstheologie der Franziskanerspiritualen des 13. und 14. Jahrhunderts nach neuen Quellen, in: ZKG 52 (1933) p.90 — 121.
Joachimstudien I — III, in:ZKG 50 (1931) p.24 — 111; 51 (1932) p.415 — 455; 53 (1934) p.52 — 116.

Bernardini, L.M., *La nozione del sopranaturale nell' antica Scuola Francescana,* Rome, 1943.

Berresheim, H., *Christus als Haupt der Kirche nach dem hl. Bonaventura.* Bonn, 1939 (Grenzfragen zwischen Phil. und Theol. Vol. 9).

Bettoni, E., *Il problema della conoscibilita di Dio nella scuola francescana*, Padua, 1950.

Beumer, J., *Rupert von Deutz und seine "Vermittlungstheologie,"* in: MThZ 4 (1953) p.255 — 270.

Beyschlag, K., *Die Bergpredigt und Franz von Assisi*. Gütersloh, 1955.

Bianchi, P., *Doctrina S. Bonaventurae de analogia universali*, Zara, 1940.

Bierbaum, M., *Bettelorden und Weltgeistlichkeit an der Universität Paris*. Texte und Untersuchungen zum literarischen Armuts- und Exemtionsstreit des 13. Jahrhunderts (1255 — 1272) Münster, 1920 (*Franz. Stud.*, 2 Beiheft).

Bignami-Odier, J., *Notes sur deux manuscrits de la Biblio-theque du Vatican contenant des traités inédits de Joachim de Flores*, in: *Mélanges d' archéologie et d' Histoire* (Ecole francaise de Rome) LIV Paris, 1937.

Bissen, J.M., *L' exemplarisme divin selon S. Bonaventure*, Paris, 1929 (Etudes IX).

Blumenkranz, M., *La survie médievale de saint Augustin a travers ses apocryphes*, in: *Augustinus Magister* II, 1003 — 1018.

Bondatti, G., *Gioachinismo è Francescanesimo nel Dugento*, Assisi, 1924.

Bonmann, O., *De authenticitate epistolae S. Francisci ad S. Antonium Padovinum*, Quaracchi, 1952.

Bonnefoy, J. Fr., *Le Saint Esprit et ses Don selon Saint Bonaventure*, Paris, 1929 (Etudes X).
    Art. *Bonaventura*, in: *Enciclopedia cattolica*, Vol. II,1837 — 1845 (Rome, 1949).

Borne, C. van den, *Doctrina Sancti Bonaventurae de inspiratione et inerrantia Sacrae Scripturae*, in: *Antonianum* 1 (1926) p.309-326.

Brezzi, *La concezione agostiniana della città di Dio*, Galatina, 1947.

Brown, R., *The Little Flowers of St. Francis*, New York, 1958.

Brunner, P. *Neuere Bonaventura-Forschungen*, in: *Theol. Rundschau*, 1930.

Callebaut, C.A., *L' entrée de S. Bonaventure dans l' Ordre des Frères Mineurs en 1243*, in:*La France Franciscaine* V (1921) p.41-51.

Callus, D.A., *The Date of Grossetestes Translation and Commentaries on Pseudo-Dionysius and the Nichomachean Ethics*, in: *Rech Th Anc Med* 14 (1947) p.186-210.
    La condenación de Sto. Tomás en Oxford, in: *Revista de Filosofia* VI (1947) p.377-416.

Cambell, J., *Les écrits de Saint Francois d' Assise devant la critique*, in: *Franz. Stud.*36 (1954) p.82 — 109; p.205 — 264.

Casutt, L., *Die älteste franziskanische Lebensform*. Untersuchungen zur regula prima sine bulla. Graz-Wien-Köln, 1955.

Carr, A., *Poverty in Perfection According to St. Bonaventure*, in: *Franc. Stud.* VII (1947) p. 313-323; 415-425.

Chénu, M.D., *Introduction a l' étude de Saint Thomas d' Aquin*. Montreal and Paris, 1950.

   La théologie comme science au XIII siècle, Paris 1943², pro manuscripto (First edition in *Arch hist doctr litt m a* 1927 (II) p.31 — 71.

   Théologie symbolique et exégese scolastique au XII et XIII siècles, in: *Mélanges Joseph de Ghellinck S.J.*, Vol. II, p.509-526 (Gembloux, 1951).

Cichitto, L., *L' escatologia di Dante e il francescanesimo*, in: *Misc. Franc.* 47 (1947) p. 217-231.

   Postille bonaventuriano-dantesche, Rome, 1940.

Clasen, S., *Kritisches zur neueren Franziskusliteratur*, in: *Wissenschaft und Weisheit* 13 (1950) p. 151-166.

   Franz von Assisi und Joachim von Fiore, ibid., 6 (1939) p.68-83.

   Die Sendung des hl. Franziskus. Ihre heilsgeschichtliche Deutung durch Bonaventura, *ibid.*, 14 (1951) p.212/25.

   Der heilige Bonaventura und das Mendikantentum, Werl, 1940.

Clusone, V. da, *Cultura e pensiero di S. Francesco d' Assisi*, Modena, 1952.

Conzelmann, H., *The Theology of St. Luke*, tr. G. Buswell, N.Y., 1960.

Cullmann, O., *Christ and Time*, tr. F. Filson, Philadelphia, 1964.

Curtius, E.R., *Europäische Literatur und lateinisches Mittelalter*, Bern, 1948.

Dady, M.R., *The Theory of Knowledge of St. Bonaventure*, Washington, 1939.

Danielou, J., *Lord of History*, tr. N. Abercrombie, Chicago, 1958.

Decker, B., *Die Entwicklung der Lehre von der prophetischen Offenbarung von Wilh. von Auxerre bis zu Thomas von Aquin*, Breslau, 1940 (Breslauer Studien zur historischen Theol., Neue Folge, vol.VII).

   Die Analyse des Offenbarungsvorganges beim hlg. Thomas im Licht vorthomistischer Prophezietraktate, in:*Angelicum* 1939, p.195-244.

Delorme, cfr. Sources under Bonaventure.

Dempsey. P., *De principiis exegeticis S. Bonaventurae*, Rome, 1945.

Dempf, A., *Sacrum Imperium*, Darmstadt, 1954² (unaltered reprint of the original 1927 edition.)

   Metaphysik des Mittelalters (in the Handbuch der Philosophie), Munich-Berlin, 1930.

   Ethik des Mittelalters, ibid., 1927.

   Ecclesia spiritualis oder Schwarmgeisterei? in: *Hochland* XXXII 2 (1935) p.170-173.

   Das Dritte Reich. Schicksale einer Idee, in:*Hochland* XXIX 1 (1931/32) p. 36-48 and 158-171.

   Etienne Gilson, in: *Phil. Jahrbuch der Gorresgesellschaft* 62 (1953) p.253-266.

Denifle, *Das Evangelium aeternum und die Commission zu Anagni*, in: ALKG I p.49-98.

Detloff, W., *Die Geistigkeit des hlg. Franziskus in der Theologie der Franziskaner*, in: *Wissenschaft und Weisheit* 19 (1956) p. 197-211.

"Christus tenens medium in omnibus." Sinn und Funktion der Theologie bei Bonaventura, ibid., 20 (1957) p.28-42; 120-140.

Dobbins, D., *Franciscan Mysticism*, New York, 1927 (*Franciscan Studies* Nr.6).

Dobschutz, E.v., *Vom vierfachen Schriftsinn*, in: *Harnack-Ehrung*, Leipzig, 1921, p.1-13.

Doctor Seraphicus . . . door V.M. Breton, A. Epping, B. van Leeuwen, N. Sanders. *Collectanea Franciscana Neerlandica* VII 3, 's Hertogenbosch, 1950.

Dondaine, H.J., *Le corpus Dionysien de l' université de Paris au XIII siecle*, Rome, 1953 (Storia e letteratura 44).

Doucet, V., *De naturali seu innato supernaturalis beatitudinis desiderio iuxta Theologos a saeculo XIII usque ad XX*. in: *Antonianum* 3 (1928) p.167-208.

Quaestiones centum ad scholam Franciscanam saec. XIII ut plurimum spectantes in cod. Florentino Bibl. Laur. Plut. 17 sin. 7. Appendix: *De quaestionibus S. Bonaventurae adscriptis in cod. Vaticano Palat. lat. 612, AFH* 26 (1933) p.183-202, 474-496 (Appendix p.487-496).

Descriptio codicis 172 *bibliothecae communalis Assisiensis, ibid.*, 25 (1932) p.257-274; 378-389; 502-524.

Duhem, P., *Le systéme de monde*; histoire des doctrines cosmologiques de Platon a Copernic, 5 vol., Paris, 1913-1917.

Ehser, K., *Zu der "Epistola de tribus quaestionibus" des hlg. Bonaventura*, in: *Franz. Stud.* 27 (1940) p.149-159.

Ehrle, F., *Der heilige Bonaventura. Seine Eigenart und seine drei Lebensaufgaben*, in: *Franz. Stud.* 8 (1921) p.109 — 124.

Beiträge zur Geschichte der mittelalterlichen Scholastik II: Der Augustinismus und der Aristotelismus in der Scholastik gegen Ende des 13. Jahrhunderts. in: ALKG V (1889) p.603-635.

Zur Geschichte der Scholastik im 13. *Jahrhundert*, in: ZkTh 13 (1889) p.172-193.

Die Spiritualen, ihr Verhältnis zum Franciscanerorden und zu den Fraticellen, in: ALKG II (1886) p.107-164.

Die 'historia septem tribulationum ordinis minorum' des fr. Angelus de Clarino, ibid., p.249-336.

Zur Quellenkunde der älteren Franziskanergeschichte. Der Catalogus ministrorum generalium des Bernhard von Bessa, in: ZkTh 7 (1883) p.323-352.

Das Studium der Handschriften der mittelalterlichen Scholastik mit besonderer Berucksichtigung der Schule des hlg. Bonaventura, in: ZkTh 7 (1883) p.1-51.

Engemann, A., *Erleuchtungslehre als Resolutio und Reductio nach Bonaventura*, in: *Wissenschaft und Weisheit* I (1934) p.211-242.

Englebert, O., *St. Francis of Assisi*, tr. by E.M. Cooper, second ed. I. Brady and R. Brown, Chicago, 1965.

Esser, K., *Mysterium paupertatis*. Die Armutsauffassung des hl. Franziskus von Assisi, in:*Wiss. und Weisheit* 14 (1951) p.177-189.

Faral, E., see Sources under William of St. Amour.

Felder, H., *Geschichte der wissenschaftl. Studien im Franziskaner-orden bis um die Mitte des* 13. *Jahrhunderts*, Freiburg, 1904.

Fortini, A., *I documenti degli archivi assisani e alcuni punti contro-versi della vita di San Francesco*, in: AFH 43 (1950) p.3-44.

Fournier, P., *Études sur Joachim de Flore et ses doctrines*. Paris, 1909.

Friederichs, J., *Zum "Vorwort des hlg. Bonaventura"* (Op. omn. II, 1-3), *Franz. Stud.* 29 (1942) p.78-89.
Die Theologie als spekulative und praktische Wissenschaft nach Bonaventura und Thomas von Aquin, Bonn, 1940.

Gass-Nitzsch. Art. *Bonaventura*, in: RE III, 282-287.

Gemelli, A., *Message of St. Francis*, Chicago, 1963.

Gennaro, G., *Francesco Cherubico*. Commento alla spiritualita di S. Francesco. Rome, 1956.

Geyer, B., *Der vierte Band der Summa des Alexander Halensis*, in: *Franz. Stud.* 31 (1949) p.1-14.
Der Begriff der scholastischen Théologie, in: *Synthesen*. Fest-schrift für A. Dyroff, 1926, p.112-125.

Ghellinck, J. de, *Le mouvement théologique du XII siècle*. Second printing, Brussels, 1948 (Museum Lessianum, Sect. hist. Nr. 10).
Patristique et argument de tradition au bas moyen âge, in: *Grabmannfestschrift*, p.403-426.
Pour l' histoire du mot "revelare", in: *Rech sc rel* VI (1916) p.149-157.
Mélanges J. d. Ghellinck, S.J., 2 vol., Gembloux, 1951, (Museum Lessianum, Sect. hist. Nr. 14).

Gilson, E., *The Philosophy of St. Bonaventure*, tr. Trethowan & Sheed, Paterson, 1965.
The Spirit of Medieval Philosophy, tr. Downes, New York, 1936.
Le philosophie au moyen âge, second printing, Paris, 1944.
Reason and Revelation in the Middle Ages, New York, 1938.
Dante und die Philosophie, Tr. E. Sommer-von Seckendorff, Frei-burg, 1953.

Glorieux, P., *Répertoire des maîtres en théologie de Paris aux XIII siècle*, 2 vol., Paris, 1933-1934 (Etudes 17 and 18).
D' Alexandre de Halès a Pierre Auriol. La suite de Maîtres fran-ciscains de Paris au XIII siècle, in: AFH 27 (1934) p.257-281.
Essai sur la chronologie de saint Bonaventure, ibid., 19 (1926) p. 145-168.
La collection authentique des sermons de saint Bonaventure, in: *R the anc med* 22 (1955) p. 119-125.
Les polémiques "contra Geraldinos," *ibid.* 6 (1934) p.5-41.

La date des Collationes de S. Bonaventure, AFH 22 (1929) p.257-272.

Goetz, W., *Die Quellen zur Geschichte des hl. Franz von Assisi*, Gotha, 1904.

Grabmann, M., *Mittelalterliches Geistesleben*. Abhandlungen zur Geschichte der Scholastik und Mystik. 2 vol. Munich, 1926 and 1936. See especially I, p.1-49, on the methods and aims of research in the area of Medieval Scholasticism and mysticism. I,p.65-103 on the natural law from Gratian to Aquinas. I,p.449-468 on the medieval Latin translations of the writings of Ps. Dionysius.

Die philosoph. und theolog. Erkenntnislehre des Kardinals Matthäus von Aquasparta, Vienna, 1906. (Theol. Studien der Leo-Gesellschaft, publ. by A. Erhard-J.M. Schindler, Vol. 14).

Die Löwener Neuscholastik und die geschichtl. Darstellung und handschriftliche Erforschung der mittelalterlichen Philosophie im Licht neuester Veröffentlichungen, in: *Philos. Jahrbuch der Görresgesellschaft* 51 (1938) p.129-154.

Die theologische Erkenntnis- und Einleitungslehre des hlg. Thomas von Aquin auf Grund seiner Schrift, "In Boethium de Trinitate" im Zusammenhang der Scholastik des 13. und beginnenden 14. Jahrhunderts dargestellt (Thomistische Studien 4) Fribourg, 1948.

Aus der Geisteswelt des Mittelalters. Martin Grabmann zum 60. Geburtstag, publ. by Schmaus-Lang-Lechner (Baeumker-Beiträge supplement-volume III), Münster, 1935; cited: *Grabmannfestschrift*.

Grundmann, H., *Studien über Joachim von Floris*, Leipzig, 1927, (Beitrage zur Kulturgeschichte des Mittelalters und der Renaissance, publ. by W. Goetz, vol. 32) Cited: *Joachim* I.

Neue Forschungen uber Joachim von Fiore, Marburg, 1950, Münstersche Forschungen, ed. J. Trier and H. Grundmann, vol. 1, cited: *Joachim* II.

Religiöse Bewegungen im Mittelalter, Berlin, 1933.

Grünewald, St., *Franziskanische Mystik*, Munich, 1932, *Zur Mystik des. hlg. Bonaventura*, in:ZAM 9 (1934) p.124-142; 219-232.

Guardini, R., *Die Lehre des hlg. Bonaventura von der Erlösung*, Düsseldorf, 1921 (cited: *Erlösungslehre*).

Eine Denkergestalt des hohen Mittelalters: Bonaventura, in: R. Guardini, *Unterscheidung des Christlichen*, Mainz, 1935, p.389-403.

Die Offenbarung, ihr Wesen und ihre Formen, Würzburg, 1940.

Hardick-Esser, *Die Schriften des hlg. Franziskus von Assisi*, Werl, 1951, (Franziskan. Quellenschriften, vol. 1), cited: *Schriften*.

Hartnett, J., *Doctrina S. Bonaventurae de deiformitate*. Mundelein, Ill., 1936.

Hayen, A., *Der hlg. Thomas von Aquin gestern und heute*, Tr. R. Scherer, Frankfurt, 1953.

Healey, E.T.H., *S. Bonaventure's De reductione artium ad theologiam*. Commentary with introduction and translation, New York, 1940.

Henquinet, F.M., *Trois petits écrits théologiques de saint Bonaventure à la lumière d' un quatrième*, inédit, in: Mélanges Auguste Pelzer, Etudes d' histoire littéraire et doctrinale de la scholastique médiévale . . . Louvain, 1947, p.195 — 216.
Un recueil de questions annoté par saint Bonaventure, in: AFH 25 (1932) p.553-555.
De causalitate Sacramentorum iuxta codicem autographum S. Bonaventurae, in: *Antoninum* 8 (1933) p. 377-424.

Hertling: *Abhandlungen aus dem Gebiet der Philosophie und ihrer Geschichte*. Eine Festgabe zum 70. Geburtstag Gg. Frh.v. Hertling, Freiburg, 1913; Cited: *Hertlingfestschrift*.

Hipler, F., *Die christliche Geschichtsauffassung*, Cologne, 1884.

B. Hirsch-Reich, *Das Figurenbuch Joachims von Fiore*, in: *Rech th anc med* 21 (1954) p.144-147.

Hirschenauer, F., *Grundlagen und Grundfragen des Pariser Mendikantenstreites*, in: ZAM 10 (1935) p.221-236.

Hoffmann, A., *Die Lehre von der Gottebenbildlichkeit des Menschen in der neueren protestantischen Theologie und bei Thomas von Aquin*, in: *Divus Thomas*, 1941, p.3-35.

Holzhey, K., *Die Inspiration der hlg. Schrift in der Anschauung des Mittelalters*. Von Karl d. Gr. bis zum Konzil von Trient. Munich, 1895.

Huck, J. Chr., *Joachim von Floris und die joachitische Literatur*. Freiburg, 1938.

Jansen, B., *Der Augustinismus des Petrus Johannis Olivi*, in: *Grabmannfestschrift*, p.878-895.

Imle, F., *Die Gabe des Intellekts nach dem hl. Bonaventura*, in: *Franz. Stud.* 20 (1933) p.34-50.
Die Theologie des hlg. Bonaventura. Werl, 1931.

Joachim von Fiore, *Das Reich des hl. Geistes*. ed. A. Rosenberg, Munich, 1955.

Jörgensen, J., *St. Francis of Assisi*, tr. T. Sloane, London, 1913.

Ivanka, E. von, *La signification historique du "Corpus areopagiticum,"* in: *R sc rel* 36 (1949) p.5-24.

Kamlah, W., *Apokalypse und Geschichtstheologie*. Die mittelalterliche Auslegung der Apokalypse vor Joachim von Fiore. Berlin, 1925 (Historische Studien, publ. by E. Ebering, vol. 285).
Christentum und Geschichtlichkeit, Stuttgart-Cologne, 1951².

Kaup, J., *Christus und die Kirche nach der Lehre des. hl. Bonaventura*, in: *Franz. Stud.* 26 (1939) p.333-344.
Zur Konkurslehre des Petrus Olivi und des hlg. Bonaventura, ibid. 19 (1932) p.315-326.

Die theologische Tugend der Liebe nach der Lehre des hlg. Bonaventura, Münster, 1927.

Keicher, O., *Zur Lehre des älteren Franziskanertheologen vom "intellectus agens"* in: *Hertlingfestschrift*, p.173-182.

Krizovljan, H.a, *Controversia doctrinalis inter magistros franciscanos et Sigerum de Brabant*, in: *Coll. Franc.* 27 (1957) p.121-165 (Bonaventure, p.127-142.)

Lee, M. van, *Les idées d' Anselme de Havelberg sur le développement des dogmes*, in: *Analecta Praemonstratensia*, 1928, p.5-35.

Lemaître, H. -Masseron, S., *Saint Francois d' Assise. Son oeuvre, son influence*, Paris, 1927 (With contributions by other authors).

Lemmens, L., *Der heilige Bonaventura*. Kempten-Munich, 1909.

Léon, A., *Saint Francois d' Assise et son oeuvre*. Paris, 1928.

Longpré, E., *La théologie mystique de S. Bonaventure*, AFH XIV (1921) p. 36-108; also (Quaracchi, 1921).

Art. *Bonaventure*, in:*Dict. d' histoire et de géographie ecclésiastiques*, T IX, Paris, 1937. p.741-788.

S. Bonaventure et Cologne, in: *Wissenschaft und Weisheit* (1934) p.289-97.

Lubac, H., *'Typologie' et 'Allegorisme'* in: *Rech Th anc med.* 14 (1947) p.180-226.

Luyckx, B.A., *Die Erkenntnislehre Bonaventuras*, Münster, 1923 (Baeumker-Beiträge, XXIII, 3-4).

Macdonald, J., *Authority and Reason in the Early Middle Ages*, Oxford, 1933.

Marrou, H.J., *Saint Augustin et la fin de la culture antique.* Paris, 1938. *Retractatio*, Paris, 1949.

The Meaning of History, tr. R. Olsen (Baltimore, 1966).

La théologie de l' histoire, in: *Augustinus Magister* III, p.193-204.

Meier, L., *Bonaventuras Selbstzeugnis über seinen Augustinismus*, in: *Franz. Stud.* 17 (1930) p.342-355.

St. Bonaventura, ein Meister der Sprache; ibid, 16 (1929) p.15-28.

Milano, Giov. da, *La dottrina del miracolo nelle opere di San Bonaventura*, Milano, 1938.

Mirgeler, A., *Ernst Benz: Ecclesia spiritualis* ... in: ZKG 55 (1936) p.286-294.

Mondreganes, P.A., *De mundi creatione ad mentem Sancti Bonaventurae*, in: *Coll. Franc.* 1 (1931) p.3-27.

Moormann, J., *The Sources for the Life of S. Francis of Assisi*, Manchester, 1950.

Nigg, W., *Grosse Heilige*, Zürich, 1952[4].

Vom Geheimnis der Mönche, Zürich-Stuttgart, 1952.

Nitzsch, see under Gass.

Oepke, A., Art. Apokalypto in: Th.W. III 565-597.

Ott, L., *Petrus Lombardus*. Persönlichkeit und Werk, in: MThZ 5 (1954) p.99-113.

Pagnani, G., *Contributi alla questione dei Fioretti de S. Francesco*, in: AFH 49 (1956) p.3-16.

Paré, Th., *Le nom de famille de S. Bonaventura*, in: Franc. Stud. 11 (1951) p.347-363.

Pelster, F., *Literargeschichtliche Probleme im Anschluss an die Bonaventura- Ausgabe von Quaracchi*, in: ZkTH 48 (1924) p.500-532.
Literaturgeschichtliches zur Pariser theologischen Schule aus den Jahren 1230-1256, in: Scholastik 5 (1930) p.46-78.

Pergamo, B., *De quaestionibus ineditis Fr. Odonis Rigaldi, Guilelmi de Melitona et Codicis Vat. lat. 782 circa naturam theologiae deque earum relatione ad Summam theologicam Fr. Alexandri Halensis*, in: AFH 30 (1937) p. 3-54 and 301-364.

Quaglia, A., *Perché manca un' edizione critica dei Fioretti di San Francesco*, in: Studi Franc. 52 (1955) p.216-223.

Rahner, K., *Der Begriff der ecstasis bei Bonaventura*, in: ZAM 9 (1934) p.1-19.

Ratzinger, J., *Volk und Haus Gottes in Augustins Lehre von der Kirche*, Munich, 1954 (MThSt II 7), cited: *Volk und Haus Gottes*.
Herkunft und Sinn der Civitas-Lehre Augustins. Begegnung und Auseinandersetzung mit W. Kamlah, in: *Augustins Magister* II 965-979.

Reeves, M., Hirsch-Reich, B., *The Seven Seals in the Writings of Joachim of Fiore*, in: Rech th anc med 21 (1954) p.211-247.
The Figurae of Joachim of Fiore, Genuine and Spurious Collections, in: Medieval and Renaissance Studies 3 (1954) p.171-199.

Reeves, M., *The Liber Figurarum of Joachim of Fiore*, ibid., 2 (1950) p.57-81.

Righi, O., *Il pensiero e l' opera de San Bonaventura*, Florence, 1932.
S. Bonaventura entro nell' Ordine franciscano in Parigi o nella provincia Romana, in: Misc. Franc. 36 (1936) p.505-511.

Robert, P., *Hylémorphisme et Devenir chez S. Bonaventure*. Montreal, 1936.
Le problème de la philosophie bonaventurienne, in: Laval théologique et philosophique 6 (1950) p.145-163 and 7 (1951) p.9-58.
St. Bonaventure, Defender of Christian Wisdom, in: Franc. Stud. 3 (1943) p.159-179.

Rondet, H., *Études Augustiniennes*, Paris, 1953.

Roques, R., *La notion de hiérarchie selon le Pseudo-Denys*, in: Arch hist doctr litt m a 24 (1949) p.183-222; 25/26 (1950/51) p.5-44.
L' univers dionysien, Paris, 1954.

Rosenberg, see under Joachim of Fiore.

Rosenmöller, B., *Religiöse Erkenntnis nach Bonaventura*. Münster, 1925 (Baeumker-Beiträge XXV 3-4).

Russo, F., *Saggio di bibliografia gioachimita*, in: Archivo storico per la Calabria e la Lucania VI (1936) p.102-141.
Bibliografia Gioachimita (Biblioteca de Bibliografia italiana 28). Florence, 1954.

Salman, D.H., *Jean de la Rochelle et les débuts de l' averroisme latin*, in: *Arch hist doctr litt m a* 22/23 (1947/48) p.133-144.

Scaramuzzi, D., *L' immagine de Dio nell' uomo nell ordine naturale secondo San Bonaventura*, Padua-Milan, 1942.

Sauer, E., *Die religiöse Wertung der Welt in Bonaventuras Itinerarium mentis in Deum*, Werl, 1937 (Franziskanische Forschungen, vol. 4).

Sciamannini, R., *Allegorismo dinamico in San Bonaventura*, in: *La città di Vita* I (1946) p.446-451.

Schmaus, M., *Der liber propugnatorius des Thomas Anglicus und die Lehrunterschiede zwischen Thomas von Aquin und Duns Scotus II. Teil. Die trinitärischen Lehrdifferzen* (Baeumker-Beiträge vol. XXIX), Munich, 1930.

Scholz, H., *Glaube und Unglaube in der Weltgeschichte. Ein Kommentar zu Augustins de civitate dei*, Leipzig, 1911.

Schönhöffer, *Die Fioretti oder Blümlein des hlg. Franziskus. Auf Grund lateinischer und italienischer Texte*, ed. H. Schönhöffer, Freiburg, 1921 (valuable because of the use of manuscripts).

Schorn, A., *Über die Gabe der Weisheit nach Bonaventura*, in: *Wissenschaft und Weisheit* 9 (1942) p.41-54.

Schreiber, G., *Studien über Anselm von Havelberg zur Geistesgeschichte des Hochmittelalters*, in: *Anal Praem* 18 (1942) p.1-90. *Anselm von Havelberg und die Ostkirche*, in: ZKG 60 (1942) p.354-411.

Semmelroth, O., *Die 'theologia symbolike' des Ps. Dionysius Areopagita*, in: *Scholastik* 27 (1952) p.1-11. *Die Lehre des Ps.-Dionysius Areopagita vom Aufstieg der Kreatur zum göttlichen Licht*, ibid., 29 (1954) p.24-52.

Sepinski, A., *La psychologie du Christ chez S. Bonaventure*, Paris, 1948.

Seppelt, Fr. X., *Der Kampf der Bettelorden an der Universität Paris in der Mitte des 13. Jahrhunderts*, I. Teil, Kirchengeschichtliche Abhandlungen, publ. M. Sdralek III 1905, p.197-241; II Teil, ibid., VI 1908, p.73-140.

Silic, R., *Christus und die Kirche. Ihr Verhältnis nach der Lehre des hlg. Bonaventura*. 1938 (Breslauer Studien zur hist. Theol., Neue Folge, vol. 3).

Smits Cr. -Sagaert, O. — Lampen, W.,-Soens, M., *Natuur en Bovennatuur. Collectanea Franciscana Neerlandica* III 3. 's Hertogenbosch, 1937.

Smeets K., Art. *Bonaventure* in: DThC II, p.962-986.

Söhngen, G., *Bonaventura als Klassiker der analogia fidei*, in: *Wissenschaft und Weisheit* 2 (1935) p.97-111. *Die Einheit in der Theologie*, Munich, 1952.

Soiron, Th., *Vom Geist der Theologie Bonaventuras*. in: *Wissenschaft und Weisheit* I (1934) p.28-38.

Spargo, E.J.M., *The Category of the Aesthetic in the Philosophy of St. Bonaventure*. New York (and F. Schöningh, Paderborn) 1953 (Franciscan Institute Publ., Philosophy Series, No.11)

Spick, C., *Esquisse d' une Histoire de l' Exégèse latin au Moyen Age*, Paris, 1944.

Spörl, J., *Grundformen hochmittelalterlicher Geschichtsanschauung*, Munich, 1935.

Squadrani, J., S. *Bonaventura christianus philosophus*, in: *Antonianum* 16 (1941) p.103-130 and p.253-304.

Stohr, A., *Die Trinitätslehre Bonaventuras*. I Teil. Die wissenschaftliche Trinitätslehre. Münster, 1923 (Münsterische Beiträge, vol 3).

Szabo, J., *De ss. Trinitate in creaturis refulgente doctrina S. Bonaventurae*, Rome, 1955.

Tavard, G.H., *St. Bonaventure's Disputed Questions "De theologia"* . . . see Sources under Bonaventure.

La théologie d' après le "Breviloquium" de saint Bonaventure, in: *L' année théol.* 10 (1949) p.201-214.

Transiency and Permanence. The nature of theology according to St. Bonaventure, New York (Paderborn) 1954.

Thomas of Celano, *Leben und Werke des hl. Franzikus von Assisi*. Introduction, translation, and notes by P. E. Grau, OFM., Werl, 1955.

Thonnard, F.J., *Augustinisme et aristotélisme au XIII siècle*, in: *L' année théol.* 4 (1944) p.442-466.

Tectaert, A., *Le Répertoire des maîtres en théologie de Paris*. Quelques remarques et corrections, in: *Eph Th Lov* 10 (1934) p.617-624.

Théry, P.G., *Thomas Gallus et les concordances bibliques*, in: *Grabmannfestschrift*, p.427-446.

Thomas Gallus, in: *Arch hist doctr m a* 14 (1939) p.141-208.

Chronologie des oeuvres de Thomas Gallus, abbé de Verceil, in: *Divus Thomas*, Piacenza 37 (1934) p.265-277; 365-385; 469-496.

Documents concernant Jean Sarrazin. Reviseur de la traduction érigénienne du Corpus Dionysiacum, in: *Arch hist doctr litt m a* 25/26 (1950/51) p.45-87.

Tinivella, F., *De impossibili sapientiae adeptione in philosophia pagana iuxta Collationes in Hexaemeron S. Bonaventurae*, in: *Antonianum* XI (1936) p.27-50; 135-186; 277-318.

Tondelli, L., *Il libro delle figure dell' abate Gioachino da Fiore*. Vol. I Introduzione e commento. Le sue rivelazione dantesche. Vol. II Testo e XXIII Tavole (X a colori). Torino, o. J. (1939); second edition, 1953 (Citations according to the first edition since the second was unfortunately unavailable).

Van Steenberghen, F., *Le mouvement* . . . see under Forest, (General Works).

Siger de Brabant d' après ses oeuvres inédites. Vol. I Les oeuvres inédites, Louvain, 1931; II Siger dans l' histoire de l' aristotelisme. 1942 (Les Philosophes Belges, Vol. XII and XIII).

Aristotle in the West. The origins of Latin Aristotelianism, Louvain, 1955.

The Philosophical Movement in the Thirteenth Century. Belfast-Lectures. Edinburgh, 1955.

Veuthey, L., *Bonaventurae philosophia christiana*. Rome, 1943.
Scientia et sapientia in doctrina Sancti Bonaventurae, in: *Misc. Franc* 43 (1943) p.1-13.

Vinca, A. da, *L' Aspetto filosofico dell' aristotelismo di San Bonaventura*, in: *Coll. Franc.* 19 (1949) p.5-44.

Werner, M., *Die Entstehung des christlichen Dogmas*. Bern-Tübingen, 1941.

Zarb, S., *Le fonti agostiniane del trattato sulla profezia di S. Tomaso d' Aquino*, in: *Angelicum* 15 (1938) p.169-200.

Ziesché, K., *Die Naturlehre Bonaventuras*, in: *Phil. Jahrbuch der Görresgesellschaft* 21 (1908) p.56-89; 159-189.

SOURCES

Alcher of Clairvaux (= Ps.-Augustinus), *De spiritu et anima*, PL 40, 779-832.

"Alexander of Hales", *Summa theologica*, Vol. I-IV, Quaracchi, 1924-1948 (Vol. I 1924, II 1928, III 1930, IV 1948; Prolegomena, 1948; brief remarks on the problem of authenticity by Geyer in *Franz. Stud.* 31 [1949] p.1-14).

Angelo of Clareno, *Historia septem tribulationum ordinis minorum*, text of the third and seventh *tribulatio* edited by F. Ehrle, in: ALKG II (1886) p.127-164, 256-336.

Anselm of Havelberg, *Dialogi* PL 188,1139 — 1248.

Augustine, *Opera omnia* PL 32-45; CSEL in as far as it is available (cfr. Dekkers, *Clavis patrum* . . . 50ff).
Tractatus in Joannem and
De civitate Dei according to CC (Turnhout, 1954f).

Bernard of Bessa, *Catalogus Ministrorum generalium ordinis fratrum minorum*, ed. Ehrle in: ZkTh 7 (1883) p.338-352.

Bonaventure, *Opera omnia*, 10 vol. Quaracchi, 1882-1902.
Collationes in Hexaemeron et Bonaventuriana quaedam selecta, ed. F. Delorme. BFSchMA VIII, Quaracchi 1934 (contains another recension and other works which have been unavailable in print), cited: Delorme.
Quaestiones disputatae de theologia = G.H.Tavard, *St. Bonaventure's Disputed Questions "De theologia"*, in: *Rech th anc med* XVII (1950) p.187-236. text p.210-236.
(Saint Bonaventure,) *Questions Disputées "De caritate, De novissimis."* Edition critique par P. Glorieux, Paris 1950 (La France Franciscaine, Document II).
Quaestiones de prophetia, Codex 186 of the Bibliotheca communale of Assisi f 10 v b — 13 v a; *ibid.* f 30 ra — 31 ra, 31 va — 32ra.
Quaestiones de visione intellectuali et corporali et de divinatione; extensive excerpts in B. Decker, *Die Entwicklung der Lehre* . . . (cfr. literature); concerning other unedited *Quaestiones* of Bonaventure, cfr. G.H. Tavard, *op. cit.*, and the work of Doucet and Henquinet listed under literature.

Dante Alighieri, *La divina Commedia*, ed. L. Olschki, Heidelberg, 1918.

Ps. Dionysius Areopagita, *Opera omnia* PG 3; see below under Johannes Scotus Eriugena and Thomas of Vercelli.

Dionysiaca, Recueil donnant l' ensemble de traductions latines des ouvrages attribués au Denys de l' Areopage . . . ed. by Ph. Chevallier and others. 2 vol. Paris 1937 and 1950. Cited: *Dionysiaca* I and II.

Floretum sancti Francisci Assisiensis. Liber aureus qui italice dicitur i Fioretti di san Francesco, ed. P. Sabatier, Paris, 1902. See literature under Schönhöffer.

Franziskus, Analekten zur Geschichte des Franciscus von Assisi. Publ. by H. Böhmer, Tübingen-Leipzig, 1904. See literature under Hardick-Esser.

Gerard of Borgo San Donnino, *Erhaltene Reste des Introductorius in Evangelium aeternum im Protokoll der Commission zu Anagni*, publ. by H. Denifle, in: ALKG I (1885) p.99-142.

Gerard of Abbeville, *Giraudi sermo factus apud Fratres Minores*, in: Bierbaum, *Bettelorden und Weltgeistlichkeit* . . . p.208-219.

Objections against the tract "Manus que contra Omnipotentem", etc., *ibid.* p.169-207.

Tractatus Gerardi de Abbatisvilla "Contra adversarium perfectionis christianae," publ. by S. Clasen, in: AFH 31 (1938) p.284-329 and AFH 32 (1939) p.89-200.

Ps. Hermes, *Liber XXIV philosophorum*. Ed. by Cl. Baeumker, in: Cl. Baeumker, *Studien und Charakteristiken zur Geschichte der Philosophie, insbes. des Mittelalters*, publ. by M. Grabmann, Baeumker-Beiträge XXV 1-2, Münster, 1927, p.194-214.

Honorius of Autun, *Expositio in Cantica canticorum*, PL 172,347-496.

Hugo of St. Victor, *Opera*, PL 175-176.

Johannes Scotus Eriugena, *Versio operum S. Dionysii Areopagitae*, PL 122, 1023-1194.

Joachim of Fiore: *Divini vatis Abbatis Joachimi liber concordiae novi ac veteris Testamenti*. Venice, 1519.

Expositio in apocalypsin. Venice, 1527.

Psalterium decem chordarum. Venice, 1527.

Liber figurarum, ed. L. Tondelli (see literature under Tondelli).

(Gioacchino da Fiore) *Tractatus super quatuor evangelia*, ed. Ernesto Buonaiuti. Fonti per la Storia d' Italia Scrittori secolo XII Rome, 1930.

De articulis fidei, ed. Buonaiuti, *ibid.*, Rome, 1936.

Joachimi Abbatis liber contra Lombardum (Scuola di Gioacchino da Fiore), ed. Carmelo Ottaviano. Rome, 1934.

Ps. Joachim of Fiore, *Scriptum super Hieremiam prophetam*, Venice 1516.

Scriptum super Esaiam prophetam. Venice, 1517.

Nicolas of Lisieux, *Liber de ordine praeceptorum ad consilia*, in: Bierbaum, *Bettelorden und Weltgeistlichkeit* . . . p.220-234.

Peter John Olivi, *Quaestiones in secundum librum Sententiarum*, ed. B. Jansen, 3 vol. (BFSchMA IV-VI), Quaracchi, 1922 — 1926.

Peter Lombard, *Libri IV Sententiarum*, in: Bonaventurae opera omnia, Vol. I — IV.[1]

Robert of Melun: *Oeuvres de Robert de Melun*, ed. by R. M. Martin,

[1] After much thought, I have decided that it would be proper in a study on Bonaventure's thought to cite the same text of Lombard's *Sentences* which is given in Bonaventure's works. For another text, cfr. the two-volume edition which appeared in a second printing by Quaracchi in 1916.

Vol. III *Sententie.* Vol. 1, Louvain, 1947; Vol. 2, Louvain, 1952 (ed. R.M. Martin and R.M. Gallet).

Rupert of Deutz, *De sancta trinitate et operibus eius.* PL 167.
Commentarium in Apocalypsin. PL 169,827 — 1214.

Speculum perfectionis ou mémoire de frére Léon. Tome I: Texte latin; préparé par P. Sabatier. Manchester, 1928 (British Society of Franciscan Studies, vol. 13).

Thomas Aquinas, *Summa theologiae,* Bibliotheca de autores Cristianos, Madrid, 1951-1952 (Text of the Leonine edition). Cfr. literature under Balthasar.

Scriptum in libros Sententiarum. Venice, 1747-50.

Quaestiones disputatae, ed. Mandonnet, Paris, 1925 (3 vol.).

Opuscula, Vol. 4, ed. Mandonnet, Paris, 1927. (Contains the *Liber contra impugnantes Dei cultum et religionem*).

Thomas of Celano, *Sancti Francisci Assisiensis vita et miracula additis opusculis liturgicis,* ed. Eduardus Alencon. Rome, 1906.

Thomas of Vercelli, (Thomas Gallus) Paraphrase of the works of Dionysius Areopagita, in: *Dionysiaca* I, p.673-717.

Thomas of York, *Traktat zur Verteidigung der Mendikanten gegen Wilhelm von Saint-Amour* (Inc Manus. que contra omnipotentem tenditur), attributed to Bertrand of Bayonne ed. by Bierbaum, *Bettelorden und Weltgeistlichkeit* . . . p.37—168. Concerning attribution of the work to Thomas of York, see: Pelster in AFH 1922, p.3 — 22 and Longpré, AFH 1926, p.875 — 930).

William of St. Amour, *Tractatus brevis de periculis novissimorum temporum,* in: Bierbaum, *Bettelorden und Weltgeistlichkeit* . . . p.1 — 36.

Responsiones. Cfr. E. Faral, *Les "Responsiones" de Guillaume de Saint-Amour,* in: *Arch hist doctr litt m a* 25/26 (1950/51) p.337-394, text p.340-361.

Annotationes zu Bonaventuras Quaestio reportata de mendicitate, in: *Bonaventura, Collationes* . . . *et Bonaventuriana quaedam selecta,* ed. F. Delorme (cfr. above) p.332-356.

Liber de antichristo et eius ministris, printed under the name of Nicholas of Oresme by E. Martène-U. Durand, *Veterum scriptorum et monumentorum* . . . *amplissima collectio,* Tomus IX, p.1271 — 1446, Paris, 1733.

LIST OF ABBREVIATIONS

Anal Praem	= Analecta Praemonstratensia
AFH	= Archivum Franciscanum Historicum
ALKG	= Archiv für Literatur- und Kirchengeschicte des Mittelalters. ed. by Denifle und Ehrle, Berlin, 1885 ff.
Arch hist doctr litt m a	= Archives d'histoire doctrinale et litteraire du moyen âge
Baeumker-Beiträge	= Beiträge zur Geschichte der Philosophie des Mittelalters. Texte und Untersuchungen, begrundet von Cl. Baeumker, Münster i. W. 1891 ff.
BFSchMA	= Bibliotheca Franciscana Scholastica Medii Aevi, Quaracchi 1903 ff.
CC	= Corpus Christianorum. Series Latina, Turnhout 1953 ff.
Coll Franc	= Collectanea Franciscana.
CSEL	= Corpus scriptorum ecclesiasticorum Latinorum. Wien 1866 ff.
DThC	= Dictionnaire de théologie catholique.
Eph Th Lov	= Ephemerides Theologicae Lovanienses.
Etudes	= Etudes de la philosophie médiévale. Directeur E. Gilson.
Franc Stud	= Franciscan Studies. Published by the Franciscan Institute St. Bonaventure University, St. Bonaventure, New York.
Franz Stud	= Franziskanische Studien.
Forschungen	= Forschungen zur christl. Literatur- und Dogmengeschichte, ed. by A. Ehrhard u. J. P. Kirsch, Paderborn.
LThK	= Lexikon für Theologie und Kirche, ed. by M. Buchberger.
Misc Franc	= Miscellanea Franciscana.
MThSt	= Münchener theológische Studien, ed. by F. X. Seppelt, J. Pascher, K. Mörsdorf.
MThZ	= Münchener theologische Zeitschrift.
New Scholast	= The New Scholasticism.
PG	= Migne, Patrologia Graeca.
PL	= Migne, Patrologia Latina.
RAM	= Revue d'Ascétique et de Mystique.
RE	= Realencyklopädie für protestantische Theologie[3], ed. by A. Hauck, Leipzig, 1896 ff.
RGG[2]	= Religion in Geschichte und Gegenwart, 2. Aufl., ed. by Gunkel-Zscharnack, 1927 ff.

Rech sc rel	= Recherches de science religieuse.
Rech Th Anc Med	= Recrerches de théologie ancienne et medievale.
R Hist Rel	= Revue de l'histoire des religions.
ThW	= Theologisches Wörterbuch zum N. T., begründet von R. Kittel, Stuttgart, 1933 ff.
ZAM	= Zeitschrift für Aszese und Mystik.
ZKG	= Zeitschrift für Kirchengeschichte.
ZkTh	= Zeitschrift für katholische Theologie (Innsbruck).

For citations from source-material, the ordinary abbreviations are used. In the case of citations from the *Sentence Commentary* of Bonaventure, the number of the volume in the Quaracchi edition is not indicated since the volume number corresponds to the number of the book of *Sentences* involved (I Sent = Vol. I, II Sent = Vol. II, etc.).

INDEX OF NAMES

INDEX OF TOPICS

DATE DUE

	SEP 2 3 2007	
30 505 JOSTEN'S		